Contents

This material is based upon work supported by the National Science Foundation under award number ESI-9255262. Any opinions, findings, and conclusions or recommendations expressed in this publication are those of the authors and do not necessarily reflect the views of the National Science Foundation.

Key Curriculum Press
P.O. Box 2304
Berkeley, California 94702

10 9 8 7 6 5 4 3 2 1   00 99 98 97 96
ISBN 1-55953-250-5
Printed in the
United States of America

Authors

Dan Fendel and Diane Resek
San Francisco State University
with
Lynne Alper and Sherry Fraser
Teacher-Educators

Publisher

Steven Rasmussen

Editorial Director

John Bergez

Project Editor

Casey FitzSimons

Additional Editorial Development

Dan Bennett, Bill Finzer, Crystal Mills

Editorial Production

Caroline Ayres, Debbie Cogan,
Greer Lleaud, Jason Luz

Editorial Assistants

Jeff Gammon, Romy Snyder

Teacher Reviews

Dave Calhoun, John Chart, Dwight Fuller,
Donna Gaarder, Dan Johnson, Jean Klanica,
Cathie Thompson

Multicultural Reviews

Edward Castillo, Ph.D., Sonoma State University
Genevieve Lau, Ph.D., Skyline College

Cover and Interior Design

Terry Lockman
Lumina Designworks

Cover Photography and Cover Illustration

Hillary Turner and Tom Fowler

Production

Luis Shein

Production Coordination

Susan Parini

Technical Graphics

Greg Reeves

Illustration

Tom Fowler, Evangelia Philippidis,
Diane Varner, Martha Weston,
April Goodman Willy

Interactive Mathematics Program

I M P ™

Integrated High School Mathematics

Y E A R 1

Dan Fendel and Diane Resek
with
Lynne Alper and Sherry Fraser

KEY CURRICULUM PRESS
Innovators in Mathematics Education

The Game of Pig

The Overland Trail

The Pit and the Pendulum

Shadows

Days 1–5: What Is a Shadow? 397

Days 6–9: The Geometry of Shadows 414

Days 10–16: Triangles Galore 424

them in meaningful contexts so that you'll see how they relate to one another and to our world.

Each unit in this four-year program has a central problem or theme, and focuses on several major mathematical ideas. Within each unit, the material is organized for teaching purposes into "Days," with a homework assignment for each day. (Your class may not follow this schedule exactly, especially if it doesn't meet every day.)

At the end of the main material for each unit, you will find a set of "supplemental problems." These problems provide additional opportunities for you to work with ideas from the unit, either to strengthen your understanding of the core material or to explore new ideas related to the unit.

Although the IMP program is not organized into courses called Algebra, Geometry, and so on, you will be learning all the essential mathematical concepts that are part of those traditional courses. You will also be learning concepts from branches of mathematics—especially statistics and probability—that are not part of a traditional high school program.

To accomplish this goal, you will have to be an active learner. Simply reading this book will not allow you to achieve your goal, because the book does not teach directly. Your role as a mathematics student will be to experiment, investigate, ask questions, make and test conjectures, and reflect, and then communicate your ideas and conclusions both verbally and in writing. You will do some work in collaboration with your fellow students, just as users of mathematics in the real world often work in teams. At other times, you will be working on your own.

We hope you will enjoy the challenge of this new way of learning mathematics and will see mathematics in a new light.

Dan Fendel Diane Resek Lynne Alper Sherry Fraser

Note to Students

You are about to begin an adventure in mathematics, an adventure organized around interesting, complex problems. The concepts you learn grow out of what is needed to solve those problems.

This curriculum was developed by the Interactive Mathematics Program (IMP), a collaboration of teachers, teacher-educators, and mathematicians who have been working together since 1989 to reform the way high school mathematics is taught. About one hundred thousand students and five hundred teachers used these materials before they were published. Their experiences, reactions, and ideas have been incorporated into the final version you now hold.

Our goal is to give you the mathematics you need to succeed in this changing world. We want to present mathematics to you in a manner that reflects how mathematics is used and reflects the different ways people work and learn together. Through this perspective on mathematics, you will be prepared both for continued study of mathematics in college and for the world of work.

This book contains the various assignments that will be your work during Year 1 of the program. As you will see, these assignments incorporate ideas from many branches of mathematics, including algebra, geometry, probability, graphing, statistics, and trigonometry. Other topics will come up in later parts of this four-year program. Rather than present each of these areas separately, we have integrated them and presented

Patterns

Getting Started

The first unit of Year 1, *Patterns,* is an introduction to the Interactive Mathematics Program. Instead of a single central problem, this unit has many shorter problems that will help

you focus on new ways of learning and communicating about mathematics.

In the opening days of this unit, you will get started using a powerful tool, the graphing calculator, and be introduced to your first Problem of the Week (POW).

Andy Schultz investigates what his graphing calculator can do.

A Brief IMP Sampler

You are about to embark on a new way of learning mathematics. One of the special features of this program is that you will learn mathematics through the context of problems, and you will see how the mathematics that you are learning is used.

Most units of the curriculum have a central problem, and you will spend about six to eight weeks developing the concepts and skills needed to solve that problem.

Some of these problems are fairly realistic, while others are a bit more fanciful. Here is a sampling of these central problems.

The Game of Pig (Year 1)

This unit centers around a dice game, with the goal of finding the best possible strategy. You will learn basic ideas about probability, as well as more complex ideas such as conditional probability and expected value.

Do Bees Build It Best? (Year 2)

This unit studies the geometry of the honeycomb and asks whether the shape that bees use for storing honey is the most efficient. You will learn about area, volume, surface area, and the Pythagorean theorem.

Cookies (Year 2)

This unit concerns a bakery that is trying to decide how many cookies of each kind to make. They have

Continued on next page

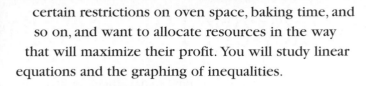

certain restrictions on oven space, baking time, and
so on, and want to allocate resources in the way
that will maximize their profit. You will study linear
equations and the graphing of inequalities.

Small World, Isn't It?

This unit looks at the world's population
growth over the centuries and the challenge
of making predictions about future growth.
You will learn about exponential functions
and study rates of change, including
derivatives (which are a fundamental
concept in calculus).

High Dive (Year 4)

This unit involves a circus act in which
a diver falls off a turning Ferris wheel
into a moving tub of water. You will learn
how to use trigonometry to
describe circular motion and
about the physics of falling
objects.

Homework 1   Past Experiences

1. Reflect on your past experiences in learning and using mathematics. With these experiences in mind, write your "mathematics autobiography."

2. Now consider all the classes you have taken over the years, both in mathematics and in other subjects. Think about those classes that were your favorites and those you liked least.

   Then write a paragraph or two about experiences you had while working in classes that you liked and about experiences in classes that you did not like.

3. Compare experiences you have had working in a group with experiences you have had working alone. What were the advantages and disadvantages of each? Which do you prefer, and why?

Calculator Exploration

Work with a partner on this activity. Your task together is to learn whatever you can about how your graphing calculator works. Write down what you discover.

Your discoveries might be as simple as how to do arithmetic operations or as involved as how the calculator works with statistics. You and your partner will determine what to investigate.

Tomorrow, you and your partner will be asked to share with the class what you learned.

Learn as much as you can so you'll have something new to add even if your favorite discovery is presented by another pair.

Although user manuals may be available, don't think that you must use one. The idea is for you to explore the calculator your own way. *Remember to write down everything you discover!*

Homework 2

Who's Who?

Steve, Felicia, and Pat—a ninth grader, a tenth grader, and an eleventh grader, but not necessarily in that order—were seated around a circular table, playing a game of Hearts.

Each passed three cards to the person on the right. Felicia passed three hearts to the ninth grader. Steve passed the queen of spades and two diamonds to the person who passed cards to the eleventh grader.

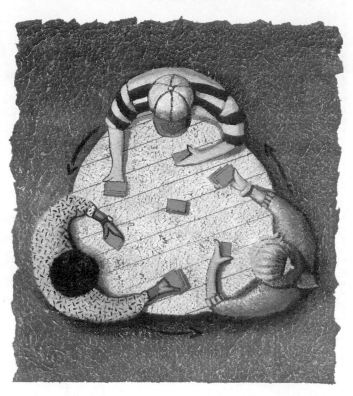

Who was the ninth grader? The tenth grader? The eleventh grader? How were they seated?

1. *Process:* Describe what you did in attempting to solve this problem. Write about such things as

   • how you got started

   • where you got stuck, and how you got unstuck

   • how you knew when to stop

   • efforts that didn't work out or that seemed like a waste of time

   Write about your process of working on the problem *even if you didn't solve the problem.*

2. *Solution:* State your solution as clearly as you can. Explain how you know that your solution is correct and complete.

Your explanation should be written in a way that will be convincing to someone else—even someone who initially disagrees with your answer. Merely stating the answer is not enough.

From *Mathematics: Problem Solving Through Recreational Mathematics* by Averbach and Chein. Copyright © 1980 by W.H. Freeman and Company. Adapted with permission.

Homework 3   Describing Patterns

Mathematics often involves looking for patterns in various situations.

This assignment involves collections of shapes or numbers called **sequences.** Each shape or number is called a **term** of the sequence, and the terms are separated by commas.

Examine each sequence of shapes or numbers below and look for a pattern.

Then write down a description of the pattern and a method for finding the next few terms of the sequence. Give at least the next three terms.

Note: There may be more than one pattern that fits a given initial sequence.

1. 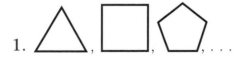 , . . .

2. 1, 1, 2, 1, 3, 1, 4, 1, 5, 1, 6, 1, . . .

3.  , . . .

4. 1, 2, 4, . . .

5. 1, 3, 5, 7, 5, 3, 1, 3, . . .

6. 1, 3, 7, 15, 31, . . .

7. Make up a picture sequence of your own. Describe it by giving the first few terms and telling how you would find more terms.

8. Make up a number sequence of your own. Describe it by giving the first few terms and telling how you would find more terms.

The Standard POW Write-up

About Problems of the Week

Problems of the Week (POWs) are an important part of the Interactive Mathematics Program. They will give you experience in carrying out extended investigations of complex problems.

These problems will not necessarily be connected to the rest of the unit.

Despite the name, you will sometimes have more than one week to work on a POW. But you should begin work on these problems as soon as you get them, since they take more time than an ordinary homework assignment. You will benefit from working a little bit every night on these problems, leaving them for a while and then coming back to them.

Problems of the Week give you a chance to work on your mathematical writing. You will be expected to explain your thinking more fully in these assignments than in regular class activities or homework. Be sure to leave ample time for this writing.

Most Problems of the Week are accompanied by "write-up" directions, often using the categories listed below. If a given Problem of the Week just lists a category by name, you should refer to the descriptions below to learn what type of write-up is expected for that category.

Some POW write-ups introduce other categories or give more specific information about a particular category, in order to make the write-up suit the particular problem.

Continued on next page

The Standard POW Write-up Categories

1. *Problem Statement:* State the problem clearly in your own words. Your problem statement should be clear enough that someone unfamiliar with the problem could understand what it is that you are being asked to do.

2. *Process:* Describe what you did in attempting to solve the problem, using your notes as a reminder. Include things that didn't work out or that seemed like a waste of time. Do this part of the write-up even if you didn't solve the problem.

   If you get assistance of any kind on the problem, you should indicate what the assistance was and how it helped you.

3. *Solution:* State your solution as clearly as you can. Explain how you know that your solution is correct and complete. (If you obtained only a partial solution, give that. If you were able to generalize the problem, include your general results.)

   Your explanation should be written in a way that will be convincing to someone else—even someone who initially disagrees with your answer.

4. *Extensions:* Invent some extensions or variations to the problem. That is, write down some related problems. They can be easier, harder, or about the same level of difficulty as the original problem. (You don't have to solve these additional problems.)

5. *Evaluation:* Discuss your personal reaction to the problem. For example, you might respond to the questions below.

   • Did you consider it educationally worthwhile? What did you learn from it?

   • How would you change the problem to make it better?

   • Did you enjoy working on it?

   • Was it too hard or too easy?

POW 1   *The Broken Eggs*

The Situation

A farmer is taking her eggs to market in her cart, but she hits a pothole, which knocks over all the containers of eggs.

Though she herself is unhurt, every egg is broken.

So she goes to her insurance agent, who asks her how many eggs she had. She says she doesn't know, but she remembers some things from various ways she tried packing the eggs.

She knows that when she put the eggs in groups of two, there was one egg left over. When she put them in groups of three, there was also one egg left over. The same thing happened when she put them in groups of four, groups of five, or groups of six.

But when she put them in groups of seven, she ended up with complete groups of seven with no eggs left over.

Your Task

Your task is to answer the insurance agent's question. In other words,

What can the farmer figure out from this information about how many eggs she had?

Is there more than one possibility?

Write-up

1. *Problem Statement*
2. *Process*
3. *Solution*
4. *Evaluation*

Homework 4   POW Beginnings

1. Write the *problem statement* portion of your write-up for
   POW 1: The Broken Eggs.

2. Some students think at first that the answer is 49. Explain why
   this is not correct.

Days 5–9

From Numbers to Functions

In your education in previous years, "mathematics" may have meant mostly arithmetic. By contrast, in the first few days of *Patterns* you haven't been asked to do much of that.

Joe Gonzales presents his results about an In-Out table.

In *Homework 3: Describing Patterns,* you had to look at some sequences of numbers and make sense of them. As you work on *POW 1: The Broken Eggs,* you will have to think about how numbers behave, rather than just do computations. These problems reflect the perspective that mathematics is not just number-crunching, even when it is about numbers.

Now the unit introduces a powerful tool—the **In-Out table**—for organizing and analyzing numerical information. The In-Out table is a useful way to work with the concept of **function,** which is one of the most important ideas in all of mathematics.

Homework 5   Inside Out

1. Supply the missing entries in the following In-Out tables.

    Then write a rule for each table that tells what to do with the *In* to get the *Out.*

    Express each rule as a complete sentence, such as "The *Out* is one more than four times the *In*." Be as clear as you can.

a.

In	Out
2	4
3	6
11	22
27	?
?	18

b.

In	Out
2	7
4	13
7	22
10	31
12	?
?	76

c.

In	Out
house	4
cup	2
writer	5
elephant	7
spin	?
mathematics	?
?	3
?	8
?	0

d.

In	Out
	3
	11
	15
?	7

e.

In	Out
division	I
ever	E
opportunity	O
toast	A
safe	E
people	O
mathematics	?
?	(can't be done)

Continued on next page

2. Create two In-Out tables based on rules of your own.

Use a separate sheet of paper for this. Put the two tables on one side of the paper and the two rules on the back.

Homewor 6

Gettin' On Down to One

This problem is about a certain pair of rules for generating a sequence of numbers.

You can start with any positive whole number (1, 2, 3, 4, and so on) as the first term. After that, you find each term by applying one of two rules to the current term.

The decision about which rule to apply depends on whether the current term is an odd number or an even number.

- If the current term is an odd number, the rule is

  Multiply the current term by 3 and then add 1 to get the next term in the sequence.

- If the current term is an even number, the rule is

  Divide the current term by 2 to get the next term in the sequence.

Continued on next page

For example, suppose the starting number is 7. Since this is an odd number, you use the first rule: multiply by 3 and then add 1. That gives 22, so the second term in the sequence is 22. Since 22 is even, you now use the second rule: divide by 2. That gives 11, so the third term in the sequence is 11. And so on.

Following the correct rule each time, starting with 7, you generate the sequence

$$7, 22, 11, 34, 17, 52, 26, 13, 40, 20, 10, 5, 16, 8, 4, 2, 1, 4, 2, 1, 4, 2, 1, 4, 2, 1, \ldots$$

Notice that any time this procedure gets to 1, the sequence will then go 4, 2, 1 again, over and over. So you should consider the sequence to be finished if it reaches 1.

In the case above, where you started with 7, it took 16 steps to reach 1. (The starting number itself is not counted as a step.)

1. Use the pair of rules above to generate and record sequences for each of these starting numbers.

   a. 6   b. 9   c. 21   d. 33

2. In Questions 1a through 1d, you should have found that each sequence eventually reached 1. Find out, for each case, how many steps it took to reach 1.

3. The only starting number that gets to 1 in only one step is 2, and the only starting number that gets to 1 in only two steps is 4.

   Which starting numbers will get down to 1 after only three steps? Four steps? Five steps? Explore.

4. Describe a way to find starting numbers that will produce very long sequences, such as 100 steps.

5. What other observations can you make about how this procedure works?

Marcella's Bagels

Have you ever been really in the mood to eat a bagel?

There are some pretty amazing things that can get in the way of this pursuit.

Marcella was walking home from the beach one day. She had just bought a big bag of bagels and was going to share them with her daughter Sonya. (Sonya loves bagels.)

On the side of the road she saw two people collecting food for needy families. Well, Marcella decided that she had quite a few bagels in her bag. Sonya didn't need that many bagels.

"Here," said Marcella, "you can have half of my bagels for the needy." The people were very happy to get all of those bagels.

Marcella thought for a moment and then said, "Aw, take one for each of yourselves." So there went two more.

Continued on next page

As Marcella walked along the beach, some surfers came out of the water. They saw, and even smelled, the fresh bagels she had. "Could you by any chance spare a few bagels?" they pleaded. "We are so-o-o hungry after riding all of those gnarly waves."

As you might imagine, Marcella was not thrilled. But she had a good heart and recognized hunger after physical exertion, so she handed her bag to the surfers. They took half of her bagels and then, just as they were about to hand the bag back, they took two more.

Now Marcella was a very reasonable person who liked to help others. She thought she still had enough bagels left to make Sonya happy. She walked on.

As you may already have guessed, Marcella didn't get far before she had another encounter. Just before she reached home, her friend Susan approached. After exchanging greetings, Susan explained that she was on her way to get some bagels for her family. Susan seemed to be in a bit of a rush.

Generosity overtook Marcella and she found herself saying, "Why don't you save yourself the trip and take some of my bagels? As you can see, I've got several." So Susan took half of what Marcella had in the bag and then two more.

Marcella finished her walk home without further interruption. When she opened her once bulging bag of bagels, she discovered that there were only two left! She had a bagel lunch with her daughter Sonya, and then there were none!

After lunch, Sonya asked her mother how many bagels had been in the bag to begin with. Marcella told her the story of her walk and then said that if Sonya could figure it out herself, Marcella would take her rollerblading in the park the next day.

Sonya took awhile, but she figured it out and got her rollerblading outing.

What was Sonya's answer?

Homework 7   Extended Bagels

The *extensions* section of the POW write-up is often an important part of your written report. This section gives you the opportunity to examine what the critical elements of the problem are and how they could be changed.

In this assignment, you will work on an extension to the *Marcella's Bagels* problem. Your work should give you some ideas about how an In-Out table can be used to gain insight into a problem situation.

Here's the extension for you to work on.

> *How does the solution to Marcella's Bagels depend on the number of bagels she has when she gets home?*

In order to explore this extension, try different values for the number she has when she gets home, like 3, 4, 5, or even 0. You should assume that everything in the problem is the same as in the original problem except for this number.

Make an In-Out table of your results. That is, make a table in which the *In* is the number of bagels she has when she gets home and the *Out* is the number she must have started with. (You already know that the *Out* is 44 for the case where the *In* is 2.)

Once you have several entries for this table, look for a relationship between the *Out* and the *In*, and then try to find a rule to describe this relationship. You may find it helpful to look for a pattern within the *Out* column.

Lonesome Llama

In the land where llamas run free, llamas live in fancy houses decorated with wonderful shapes.

Most llamas live in houses that look just like the house of at least one other llama. Llamas who live in identical houses tend to play together.

But one llama has a house different from all the rest. So sometimes this llama is left all alone.

If you can help find the lonesome llama, perhaps you can introduce that llama to others.

The Cards

A set of cards will be distributed among your group members, face down. Each card in the set has a picture of a llama's house.

One card in the set is a **singleton;** that is, there is no other card with a house exactly like it.

Every card other than this singleton has at least one duplicate.

The Task

Your task *as a group* is to discover the singleton card of the lonesome llama's house.

When your group indicates that they have located the lonesome llama, the task is ended, whether or not you are correct. Therefore, be sure *everyone* is confident of your answer before you declare that you are done.

The Rules

1. You may not show any of your cards to another member.

2. You may not pass cards to another member.

3. You may not look at another member's cards.

4. You may not draw pictures or diagrams of the designs on the houses.

5. You may not put cards in a common pile.

Aside from these rules, you may work in any way you choose.

Homework 8   Group Reflection

As you can tell from the activity *Lonesome Llama*, people play many roles when they work in groups. Of course, this is true not only in math classes.

This assignment is an opportunity for you to reflect upon the way you participate in groups. Be as thoughtful as possible when you answer these questions because they are designed to help you.

This homework will not be shared with other students unless you wish it to be.

1. a. Try to remember a time when you or someone in a group you were in was left out of a discussion. Describe the situation. Did anyone try to include that person? If not, why not? If yes, then how?

   b. What might you have done to help with the situation?

2. a. What has been your experience when someone has made a mistake in your group?

   b. How do you think groups should handle mistakes by group members?

3. a. Try to remember a time when you thought of saying something, or you did not understand something, but were afraid to speak out. Describe the situation, what you wanted to say, and why you did not say it.

   b. How do you wish you had handled the situation?

4. Do you participate more or less than other group members? Why do you think you do so?

5. Discuss how the amount of homework preparation you do for class affects your participation in group discussions.

Homework 9   Uncertain Answers

By convention, mathematical expressions are simplified according to this sequence.

1. Parentheses

2. Exponents

3. Multiplication and division (left to right)

4. Addition and subtraction (left to right)

1. **Fix these equations!**

   None of the statements below is correct as written. Rewrite them, inserting parentheses so that the resulting statements are correct equations.

   a. $12 - 8 \cdot 1 + 7 = 32$

   b. $8 - 15 + 6 \div 3 = 1$

   c. $7 + 3^2 = 100$

   d. $24 + 16 \div 8 - 4 = 10$

   e. $20 \div 7 - 2 + 5^2 \cdot 3 = 79$

2. **What could it be?**

   Place parentheses in different places in the expressions below to see how many different values you can make for each expression. Find at least three different values for each problem.

   a. $7 - 5 \cdot 8 + 6 \div 2$

   b. $4 + 9 - 6 \div 2 \cdot 5 + 1$

POW 2

1-2-3-4 Puzzle

You've seen that you can change the meaning of an arithmetic expression by inserting or removing parentheses. Of course, another way to change the meaning of an expression is to rearrange its terms.

This problem is about using the digits 1, 2, 3, and 4, in any order you choose, to create arithmetic expressions with different numerical values according to the rules for order of operations.

Continued on next page

For this problem, a 1-2-3-4 expression is any expression written using each of these digits *exactly once,* according to the following rules.

- You may use any of the four basic arithmetic operations—addition, subtraction, multiplication, and division (according to the order-of-operations rules). For example, $2 + 1 \cdot 3 - 4$ is a 1-2-3-4 expression for the number 1 (since $2 + 1 \cdot 3 - 4 = 1$).

- You may use exponents. For example, $2^3 - 4 - 1$ is a 1-2-3-4 expression for the number 3.

- You may use radicals. For example, $\sqrt{4 \cdot 2 + 1}$ is equal to 3, so $3 + \sqrt{4 \cdot 2 + 1}$ is a 1-2-3-4 expression for the number 6.

- You may use factorials. For example, 4! means $4 \cdot 3 \cdot 2 \cdot 1$, so $3 + 4! + 1 - 2$ is a 1-2-3-4 expression for the number 26.

- You may juxtapose two or more digits (that is, put them next to each other) to form a number such as 12. For example, $43 - 12$ is a 1-2-3-4 expression for the number 31.

- You may use parentheses and brackets to change the meaning of an expression. For example, according to the rules for order of operations, $1 + 4 \cdot 3^2$ is a 1-2-3-4 expression for the number 37. You can add parentheses and brackets to get $[(1 + 4) \cdot 3]^2$, which is a 1-2-3-4 expression for the number 225.

Your task in this problem is to create as many 1-2-3-4 expressions as you can for each of the numbers from 1 to 25. *Remember:* In every case, the expression must use each of the digits 1, 2, 3, and 4 *exactly once.*

Write-up

1. *Problem Statement*

2. *Process:* Describe how you went about solving the problem. Which numbers did you find first? Did you find any patterns that helped you? What did you do when you got stuck?

3. *Solution:* List the numbers from 1 to 25, giving at least one 1-2-3-4 expression for each. If you got more than one expression for a given number, show as many as you found.

4. *Extensions:* Come up with some variations on this problem.

5. *Evaluation*

Investigating Sums

Some problems have a simple answer. Others have several answers. Some seem never to be finished.

Over the next several days, you will be working on a problem called *Consecutive Sums.* You and your group will

Rebekah Turner presents her group's findings from "Consecutive Sums."

probably not be able to learn all there is to know about consecutive sums in just a few days, but you can look at many specific examples, and you will probably see some general principles. As you grow mathematically, you may want to come back to this problem to see what new insights you can find.

This activity will also give you and your group a chance to apply what you learned in *Lonesome Llama* about working together.

Consecutive Sums

A sequence of two or more whole numbers is **consecutive** if each number is one more than the previous number.

For example, the numbers 2, 3, and 4 are consecutive; the numbers 8, 9, 10, and 11 are consecutive; and the numbers 23 and 24 are consecutive.

On the other hand, the numbers 6, 8, 10 are not consecutive, because each number is *two* more than the previous number. A single number by itself is not considered consecutive.

Continued on next page

A **consecutive sum** is a sum of a sequence of consecutive numbers. So each expression below is a consecutive sum.

$$2 + 3 + 4$$

$$8 + 9 + 10 + 11$$

$$23 + 24$$

These examples illustrate how to express 9, 38, and 47 as consecutive sums.

For this activity, you should consider only consecutive sums involving *positive whole numbers* (1, 2, 3, 4, and so on). These are also called the **natural numbers** or **counting numbers.**

Your task

> *Explore the idea of consecutive sums. Try to find patterns and make generalizations.*

Suggestion: Start by looking at specific cases. For instance, you might work with the numbers from 1 to 35, and try to find all the ways to write each of these as a consecutive sum. Are there numbers for which this is easy to do? Are there any that are impossible?

Note: This is a group activity. Find ways for the members of your group to work together.

Your group should produce a display of some sort on a large sheet of paper. It should show your results and include summary statements of the patterns you observed. Your group will also present some of its discoveries to the class.

Include *conjectures* (general patterns that you think *might* be true) as well as patterns that you are *certain* are true. Include any explanations you find for why your patterns are true.

Also, if you made a conjecture and later discovered that it was false, include both the original conjecture and the evidence that later convinced you that the conjecture was false.

Homework 10   Pulling Out Rules

1. Write a rule for each of the following In-Out tables.

   Express each rule as a complete sentence, describing what to do with the *In* in order to get the *Out*. Be as clear as you can.

   a.
In	Out
10	23
5	13
1	5
0	3

   b.
In	Out
1	3
3	17
10	66
6	38

   c.
In	Out
3	17
8	12
15	5
0	20

2. The next two In-Out tables don't provide very much information. In fact, there are many different rules that would fit the single pair of numbers in each table.

   Find five rules for each of these In-Out tables. As in Question 1, express each rule as a complete sentence.

   a.
In	Out
10	30

   b.
In	Out
5	25

3. Read the following problem.

   The supervisor of a community garden project organizes volunteers to help dig out weeds. The supervisor has found that the more people they have, the more weeds get pulled. That's not surprising, but the results are even better than one might think. Although one person will pull only about two bags a day, two people will pull about five bags a day, and three people will pull about eight bags a day.

Continued on next page

It is the beginning of spring, and the garden must be cleared of a huge amount of winter weeds. The supervisor estimates that there are about 30 bags' worth of weeds to be pulled. How many volunteers would the supervisor need in order to get the job done in a day?

a. Make an In-Out table showing the information provided in the problem, using *number of people* as the *In* and *number of bags of weeds pulled* as the *Out*.

b. Use this In-Out table to solve the problem and explain your reasoning.

Homework 11   Add It Up

Summation notation can be useful when working with sums of numbers, such as consecutive sums.

For instance, we can express the consecutive sum $3 + 4 + 5 + 6 + 7$ as

$$\sum_{r=3}^{7} r$$

This expression is read, "The summation, from r equals 3 to 7, of r." The symbol Σ is an uppercase letter in the Greek alphabet, called *sigma*.

Similarly, the expression

$$\sum_{i=2}^{6} i$$

means $2 + 3 + 4 + 5 + 6$. (This could also be written as

$$\sum_{n=2}^{6} n$$

It doesn't matter what letter is used.)

Continued on next page

This **sigma notation** can also be used for sums more complex than sums of consecutive numbers. For example,

$$\sum_{t=5}^{8} (4t^2 + 3)$$

represents the expression

$$(4 \cdot 5^2 + 3) + (4 \cdot 6^2 + 3) + (4 \cdot 7^2 + 3) + (4 \cdot 8^2 + 3)$$

In an expression such as

$$\sum_{t=5}^{8} (4t^2 + 3)$$

the number 5 is called the **lower limit,** the number 8 is called the **upper limit,** and the expression $4t^2 + 3$ is called the **summand.**

1. Write out each of these summation problems as a string of numbers added together.

   a. $\displaystyle\sum_{z=3}^{8} z$

   b. $\displaystyle\sum_{m=1}^{5} 2m$

   c. $\displaystyle\sum_{c=2}^{9} (4c + 7)$

2. Use summation notation to describe the number of squares in the picture.

Continued on next page

3. Use summation notation to express each of these sums.

   a. 10 + 11 + 12 + 13 + 14 + 15

   b. 3 + 6 + 9 + 12 + 15 + 18 + 21

   c. 8 + 11 + 14 + 17 + 20

4. Use summation notation to describe the total number of small squares in the picture.

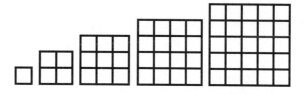

Homework 12

That's Odd!

A student who worked on the consecutive sum problem made the following conjecture, based on many examples:

> *Any odd number greater than 1 can be written as the sum of two consecutive numbers.*

If you think that this statement is false, your task is to find a counterexample. That is, find an odd number greater than 1 that *cannot* be written as the sum of two consecutive numbers.

If you think that the statement is true, your task is to create a set of general instructions for writing an odd number greater than 1 as the sum of two consecutive numbers. Your instructions should work for *any* odd number greater than 1.

Important: Remember that in *Consecutive Sums,* you are working only with *positive* whole numbers.

Days 13-14

Both Positive and Negative

You've probably heard about negative numbers before. You may even have learned some tricks or rules for how to work with them.

The Chef's Hot and Cold Cubes introduces you to an amusing new way to think about positive and negative numbers. Say goodbye to rules and start "cooking" with the integers.

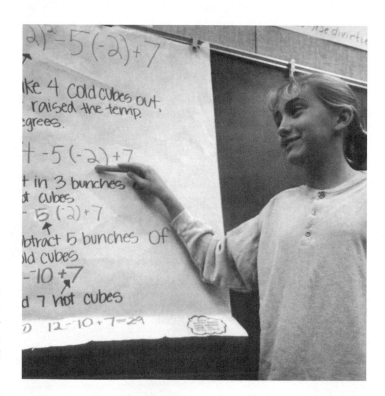

Tenley McGurk describes her group's explanation for computing with positive and negative numbers.

The Chef's Hot and Cold Cubes

You may have learned some rules for doing arithmetic with positive and negative numbers. Many people find these rules hard to remember and don't understand where the rules come from.

The following mythical story provides a context for understanding how positive and negative numbers work. Many people find it easy to remember the story many years after they first heard it, and the memory of the

Continued on next page

story enables them to reconstruct the rules. The story also helps some people make sense of the rules.

The Story

In a far-off place, there was once a team of amazing chefs who cooked up the most marvelous food ever imagined.

They prepared their meals over a huge cauldron, and their work was very delicate and complex. During the cooking process, they frequently had to change the temperature of the cauldron in order to bring out the flavors and cook the food to perfection.

They adjusted the temperature of the cooking either by adding special hot cubes or cold cubes to the cauldron or by removing some of the hot or cold cubes that were already in the cauldron.

The cold cubes were similar to ice cubes except they didn't melt, and the hot cubes were similar to charcoal briquettes, except they didn't lose their heat.

If the number of cold cubes in the cauldron was the same as the number of hot cubes, the temperature of the cauldron was 0° on their temperature scale.

For each hot cube that was put into the cauldron, the temperature went up one degree; for each hot cube removed, the temperature went down one degree. Similarly, each cold cube put in lowered the temperature one degree and each cold cube removed raised it one degree.

The chefs used positive and negative numbers to keep track of the changes they were making to the temperature.

For example, suppose 4 hot cubes and 10 cold cubes were dumped into the cauldron. Then the temperature would be lowered by 6° altogether, since 4 of the 10 cold cubes would balance out the 4 hot cubes, leaving 6 cold cubes to lower the temperature 6°. They would write

$$^+4 + {}^-10 = {}^-6$$

to represent these actions and their overall result.

Similarly, if they added 3 hot cubes and then removed 2 cold cubes, the combined result would be to raise the temperature 5°. In that case, they would write

$$^+3 - {}^-2 = {}^+5$$

And if they wrote $^-5 - {}^+6 = {}^-11$, it would mean that first 5 cold cubes were added and then 6 hot cubes were removed, and that the combined result was to lower the temperature 11°.

Continued on next page

Sometimes they wanted to raise or lower the temperature by a large amount, but did not want to put the cubes into the cauldron one at a time. So for large jumps in temperature, they would put in or take out bunches of cubes.

For instance, if the chefs wanted to raise the temperature 100°, then they might toss five bunches of 20 hot cubes each into the cauldron instead of 100 cubes one at a time. This saved a lot of time because they could have assistant chefs do the bunching.

When the chefs used bunches of cubes to change the temperature, they used a multiplication sign to record their activity. For example, to describe tossing five bunches of 20 hot cubes each into the cauldron, they would write

$$^+5 \cdot {}^+20 = {}^+100$$

where the $^+5$ meant that five bunches were being added, and the $^+20$ showed that there were twenty hot cubes in each bunch.

The chefs could also change the temperature by removing bunches. For example, if they removed three bunches of 5 hot cubes each, the result was to lower the temperature 15°, because each time a bunch of 5 hot cubes was removed, the temperature went down 5 degrees. To record this change, they would write

$$^-3 \cdot {}^+5 = {}^-15$$

where the $^-3$ meant that three bunches were being removed, and the $^+5$ showed that there were five hot cubes in each bunch.

1. Each of the problems below describes an action by the chefs. Figure out how the temperature would change overall in each of these situations and write an equation to describe the action and the overall result.

   a. Three cold cubes were added and 5 hot cubes were added.

   b. Five hot cubes were added and 4 cold cubes were removed.

   c. Two bunches of 6 cold cubes each were added.

   d. Four bunches of 7 hot cubes each were removed.

   e. Three bunches of 6 cold cubes each were removed.

2. Describe the action involving hot or cold cubes that is represented by each of the following arithmetic expressions and state how the temperature would change overall.

   a. $^+4 - {}^-3$

   b. $^-6 + {}^-4$

   c. $^-10 \cdot {}^-5$

   d. $^+4 \cdot {}^-8$

Homework 13   Do It the Chef's Way

Explain each problem in terms of the model of hot and cold cubes.

Your explanation should describe the action and state how the temperature changes overall in each case.

1. $^-6 + ^-9$

2. $^-7 - ^-10$

3. $^+5 \cdot ^-2$

4. $^-4 - ^+6$

5. $^+3 + ^-7$

6. $^-6 \cdot ^+9$

7. $^-3 \cdot ^-4$

8. $^+8 - ^-12$

9. $^-12 + ^+5$

Homework 14   You're the Chef

After a lengthy term as "Number One Chef in the World," you have decided to step down and retire to the warmer climates of the Lazy Chef Sunset Ranch. It has been a memorable time, but one with many responsibilities.

Though it was fun to be a master chef, any drastic miscalculation of the temperature could have caused catastrophic results.

Your final responsibility before retirement is to train an assistant chef to take your place. Assistant chefs spend most of their time helping children with their homework, so they know very little about changing the temperature in the cauldron. But they do know how to do arithmetic with whole numbers.

Prepare a manual for the assistant chef who will be taking your place. Be sure to include specific examples of all the different ways to raise and lower the temperature.

Days 15–19

An Angle on Patterns

Mathematics is not just about numbers. People long ago invented geometry to understand the physical space around them. (The word "geometry" comes from the Greek root words that mean "measuring the earth.")

A group of students uses pattern blocks to measure angles.

In the next few days of the unit, you'll explore angles and polygons, which are important building blocks of the geometric world. And speaking of blocks, you'll get to work with some objects called pattern blocks to help strengthen your understanding of the ideas.

You'll continue to work with In-Out tables and see how they can help you with the numerical aspects of geometry. You'll also continue the work with proof that you began in *Homework 2: Who's Who* and *Homework 12: That's Odd!*

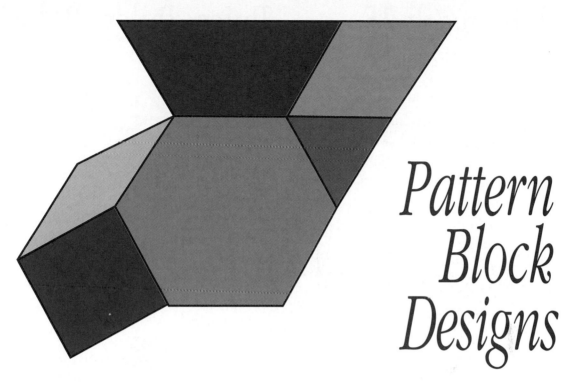

Pattern Block Designs

Your group should have access to at least a half tub's worth of pattern blocks.

1. Work together as a group to create a single group design from your blocks. You don't need to use every kind of block in your design, and you may use many of a single kind of block.

2. Explore different ways to fit several pattern blocks together so they come together at a single point. Can you do this using blocks that are all the same shape? If so, which shapes can you do this with?

Homework 15   Rules, Rules, Rules

1. There are many rules that fit the information in the In-Out table at the right.

Your task is to find at least ten different rules that work. You can use multiplication, division, addition, subtraction, and exponents, and you can use more than one operation in a single rule.

In	Out
5	16

2. The table at the right gives a bit more information than the one above, but that just makes things harder.

Find as many rules as you can that fit both rows of this table.

In	Out
1	2
2	5

Interactive Mathematics Program

POW 3 *Checkerboard Squares*

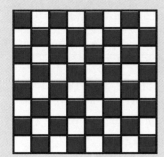

The picture at the left shows a standard 8-by-8 checkerboard, made up of 64 small squares.

But there are many other squares of various sizes within the checkerboard.

For example, the diagram at the right shows a 3-by-3 square outlined within the larger checkerboard. (This is just one of many 3-by-3 squares.)

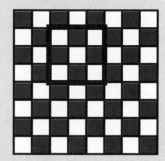

The first question of this POW is this:

1. How many squares are there altogether on the checkerboard?

When you are confident that you have counted all the squares of various sizes on the 8-by-8 checkerboard, move on to the generalization.

2. Suppose you have a square checkerboard of some other size—not 8-by-8. How can you determine how many squares are on it altogether?

You will know you are done with this problem when you feel confident that, no matter what size checkerboard you are given, you can quickly and easily compute the total number of squares.

Write-up

1. *Problem Statement*

2. *Process:* Be sure to describe any diagrams or materials you used.

3. *Solution:* Explain your answer in the case of the 8-by-8 checkerboard in complete detail. Also give results, with explanations, on any other specific checkerboard sizes you studied. Be sure to include your reasoning in discussing any generalizations you found.

4. *Extensions*

5. *Evaluation*

Pattern Block Angles

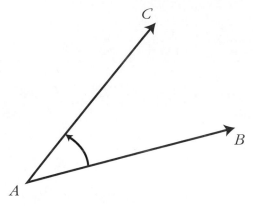

You have seen that you can think of an angle as "an amount of turn."

You can express the size of an angle as a fraction of a complete turn. For example, if you are facing north and turn to face west, you have made a quarter turn. A turn of this amount is called a **right angle.**

You can also measure angles in terms of **degrees,** where a complete turn is defined to be 360 degrees (written 360°) and so one degree is $\frac{1}{360}$ of a complete turn. Since a right angle is one fourth of a complete turn, it is measured as 90°.

An angle between 0° and 90° is called an **acute angle,** and an angle between 90° and 180° is called an **obtuse angle.**

Mathematicians formally define an angle to be a figure formed by two rays with a common initial point, such as ∠BAC shown above.

To measure such an angle, you can imagine that you are standing at the vertex *A,* facing toward *B.* You want to know how much you would need to turn in order to face toward *C.*

The angles of a polygon are simply the angles formed at each vertex by two of the polygon's sides.

The Task

Use the fact that a complete turn is 360° to find the size (in degrees) for each of the angles of each of the six different pattern blocks. Use the blocks themselves to explain your reasoning.

Homework 16   Another In-Outer

Find the missing items in each of the following In-Out machines.

In Questions 1, 4, and 5, give a description in words for how to find the *Out* from the *In*.
In Questions 2, 3, and 6, give an algebraic expression for the *Out* as a function of the *In*.

1.

In	Out
●	LBC
○	SWC
■	LBS
△	SWT
☐	?
?	LWT

2.

In	Out
2	–6
5	–15
0	0
13	?
–7	?
?	–30
?	35

3.

In	Out
1	5
3	11
7	23
10	32
–2	–4
–5	?
?	2
?	–19

4.

In	Out
Ruth	U
Johnny	I
Carol	S
Anne	O
Aaron	S
Robert	?

Continued on next page

5.

In	Out
	6
	11
	19
	?

6.

In	Out
1	–2
4	–11
–5	16
0	1
3	?
–2	?
?	10

A Protracted Engagement

Deon and Marsha thought of an interesting way to announce their long-awaited wedding.

They decided to send the invitations out in code. In the code they decided on, each letter is represented by an angle of a certain size.

An angle between 0° and 5° represents the letter *A*, an angle between 5° and 10° represents *B*, an angle between 10° and 15° represents *C*, and so on.

To avoid confusion, they never used angles that were exact multiples of 5°. The design below spells out part of their invitation.

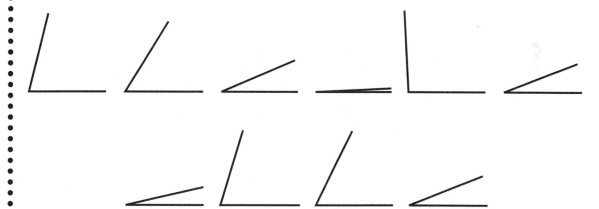

1. What does this message say?

2. Make up a message of your own that is between 10 and 20 letters long. You and other students can exchange and decipher each other's messages.

Homework 17   Diagonally Speaking

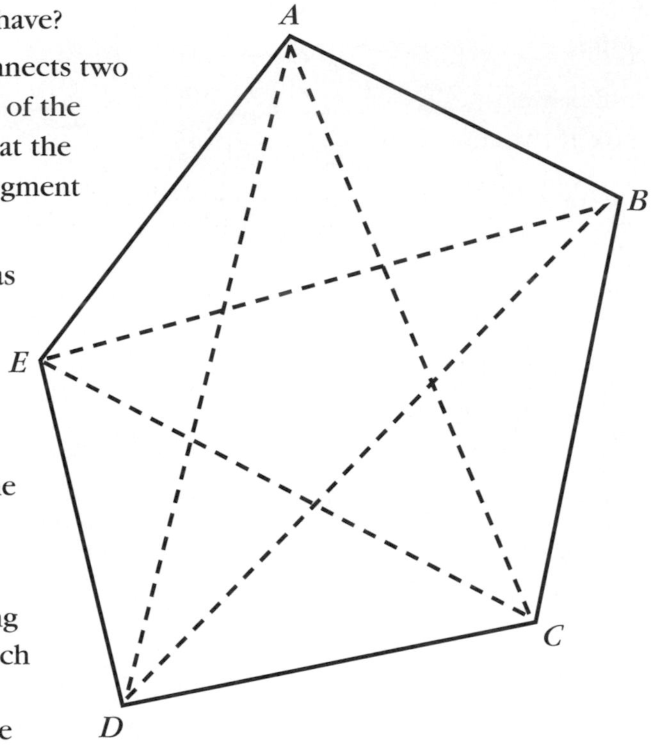

How many diagonals does a polygon have?

A **diagonal** is a line segment that connects two vertices of a polygon but is not a side of the polygon. For example, in the diagram at the right, segment *AC* is a diagonal and segment *CD* is a side of the polygon.

The diagram shows all the diagonals as dotted lines, and this polygon has five diagonals.

As you might expect, the number of diagonals in a polygon depends on the number of sides it has (which is the same as the number of vertices it has).

1. Experiment by drawing various polygons and finding out how many diagonals each has. Organize the results in an In-Out table in which the *In* is the number of sides of the polygon and the *Out* is the number of diagonals.

2. a. Look for a pattern for your In-Out table.

   b. Once you have found a pattern, use it to figure out how many diagonals a 12-sided polygon has. Try to confirm your result by actually counting the diagonals.

3. Think about *why* your pattern holds. That is, why should the number of diagonals in a polygon follow this pattern? Write down any explanations you come up with.

Degree Discovery

In the activity *Pattern Block Angles*, you found the angles of some very special polygons.

In this activity, you will use protractors to explore more general polygons and also to look at the sum of the angles.

1. Begin with triangles. Use a ruler or straightedge to draw a variety of triangles, and measure the angles for each triangle. Then find the sum of the angles for each of your triangles.

    What conclusion do your results suggest? Does this conclusion hold for the angles you found for the triangle pattern block?

2. Now do the same for quadrilaterals. Does your conclusion hold for the angles you found for the various quadrilateral pattern blocks?

Homework 18   Polygon Angles

In *Degree Discovery,* you measured the angles of various triangles and quadrilaterals. In each case, you found the sum of the angles and looked for a general conclusion.

Now experiment with polygons with more than four sides, measuring the angles and finding their sum.

What do you notice? What generalizations or conjectures can you come up with? Can you find an expression for the sum of the angles of a polygon as a function of the number of its sides?

Give your results, and explain why you think they are true.

A Proof Gone Bad

Jerry thought he had it all figured out. He was supposed to be writing a proof to show that the sum of the angles of a quadrilateral is 360°, based on the assumption that the sum for any triangle is 180°.

But when he looked over his work, it seemed to show that the sum for a quadrilateral is 720°.

Here's the proof he wrote.

Take any quadrilateral, such as the figure shown at the right (formed by the solid lines).

Then draw its diagonals (shown as dotted lines).

As you can see, this breaks the quadrilateral into four small triangles. We are assuming that the angles of each triangle add up to 180°, so the sum of the angles of the quadrilateral is 4 · 180°, which is 720°. Since this can be done with any quadrilateral, it must be true that the sum of the angles of any quadrilateral is 720°.

1. Explain what went wrong with Jerry's proof.

2. Write a correct proof based on Jerry's diagram.

Homework 19   An Angular Summary

Through your work on *Homework 18: Polygon Angles* and the discussion of that assignment, you have seen a formula that gives the sum of the angles of a polygon in terms of the number of sides it has.

1. Summarize what you know about the sum of the angles of a polygon, and explain the reasoning behind any formulas you include.

2. A **regular polygon** is a polygon that has all of its angles equal and all of its sides equal.

   a. Use the formula about angle sums to find the size of each of the angles for the following regular polygons. Explain your reasoning.

      i. A regular pentagon (five sides)

      ii. A regular octagon (eight sides)

   b. Draw each of the polygons in Question 2a, using a protractor to get the angles to be the right size. (You can decide on the lengths for the sides in each case. The sides of your pentagon do not need to have the same length as the sides of your octagon.)

Days
20-24

Putting It Together

In the last few days of *Patterns,* you'll be applying some of the ideas you've learned to problems that involve both numbers and geometry. These problems will give you a chance to see more ways to use In-Out tables, and you'll also learn how to make your graphing calculator act like an In-Out machine.

Laura Harr writes a program to make her graphing calculator act like an In-Out machine.

You'll finish the unit by putting together a portfolio of your work. An important part of your portfolio will be a "cover letter" in which you summarize the important themes of the unit.

Homework 20   Squares and Scoops

1. Suppose some squares are stacked in piles of different heights as shown in the pictures below. The In-Out table gives the number of squares for stacks of each height shown.

 a "1-high" stack   a "2-high" stack

 a "3-high" stack   a "4-high" stack

Height of the stack	Number of squares
1	1
2	3
3	6
4	10

a. Use diagrams or a continuation of the table (or both) to find the number of squares in the stacks below.
   i. A "7-high" stack
   ii. A "10-high" stack
   iii. A "40-high" stack

b. Give a general description for how to find the number of squares in an "n-high" stack.

2. Suppose you have some scoops of ice cream, and each scoop is a different flavor. How many different ways can you arrange the scoops in a stack?

One scoop —one way

The pictures show the cases of one scoop and two scoops, and the table below gives other values as well.

a. Show why the *Out* for three scoops is equal to 6.

Two scoops — two ways

b. Find a numerical pattern for the entries given in the table, and use that pattern to find the number of ways to arrange the scoops for each of the cases below.
   i. Seven scoops
   ii. Ten scoops

c. Describe how you would find the number of ways to arrange the scoops if there were 100 scoops. (You should *not* try to find this number. Just describe *how* you would find it.)

Number of scoops	Ways to arrange
1	1
2	2
3	6
4	24
5	120

Homework 21   The Garden Border

Leslie was planning an ornamental garden.

She wanted the garden to be square, 10 feet on each side, and she wanted part of this area to be used for a border of tiles. The tiles she wanted were each 1 foot by 1 foot square.

Leslie had to figure out how many tiles she needed.

Your challenge is to figure out how many tiles Leslie needed without counting the tiles individually. Write down as many ways as you can for doing this, giving the specific arithmetic involved in detail.

For each method that you find, draw a diagram that indicates how that method works.

Homework 22 Border Varieties

Leslie decided it would be nice to have a general formula for her border problem, giving the number of tiles needed as a function of the size of the garden.

She imagined a square garden which was s feet on each side, and continued to work with square tiles that were 1 foot on each side.

She asked for some help from students who had worked on the border problem for the 10-by-10 square. Since they had solved it in different ways, they also came up with different formulas for the general problem.

$$
\begin{array}{r}
10 \\
\times\, 4 \\
\hline
40 \\
-\, 4 \\
\hline
36
\end{array}
$$

For example, one student had counted ten tiles along each edge, and then subtracted 4 because the corner tiles had each been counted twice. In other words, this student's arithmetic looked like that shown at the right.

The student used the diagram at the right to explain this arithmetic and came up with the formula $4s - 4$ for the general border problem.

Continued on next page

1. Shown below is the arithmetic used by five other students in the 10-by-10 case, along with a diagram that each student used to explain the arithmetic.

   For each of these methods, find a general formula that fits that student's way of thinking about the problem. Your formula should use *s* to represent the length of one side of the garden. Make your formula match the arithmetic as closely as possible.

a.
$$
\begin{array}{r} 10 \\ +10 \\ \hline 20 \end{array}
\qquad
\begin{array}{r} 8 \\ +8 \\ \hline 16 \end{array}
$$
$$
\begin{array}{r} 20 \\ +16 \\ \hline 36 \end{array}
$$

b.
$$
\begin{array}{r} 10 \\ 9 \\ 9 \\ +8 \\ \hline 36 \end{array}
$$

c.
$$
\begin{array}{r} 8 \\ \times 4 \\ \hline 32 \end{array}
$$
$$
\begin{array}{r} +4 \\ \hline 36 \end{array}
$$

d.
$$
\begin{array}{r} 100 \\ -64 \\ \hline 36 \end{array}
$$

e.
$$
\begin{array}{r} 9 \\ \times 4 \\ \hline 36 \end{array}
$$

2. Give the arithmetic, a diagram, and a general formula for another method of solving the border problem.

Stump Your Friend

The first part of your work in this activity is to write a program for the calculator to make it act like an In-Out machine.

After you have written your program (and tested it to be sure it works properly), trade calculators with someone else. Then each of you should attempt to find the rule that the other person programmed.

That is, each of you will run the other's program, making an In-Out table and looking for the rule. (You are on your honor not to look at the program itself—that's cheating.)

When you and the person you traded with think you have found each other's rules, check with each other to see if you are right.

Then get you calculator back and trade with someone else. Continue as long as time allows.

Note: It's possible that the same rule can be written in different ways. If the rule you find is different from the rule the other person used to write the calculator program, check more examples to see if your rule always gives the same *Out* values as the program. If it does, work together to see if you can figure out why the two "different" rules are really the same.

Homework 23

Cutting Through the Layers

Imagine a single piece of string, which can be bent back and forth. In the picture at the left, the string is bent so that it has three "layers." But it is still one piece of string.

Imagine now that you take scissors and cut across the bent string, as indicated by the dotted line. The result will be four separate pieces of string, as shown at the right.

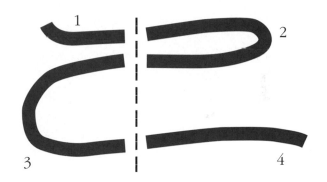

You could have made more than one cut across the bent string, creating more pieces.

In the picture at the left, two cuts have been made, creating a total of seven pieces.

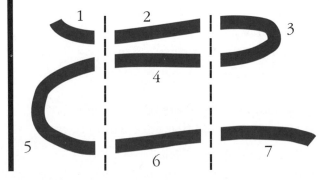

Continued on next page

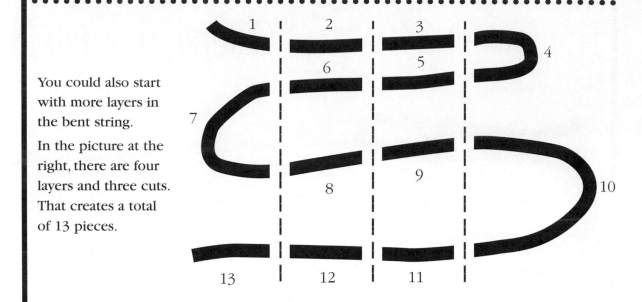

You could also start with more layers in the bent string.

In the picture at the right, there are four layers and three cuts. That creates a total of 13 pieces.

All of this information about layers, cuts, and pieces of string has been organized into the In-Out table below. Since the number of pieces depends on both the numbers of layers and the number of cuts, there are two inputs, while the number of pieces is the output.

Inputs		Output
Number of layers	Number of cuts	Number of pieces
3	0	1
3	1	4
3	2	7
4	3	13

1. Make your own pictures of string with different numbers of layers and different numbers of cuts. Count the pieces and add that information to the In-Out table.

2. Suppose the number of layers is L and the number of cuts is C. Find a rule or formula expressing the number of pieces as a function of both L and C. In other words, tell what to do with L and C to find out how many pieces there will be.

"Patterns" Portfolio

Now that *Patterns* is completed, it is time to put together your portfolio for the unit. Compiling this portfolio has three parts:

- Writing a cover letter in which you summarize the unit

- Choosing papers to include from your work in the unit

- Discussing your personal growth during the unit

Cover Letter for Patterns

Look back over *Patterns* and write a cover letter describing the central ideas of the unit. This description should include

- mathematical concepts

- ideas about what mathematics is and how mathematics is learned

- any other general themes of the unit

As part of the compilation of your portfolio, you will select activities both about In-Out tables and about angles. Your cover letter should include an explanation of why you select the particular items you do.

Selecting Papers from Patterns

Look through all of your papers for *Patterns,* and select the items described below for your portfolio.

- *Homework 1: Past Experiences*

  Include this so you can look back later and compare your experiences before this year to your experiences with the Interactive Mathematics Program.

- One or two activities on In-Out tables

  Choose activities that helped you understand what In-Out tables are and how to use them.

- *Homework 14: You're the Chef*

  You will be asked to refer to this summary of the hot-and-cold-cube model in Year 2 of the Interactive Mathematics Program.

Continued on next page

- One or two activities about angles

  Choose activities that strengthened your understanding of angles or that gave you new insight into angles and polygons.

- A Problem of the Week

  Select one of the three POWs you completed during this unit *(The Broken Eggs, 1-2-3-4 Puzzle,* or *Checkerboard Squares).* Choose a POW in which you explained your thought processes well, perhaps used several different strategies, and so on.

- Other quality work

  Select one or two other pieces of work that demonstrate your best efforts. (These can be any work from the unit, such as a Problem of the Week, homework, classwork, or presentation.)

Later you'll add the in-class and take-home assessments for *Patterns.*

Personal Growth

Your cover letter for *Patterns* describes how the unit develops. As part of your portfolio, write about your personal development during this unit. You may want to address the questions below.

✓ How do you feel you progressed

- in working together with others?

- in presenting to the class?

- in writing about and describing your thought processes?

✓ What do you feel you need to work on and how might you work on it?

You should include here any other thoughts about your experience with this unit that you want to share with a reader of your portfolio.

Appendix *Supplemental Problems*

The supplemental problems for each unit pursue some of the themes and ideas that are important in that unit.

Here are some examples from the supplemental problems for *Patterns.*

- *Whose Dog is That?* and *Infinite Proof* continue your work with proof.

- *Three in a Row* and *The General Theory of Consecutive Sums* follow up on your investigation of consecutive sums.

- *Instruct the Pro* and *From Another Angle* give you more experience measuring and thinking about angles.

Other supplemental problems for *Patterns* follow up on concepts and techniques for working with In-Out tables, integers, and calculator programming.

Whose Dog Is That?

Abigail, Bertha, Candy, Dodi, and Eudora showed up with their puppies at the Little Red School House for Dogs. During the morning break, they found that each of their pets has the same name as the husband of one of the other women.

In particular, they noticed that

- Abigail's dog is named George.

- Candy's dog is named Jerry.

- Eudora's dog is named Ike.

- Dodi's dog is named Frank.

- Abigail's husband is also named Frank.

- Bertha's husband has the same name as George's dog.

- Horace and his wife, Candy, have the best behaved dog.

Your job is to figure out the names of each woman's husband and each woman's dog.

In addition, you must explain clearly how you found your answer. If you think there is more than one possibility, give all solutions, and explain why there are no more. If you think there is only one solution, explain why there are no others.

From *Mathematics: Problem Solving Through Recreational Mathematics* by Averbach and Chein. Copyright © 1980 by W.H. Freeman and Company. Adapted with permission.

A Fractional Life

Here is a problem that is part of *The Greek Anthology*, a group of problems collected by ancient Greek mathematicians.

> Demochares has lived a fourth of his life as a boy, a fifth as a youth, a third as a man, and has spent 13 years in his dotage. How old is he?

How old is Demochares?

(*Note:* The phrase "in his dotage" refers to the period of Demochares' old age.)

Problem 6.13 from *An Introduction to the History of Mathematics,* Fifth Edition by Howard Eves, copyright © 1983 by Holt, Rinehart and Winston, Inc., reproduced by permission of the publisher.

Infinite Proof

Proof involves considering all the possible cases.

For example, in *Homework 2: Who's Who,* you saw that there is a unique solution to the problem. One way to prove this is to examine each possible combination. Since that problem has only a finite number of combinations to consider, you can consider each combination individually to see that only one of them fits the problem.

In *Homework 6: Gettin' On Down to One,* you saw that the sequences described there always seem to lead to the number 1. But no matter how many starting numbers you tried, you couldn't check them all, so your list of examples was not a proof. In fact, no one has ever proved that you "get down to 1" for every possible starting number.

This problem is about proving things about every possible case in situations where there are infinitely many cases to consider.

1. You know that there are infinitely many odd numbers. Prove that the square of *every* odd number is odd.

2. A **prime number** is a number greater than 1 whose only whole number divisors are 1 and itself. For example, 3 and 7 are both prime numbers. But 12 is not a prime number, since it has whole number divisors other than 1 and 12. For example, 4 is a divisor of 12.

Prove that *every* prime number greater than 10 must have the digit 1, 3, 7, or 9 in the ones column.

It's All Gone

A man goes into a store and says, "If you give me as much money as I have with me now, I will spend $10 in your store." The proprietor agrees, and the man spends the money.

He goes into a second store and again says, "If you give me as much money as I have with me now, I will spend $10 in your store." Again, the proprietor agrees, and the man spends the money.

In a third store, he repeats his proposition, the proprietor agrees, and the man spends the money.

At this point, the man has no money left.

How much money did this man have to begin with? Explain your answer.

More Broken Eggs

In *POW 1: The Broken Eggs,* you found a possible number of eggs that the farmer might have had when her cart was knocked over.

You may have found only one solution to that problem, but there are actually many solutions.

Your task is to look for other solutions to the problem. Find as many as you can. If possible, find and describe a pattern for getting all the solutions and explain why all solutions fit your pattern.

Here are the facts you need to know.

- When the farmer put the eggs in groups of two, there was one egg left over.

- When she put them in groups of three, there was also one egg left over. The same thing happened when she put them in groups of four, five, or six.

- When she put the eggs in groups of seven, she ended up with complete groups of seven with no eggs left over.

The Number Magician

A magician said to a volunteer from the audience, "Pick a number, but don't tell me what it is. Add 15 to it. Multiply your answer by 3. Subtract 9. Divide by 3. Subtract 8. Now tell me your answer."

"Thirty-two," replied the volunteer.

Then the magician *immediately* guessed the number that the volunteer had originally chosen.

1. What was the volunteer's number?

2. How did the magician know so quickly? (The magician couldn't possibly have worked backwards that fast.)

From *Mathematics: Problem Solving Through Recreational Mathematics* by Averbach and Chein. Copyright © 1980 by W.H. Freeman and Company. Adapted with permission.

Three in a Row

In *Homework 12: That's Odd!* you looked at the conjecture that any odd number greater than 1 can be written as a sum of two consecutive natural numbers.

In this problem, you are to examine what kinds of numbers can be written as a sum of *three* consecutive natural numbers.

1. Try to come up with a simple description of such numbers.

2. Once you come up with a conjecture on how to describe such numbers, try to prove your conjecture.

Note: Your proof might have two parts—the first showing that all numbers that fit your description *can* be written as such a sum, and the second showing that all numbers that can be written as such a sum *fit* your description.

3. Look for a generalization that holds for sums of other lengths and try to prove it. *Suggestion:* Start by looking at sums for another odd number of terms. You may want to consider consecutive sums of *integers,* and not restrict yourself to natural numbers.

Any Old Sum

This problem, like *Consecutive Sums,* is about sums of natural numbers, that is, sums of whole numbers other than zero.

But this time you aren't restricted to consecutive sums. Now your task is to look at *all* the ways various numbers can be written as a sum of natural numbers.

For example, the number 4 can be written in exactly eight ways, as shown below.

1 + 1 + 1 + 1	1 + 2 + 1
2 + 2	4
2 + 1 + 1	3 + 1
1 + 3	1 + 1 + 2

Notice that 4 by itself is counted as a way, and that 1 + 2 + 1, 2 + 1 + 1, and 1 + 1 + 2 are all counted separately.

Explore. Look for patterns. Look at ways of categorizing the different ways to write a number as a sum. Make some generalizations.

State each generalization clearly and try to explain why that generalization is always true.

Getting Involved

Imagine that you have been in the same group for about a week. During that time, everyone in your group has been doing fine except one person.

This person doesn't say a thing besides "I don't know" and won't help with presentations.

Write about

- why someone might behave that way

- what you and the group can do about it

Be specific and look for many possibilities.

Chef Divisions

Nowhere in the Chef's Manual is there any reference to hot and cold cubes and the division of negative numbers.

For example, what would the chefs mean by the expression $15 \div -3$? What might the numbers 15 or -3 in this division problem represent in terms of the hot-and-cold-cube model?

1. Explain this specific problem in terms of the model.

2. Make up some other division problems using integers and explain them using the model. Include different combinations of signs.

3. Suppose a and b were arbitrary integers. Give a general description of what an expression of the form $a \div b$ would mean. What would a tell you? What would b tell you?

1-2-3-4 Varieties

In *POW 2: 1-2-3-4 Puzzle,* you were asked to express each of the numbers from 1 to 25 as a 1-2-3-4 expression.

As you may recall, a 1-2-3-4 expression is an arithmetic expression that uses each of the digits 1, 2, 3, and 4 exactly once, according to certain rules.

Your task in this problem is to do the assignment again but with one additional rule.

• The digits 1, 2, 3, and 4 must appear in order.

For example, you can express the number 10 as 1 + 2 + 3 + 4, but not as 4 · 3 – 2 · 1 or as 3 + 2 + 1 + 4.

Are all results from 1 through 25 still possible? What is the highest result you can get?

What other problems can you make up that are variations of this POW?

The General Theory of Consecutive Sums

In the activity *Consecutive Sums,* you were restricted to positive whole numbers (1, 2, 3, 4, etc.).

But the idea of consecutive sums also makes sense for all integers. For example, "–2 + –1 + 0 + 1" is a consecutive sum for the number –2.

Your task in this activity is to investigate how your results on *Consecutive Sums* would have been different if you had been allowed to use the complete set of integers—positive, negative, and zero. (You can use the hot-and-cold-cube model to help with the arithmetic of the sums.)

In particular, you may want to look for a general rule for the number of ways in which a given integer can be expressed as a consecutive sum.

If you worked on the problem *Three in a Row,* you may find your results from that problem helpful.

Start with lots of examples. Look for patterns in your data and then think about ways in which you might explain those patterns.

Instruct the Pro

Take a clean sheet of paper and make a sketch of something made up only of line segments touching end to end, like the one at the right. (Your sketch can be more interesting than this one.)

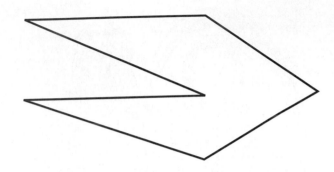

Then write instructions so that someone with a ruler and protractor could draw a diagram exactly like yours without seeing your diagram.

Suggestion: Select a point in your diagram where two segments meet, and use that point as the starting point for your instructions. You may also want to tell the person where to start on the sheet of paper. For example, you might say, "Start in the center of your page."

Diagonals Illuminated

In *Homework 17: Diagonally Speaking,* you looked at a pattern for finding the number of diagonals of a polygon.

The goal of that problem was to find a way to get the number of diagonals as a function of the number of sides of the polygon.

This activity provides two further investigations you can do to gain more insight about diagonals. The two investigations are somewhat independent of each other—you can work on one without working on the other—but your work on either problem might help you understand the remaining one.

These investigations involve some general ideas that have nothing to do with diagonals.

Continued on next page

To get a sense of these ideas, suppose you are using an In-Out table to solve the following simple problem:

A group of people are in a room. How many hands do they have?

If you make a table in which the *Ins* increase by 1 at each step, you might notice that the *Outs* are going up by 2 at each step. You can explain this pattern by the fact that when another person joins the group, two more hands are added.

In other words, the number of hands for *n* + 1 people is 2 more than the number of hands for *n* people. In this approach, each table entry is found from the previous one. This type of description of an In-Out table is called a **recursive function.**

On the other hand, you might look at the table and notice that each *Out* is exactly twice the corresponding *In.* You can explain this by the fact that each person has two hands.

In other words, the table can be described by the formula *Out* = 2 · *In.* In this approach, the *Out* is expressed directly in terms of the *In.* A formula like this is called a *closed formula.*

Now use the ideas of *recursive function* and *closed formula* in these problems.

1. You may have found a recursive function for the number of diagonals in a polygon, in which you described how the number of diagonals grows as the number of sides increases by one side at a time. But a recursive function can be difficult to work with if the polygon has many sides.

   For example, you probably wouldn't want to use a recursive function to find the number of diagonals for a 1000-sided polygon.

   Your task in this problem is to find a closed formula for the In-Out table from *Homework 17: Diagonally Speaking.* That is, look for a formula that will allow you to find the number of diagonals for *any* polygon directly in terms of the number of sides, without having to work your way through all the cases of polygons with fewer sides.

2. Whatever method you discovered for finding the number of diagonals, you probably found it by looking at some examples and seeing a pattern.

   That's an excellent approach, but it doesn't necessarily tell you *why* the pattern holds. If you aren't sure why it holds, then you don't have much of a guarantee that the pattern *always* holds.

   Your task in this problem is to *explain* why your method for finding the number of diagonals must work. Whether you are using a *recursive function* or a *closed formula,* you will need to think about what a diagonal is and not just look at the numerical pattern of your data.

From Another Angle

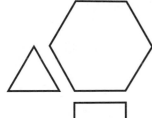

As you saw in *Homework 19: An Angular Summary,* a regular polygon is a polygon in which all the angles are equal and the sides are equal.

For example, the three pattern blocks shown at the left are in the shape of regular polygons.

The problems below involve both pattern blocks and regular polygons. In doing these problems, you may use any formulas you know for the sum of the angles of a polygon.

1. Make an In-Out table where the *In* is the number of sides of a regular polygon and the *Out* is the size of each angle of such a polygon.

    For example, if a regular polygon has three sides, each angle of that polygon is 60°, since the three angles must add up to 180°.

    Look for a rule for your table.

2. Investigate whether any other regular polygons, besides those shown above, can be made from pattern blocks.

    a. For each polygon that can be made, draw a picture to show how it can be made.

    b. Explain why your answer to part a is complete. That is, explain why no other regular polygons can be made.

    (Careful! One polygon that can be made has more than six sides.)

You may want to use pattern blocks to do this assignment. For your convenience, pictures of all six pattern blocks are shown here.

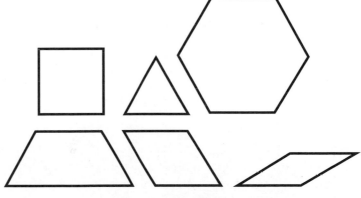

A complete set of pattern blocks (drawn to scale).

Lots of Squares

Can you divide a square into a certain number of smaller squares? That may depend on exactly how many smaller squares you want.

The first diagram at the right shows that any square can be divided into four smaller squares. The second diagram shows that any square can be divided into seven smaller squares.

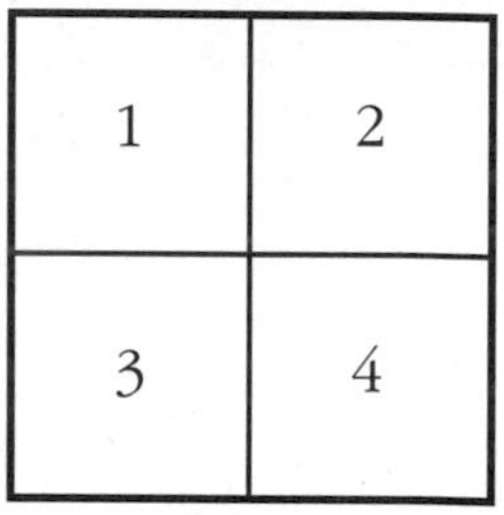

Notice that these smaller squares don't have to be the same size as each other, but keep in mind that the smaller portions must all be squares, not simply rectangles.

The task of this activity is to investigate what numbers of smaller squares are possible. For example, you can probably see that there is no way to divide a square into just two smaller squares. (Try it and convince yourself that it's impossible.)

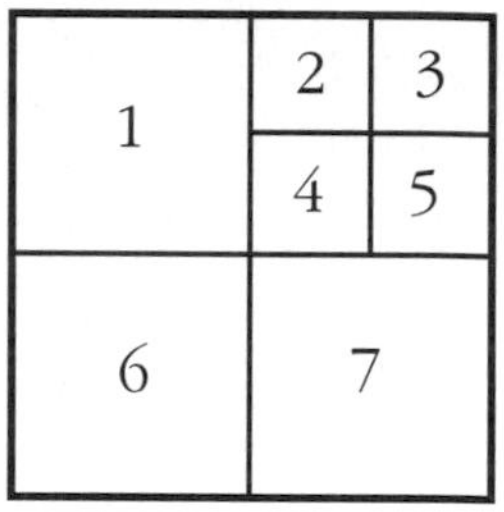

1. Start with specific cases. Is it possible to divide a square into three smaller squares? Five? Six? Eight? (The cases of four and seven smaller squares are shown in the diagrams, although you may want to look for other ways to do them.)

   Continue this process, at least up to the case of 13 smaller squares.

Now reflect on what you've done, and just *imagine* continuing this process. Would there be any numbers beyond 13 for which you *couldn't* divide a square into that many smaller squares? What patterns can you find in the cases you've done that help with this question?

2. a. What is the largest "impossible" case?

   b. Prove your answer to Question 2a. That is, prove that all cases beyond the one you named in Question 2a are possible.

From One to N

In Question 1 of *Homework 20: Squares and Scoops,* you looked at the number of squares in an "*n*-high" stack.

You may have seen that this number could be found by getting the sum $1 + 2 + \cdots + n$. For example, the number of squares in a 5-high stack is $1 + 2 + 3 + 4 + 5$.

The sum $1 + 2 + \cdots + n$ occurs often in mathematics problems. (You may have used a similar sum in *Homework 17: Diagonally Speaking.*)

Your task in this activity is to find a simple expression in terms of *n* that allows you to find this sum without repeated addition. (What you are looking for is called a *closed formula,* as explained in the problem *Diagonals Illuminated.*)

If you find such an expression, look for a proof that your answer is correct. Don't just say, "It works"; you need to guarantee that it works for *every* value of *n*.

Different Kinds of Checkerboards

In *POW 3: Checkerboard Squares,* you found a way to compute the total number of squares that can be formed as a combination of squares on an *n*-by-*n* checkerboard.

But what if the checkerboard itself isn't necessarily square? For example, how many squares are there altogether on the 4-by-6 checkerboard shown at the left?

Here are two examples of squares that can be formed on that checkerboard.

Start with this 4-by-6 example, and then look for ways to generalize what you find.

Your goal is to find a method to compute the total number of squares that can be formed from squares on an *m*-by-*n* checkerboard.

Programming Down to One

In *Homework 6: Gettin' On Down to One,* you examined a process for generating sequences of numbers. Here's a summary of that process.

You begin with a starting number. You find each number after that by applying one of two rules to the current number.

The decision about which rule to apply depends on whether the current number is odd or even.

• If the current number is odd, the rule is

> *Multiply the current number by 3 and then add 1 to get the next number.*

• If the current number is even, the rule is

> *Divide the current number by 2 to get the next number.*

The task in this assignment is to write a program that will generate the sequence for you.

There are several types of programs that you could write for this task. Here are three possibilities.

Continued on next page

Option 1

The program asks the user for a number, and then tells the user what the next number is.

For example, the screen for such a program might look like the display at the right.

The user of the program enters the number 13. The program does the rest.

```
Give me a number.
? 13
The next number in
the sequence is 40
```

Option 2

The program asks the user for a number, and then generates a sequence of terms based on the two rules.

For example, the screen for such a program might look like the display at the right.

Again, everything except the number 13 following the question mark is done by the program.

```
Give me a number.
? 13
The sequence goes
13, 40, 20, 10,
5, 16, 8, 4, 2, 1
```

Option 3

The program asks the user for a number, and then tells the user how many steps it takes to get to 1, without actually showing the terms.

For example, the screen for such a program might look like the display at the right.

Again, everything except the number 13 following the question mark is done by the program.

```
Give me a number.
? 13
The sequence gets
to 1 in 9 steps.
```

Whatever option or options you work on, your program will have to determine which of the two rules to use, depending on whether a given number is odd or even.

You may want to consult a manual to find out how to display words on the screen, how to put the decision about which rule to use into your program, and so on.

More About Borders

The problem in *Homework 22: Border Varieties* involved finding the number of tiles needed to form a border around an s-by-s square.

In this activity, you will explore some variations or extensions of that problem.

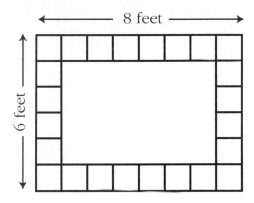

1. Suppose Leslie's garden isn't square. For example, if she has a garden that is 6 feet by 8 feet, the tiles would look like the diagram at the right.

   Explore examples like this, and then develop an expression for the number of tiles needed for the border of a garden that is *m* feet by *n* feet.

2. Suppose that each tile costs $3. Suppose also that Leslie buys topsoil for the part of the garden that is not tiled, and it costs 20¢ for each square foot of ground to be covered with topsoil.

   Develop an expression in terms of *m* and *n* for Leslie's total cost for tiles and topsoil for a garden that is *m* feet by *n* feet.

3. Consider the problem of creating a border 2 feet wide. For example, for a garden 10 feet by 10 feet, the border would look like the diagram at the right.

   How many tiles would be needed?

   And, in general, how many tiles would be needed for a border like this for a square garden that is *s* feet by *s* feet? And what about for a rectangular garden that is *m* feet by *n* feet?

   And what would Leslie's costs be, based on the information in Question 2?

4. Generalize the problem even further by considering a border that is *r* feet wide all around.

Programming Borders

The problem *More About Borders* poses a variety of questions generalizing the ideas in the original border problem.

If you were running an outdoor supply store, you might often be asked questions like these, and you might not want to figure out the amount of tiling or topsoil needed each time.

Perhaps technology can help. Write a program that answers some or all of the questions posed in *More About Borders*.

At the ultimate level of detail, the program might run something like the display at the left.

As usual, everything but the numbers that follow the question marks is done by the program. The numbers 7, 10, and 2 are entered by the user.

```
How wide is the
garden?

? 7

How long is the
garden?

? 10

How wide is the
border?

? 2

You will need 52
tiles and will
have to cover 18
square feet with
topsoil.

This will cost
192 dollars.
```

Explaining the Layers

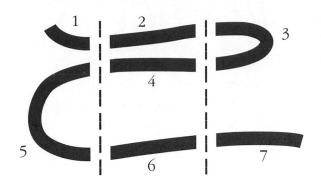

In *Homework 23: Cutting Through the Layers,* you looked at diagrams like the one at the left.

In these diagrams, a single piece of string is bent back and forth into several "layers," and then a number of cuts are made across the bent string. The problem is to figure out how many pieces of string you get.

For example, the diagram above shows three layers of string and two cuts, resulting in seven pieces of string after the cuts.

Your task in that assignment was to find a formula for the number of pieces of string in terms of the number of layers (represented by L) and the number of cuts (represented by C).

Your task in this problem is to write an explanation, in terms of the problem situation, for why your formula works for any number of layers and any number of cuts.

POW-Style Write-up of "Marcella's Bagels"

Problem Statement: Marcella is carrying a bag of bagels on her way home. Various people stop her three times along the way, each time taking *half of her bagels plus two more* from her bag. By the time she gets home, she has only two bagels left! Sonya gets a trip to the park if she can determine how many bagels Marcella had to start with.

Process: When I got home, I started to tell the story to my little brother. All he wanted to know was where the bagels were. He was no help!

I asked myself, what if Marcella had 100 bagels to start with? The first group would have taken 50 and then 2 more, leaving Marcella with 48. Then the second would have taken half of that, 24, and 2 more, leaving her now with 22; the third person would have taken 11 and 2, and she would have 9 left. Too many!

At this point, sitting at the kitchen table, I noticed the kidney beans in the glass jar. I got the jar and spilled out a bunch on the table. My dad was used to my using beans for my math homework.

I put 2 beans in front of me to represent the 2 bagels that Marcella had left at the end.

Since the third person, Susan, had taken half plus 2 more, I added 2 more beans to my pile to represent the 2 extra Susan had taken. Now I had 4.

But I knew that this was half of what Marcella had before Susan came along; so I doubled the 4, giving me 8. That's how many Marcella had after she left the group of surfers.

Continued on next page

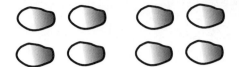

But the surfers also had taken half plus 2 more; so I put the 2 back, now giving Marcella 10. This was what she had after the surfers had taken half.

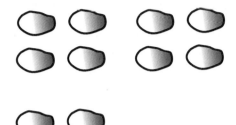

So she must have had 20 bagels before they came along.

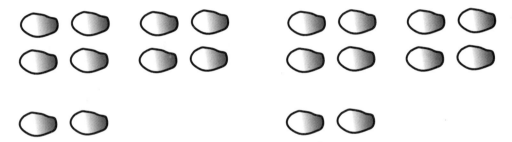

The group collecting for the needy had done the same as the other two—taken half plus 2 more—so I added the 2 more, giving Marcella 22.

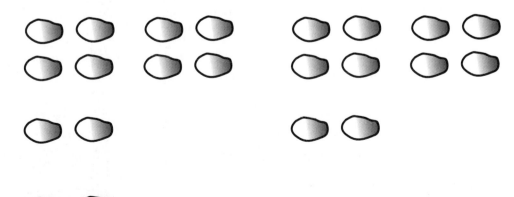

Continued on next page

And finally, I doubled that.

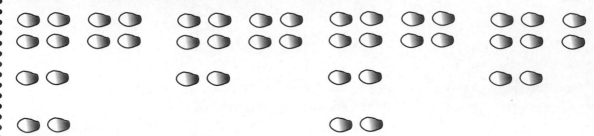

This gave her 44 beans.

Solution: So I figure since each bean represents a bagel, Marcella must have started out with 44 bagels.

At this point my younger brother asked me how come I was playing with food again. So, for the second time, I told him the story about Marcella and the bagels and acted it out with him with the beans as I talked.

$$44 \rightarrow 22 \rightarrow 20 \rightarrow 10 \rightarrow 8 \rightarrow 4 \rightarrow 2$$

It really helped to use the beans to be Marcella's bagels. I could also tell that I got the answer because I acted it out, and I came out with 2, which is what she had left. I don't know if another answer would work, but I don't think so since I worked backwards and didn't have any choices along the way. It wasn't like Marcella had fewer than 5 bagels, or more than 1 bagel. She had *exactly* 2 bagels left.

Drawing the pictures I did, I could now explain my process to someone else, using dots. Each dot was a bean, which was really a bagel.

Extensions: What if Marcella had 5 bagels left? What would that mean about how many she had at the start? Or what if she ended with 2 but each group she met took a third and then 3 more? Or what if she met even more people on her way home?

Evaluation: Not too hard, maybe even a little easy once I used the beans. It was fun trying to explain it to my brother. I think I learned something about experimenting and trying things out. I'd like the problem better if Marcella weren't such a softie!

The Game
of Pig

Days 1-2

A Game of Chance and Strategy

The theory of probability was developed in the seventeenth century, primarily to answer questions posed by gamblers. Mathematicians of the time saw that strategies can be developed to optimize the chances of success, even in situations involving luck. Today, probability is used in a variety of applications, ranging from scientific research to making practical business decisions.

In *The Game of Pig* you'll explore the world of probability with a dice game called Pig. In the opening days of this unit, you'll experiment as the first step toward finding the best strategy for the game.

Leah Allen and Crystal Kovarik begin the unit by playing the game of Pig in order to develop the best strategy.

The Game of Pig

The Game

To play this game, you need an ordinary six-sided die, labeled 1 through 6.

Each turn of the game consists of one or more rolls of the die. You keep rolling until you decide to stop or until you roll 1. You may choose to stop rolling at any time.

Continued on next page

Scoring

If you choose to stop rolling *before* you roll 1, your score for that turn is the sum of all the numbers you rolled on that turn.

However, if you roll 1, your turn is over, and your score for that turn is 0.

Examples

- You roll 4, 5, and 2, and then decide to stop. Your score for this turn is 11.

- You roll 3, 4, 6, and 1. The turn is over because you rolled 1, and your score for this turn is 0.

Each turn is scored separately. With each turn you play, you add the score for that turn to the total of your previous turns.

Your Assignment

1. Play several turns as a whole group. As you play, talk about how you are deciding whether or not to roll again.

2. Split into two smaller groups and play some more turns.

3. Make a list of some strategies that you found yourselves using. Be prepared to discuss these with the entire class.

Homework 1   Pig at Home

Play Pig with someone at home. If you don't have a die, you can put numbers on a wooden cube, or you can write the numbers 1 through 6 on cards and put them in a bag. If you use cards, mix the bag well each time before drawing out a card, and replace the card after each draw.

Then write about your experience playing Pig. Include in your write-up:

- Who you played with

- How you taught them to play

- What strategies each of you used and which seemed most effective

- Whether you played "with each other" or "against each other," and why

POW 4 *A Sticky Gum Problem*

This Problem of the Week starts with some specific problems, and then asks you to generalize what you've learned from them.

Here's the first problem.

1. Ms. Hernandez comes across a gum ball machine one day when she is out with her twins. Of course, the twins each want a gum ball. What's more, they insist on being given gum balls of the same color. (They don't care what color the gum balls are, as long as they're the same color.)

Ms. Hernandez can see that there are only white gum balls and red gum balls in the machine. The gum balls are a penny each, and there is no way to tell which color will come out next. Ms. Hernandez decides she will keep putting in pennies until she gets two gum balls of the same color.

Why is three cents the most she might have to spend in order to satisfy her twins?

The next two problems are similar to Question 1.

2. The next day, Ms. Hernandez passes a different gum ball machine. This one has three colors—red, white, and blue.

What is the most Ms. Hernandez might have to spend at this new gum ball machine in order to get matching gum balls for her twins?

Continued on next page

3. Here comes Mr. Hodges with his triplets past the three-color gum ball machine described in Question 2. Of course, his children also insist that they all get the same color gum ball. What is the most Mr. Hodges might have to spend?

After you have answered the questions above, create some examples of your own. You may want to begin with more examples about the Hernandez twins, using different numbers of colors. Or you may want to create other examples using the three-color gum ball machine and larger sets of children.

As you create and solve examples of your own, look for a way to organize the information and look for patterns. Your ultimate goal is to find a formula so that, if someone tells you the number of colors and the number of children, your formula will tell you the maximum that the parent might need to spend.

Write-up

Your write-up for this Problem of the Week should begin with a discussion of Questions 1 through 3. Explain your answers to each of these problems and describe the process by which you solved them.

Then discuss the problems you made up and their solutions. Explain how you organized your information and what patterns you found.

Finally, state any general ideas you were able to formulate. Include conjectures you may have about the general problem, even if you can't prove them. For each general statement, include an explanation of why you think it's true and examples to illustrate it, as well as a description of the process by which you arrived at the idea.

Adapted from "A Sticky Gum Problem" in *aha! Insight* by Martin Gardner, W. H. Freeman and Company, New York City/San Francisco, 1978.

Pig Strategies

Continue working in your groups on developing strategies for Pig.

1. Share with group members the strategies you each used in *Homework 1: Pig at Home*.

2. Discuss these strategies, and decide on the strategy you think is the best that you have found so far. (It may be one of those written for homework, or it may be something new.)

3. Write this "best strategy" in such a way that another group would be able to play Pig using this strategy.

Homework 2   Waiting for a Double

In many games that use dice, such as backgammon, you roll two dice at a time. Often special rules apply when you roll a double. (A **double** means having the same number show on both dice).

So you might want to know how long it takes to get a double. Here is an experiment to consider.

> You roll a pair of dice, and continue rolling until you get a double. You record the number of rolls it took to get a double.

Example:

First roll	Dice come up 3 and 4.
Second roll	Dice come up 2 and 5.
Third roll	Dice come up 5 and 3.
Fourth roll	Dice come up 2 and 2.

It took four rolls to get a double.

Continued on next page

1. Predict the *average* number of rolls it will take to get a double. Write a sentence or two explaining why you made that prediction.

2. Do the experiment ten times. That is, for each experiment, roll a pair of dice until you get a double, counting how many rolls it takes. Write down the number of rolls needed each time.

3. Use the data you gathered in Question 2 to answer these questions.

   a. What was the largest number of rolls it took to get a double? What was the smallest?

   b. What was the average of the ten experiments?

4. How close is the average you found in Question 3b to the prediction you made in Question 1? Would you revise your prediction now, based on your experiments? Why or why not?

Days 3-6

Flip, Flip

You've seen that the game of Pig is rather complicated. Although you may already have a favorite strategy, you're still a long way from completely understanding the game. That understanding probably won't come until the end of this unit. To reach this goal, you're going to have to learn more about the theory of probability.

Flipping coins is one of the most common ways to investigate ideas about probability. In *The Gambler's Fallacy*, you'll use coin flips to arrive at a conclusion that may surprise you. Then you'll move on to the formal definition of probability. As you'll see, people study probability through both experimentation and theoretical analysis.

Laurel Akers prepares a bar graph in order to record the results of her coin flipping experiment.

Interactive Mathematics Program

The Gambler's Fallacy

Introduction

In the game of roulette, a ball is spun around a roulette wheel, and it lands either in a red slot or in a black slot. (There is also a very small chance that it will land in a green slot, but, in this problem, we will simplify things by ignoring that fact.)

The chance of the ball landing in a red slot is the same as its chance of landing in a black slot.

Some gamblers use the following strategy for winning at roulette: They watch a wheel and if it gets a certain number of reds in a row, they bet on black, since they figure it is black's turn. Similarly, if they see a string of blacks coming up, they bet on red, since they figure red will be more likely than black after a string of blacks.

A Historical Example

In a famous incident in 1913, at the Casino in Monte Carlo, black came up a record 26 times in a row. By about the fifteenth time, people started betting overwhelmingly on red, believing that it was now "red's turn." As a result, the Casino made an enormous sum of money.

Continued on next page

The Experiment

Do this experiment with a partner.

> Flip a coin 25 times and record each flip as heads (H) or tails (T), according to the outcome.

When you have completed all 25 flips, you will have a list of 25 letters, made up of H's and T's.

Now start from the beginning of this list and find the first instance of three flips in a row that are identical (either three heads in a row or three tails in a row). We will call three identical flips in a row a **triplet**.

Record whether the flip that followed this first triplet was the *same* as the letters in the triplet or *different*. Then move to the next triplet and again record whether the flip that followed it was the same as, or different from, the letters in the triplet. Continue in this way through your whole list. (*Note:* You should ignore a triplet at the end of your 25 flips, since there is nothing following it.)

Then find out how many "same's" and how many "different's" you got.

Be careful! If you have four identical flips in a row, that gives you two triplets. For example, suppose you have H H H H T as part of your record. As shown below, the first three H's form a triplet that is followed by an H (which is the *same* as the triplet); the second, third, and fourth H's also form a triplet, and this triplet is followed by a T (which is *different* from the triplet).

This triplet is followed by H, which
is the same as the triplet.

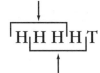

This triplet is followed by T, which
is different from the triplet.

Similarly, if you have five identical flips, and then a different flip (such as T T T T T H), that gives three triplets: The first two triplets are followed by a flip the *same* as the letters in that triplet, while the third triplet is followed by a letter that is *different* from the letters in the triplet.

Homework 3

Expecting the Unexpected

You know that if you flip a coin a bunch of times, you might get more heads than tails or more tails than heads, even though heads and tails are equally likely.

This activity asks you to experiment with this phenomenon and think about what is likely.

1. First gather some data by flipping a coin 50 times and recording the number of heads. Then do this 50-flip experiment again and record the result.

2. Each of your classmates will also do this 50-flip experiment twice, recording the number of heads each time.

   a. What do you think will be the largest number of heads that anyone will get in a 50-flip experiment? The smallest number of heads?

   b. About how many of the experiments do you think will give exactly 25 heads?

Homework 4

Coincidence or Causation?

Most people accept the idea that a coin doesn't "remember" its previous flips, and therefore the coin's "history" doesn't affect the probability of a given result in the future.

But there are times when previous events *do* affect future events.

In each of the following situations, you are to decide whether you think the past will or will not have a certain influence on the future.

In each case, state your decision and write a paragraph explaining why you believe that it is correct.

1. A baseball player has averaged hitting a home run once every seven games for most of the season. She has just hit a home run in each of the last three games.

   Are her chances of hitting a home run in the next game greater than, less than, or no different from usual?

2. It seems to Mr. Bryant that every time he comes along Pine Street to the traffic light at the intersection with Lincoln Avenue, the light is red. He is so infuriated with this situation that he contacts the city planner. The city planner reports that the light is set so that cars on Pine Street and cars on Lincoln Avenue are given equal time to pass through the intersection.

   If you are driving right behind Mr. Bryant one morning and come to that traffic light, do you think that your chances of getting a red light are greater than, less than, or equal to those given by the city planner?

Continued on next page

3. The Happy Days Ice Cream Cone Company claims that, on the average, only about 1 out of every 100 boxes of their famous ice cream cones will contain a broken cone. The company gladly replaces any box containing a broken cone.

You go to the store and purchase a box of Happy Days Ice Cream Cones. Upon arrival at home, you discover that one of the cones is broken. Feeling somewhat cheated, you return the box to the place of purchase and exchange it for a new box. Just to be sure, you immediately check the new box for broken cones.

Are the chances that the box contains no broken cones different from 1 out of 100?

What Are the Chances?

Part I: Finding Probabilities

Decide on the probability for each event below. (Some of the probabilities will be approximate.)

Describe how you decided on the probability for the events, including whether your answer was based on a theoretical model or on observed results.

A. Reaching into a bag with three red gum balls, two blue gum balls, and four black gum balls, and pulling out a blue gum ball

B. Snow falling sometime in July in Florida

Continued on next page

C. Snow falling sometime in July in New Zealand

D. Flipping a coin twice and getting different results

E. Rolling a die and getting a prime number

F. Going to a store and finding that they don't have your size in the T-shirt you like best

G. A student in your mathematics class wearing sneakers

H. Rolling two dice and getting doubles

I. Rolling a pair of dice and getting doubles by the third roll

Part II: Probabilities on the Number Line

Make a number line like the one below and put the letter of each of the events above in the proper place on the number line to indicate its probability.

Homework 5

Paula's Pizza

Paula's favorite pizza place offers six toppings—sausage, onions, mushrooms, pepperoni, olives, and peppers.

Paula ordered a pizza with mushrooms and olives.

Unfortunately, the server only wrote down that Paula ordered two toppings, and didn't write down which two they were. The chef doesn't know Paula, and decided to pick two toppings at random.

1. How many different two-topping pizzas are possible altogether?

2. What is the probability that Paula will get the pizza that she ordered? What is the probability that she'll get something different?

3. Paula actually likes all of the toppings except sausage and pepperoni. What is the probability that she will get a pizza she likes? What is the probability that she'll get a pizza she doesn't like?

Homework 6

0 to 1, or Never to Always

For each of the probabilities below, think up two situations that have the given probability.

In one of those two situations, the probability should be based on a theoretical model. In the other situation, the probability should be based on observed results. (You can be imaginative about this.)

1. Probability = 0

2. Probability = $\frac{2}{7}$

3. Probability = 75%

4. Probability = 1

5. Probability = 2.3

6. Probability = .01

**Days
7-11**

Pictures of Probability

You've seen that probabilities can be expressed with fractions, percentages, or decimals, so you can see that numbers play an essential role in talking about probability.

Pictures are another important tool used to understand mathematics. In this portion of the unit, you will blend geometry with probability, using area diagrams to think about the probabilities of different events. Your next POW, *POW 5: What's on Back?*, will also involve probability, and you may find that working with area diagrams helps solve the problem.

*Jessica Ehlers is using
area models to determine
probabilities.*

Interactive Mathematics Program

Rug Games

Imagine that each diagram in this activity represents a rug. A trap door opens directly over the rug and a dart falls down, landing at random somewhere on the rug.

"At random" means that every point on the rug has as good a chance of getting hit as every other point.

1. If you were trying to predict which part of this rug will get hit, which color would you choose, gray or white? What is the probability of being hit for each color?

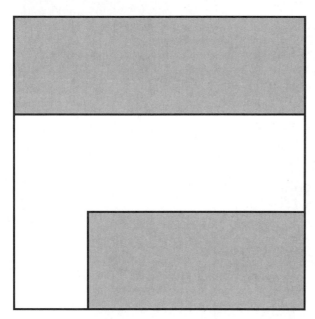

Continued on next page

2. For each of the rugs below, decide which color you would predict as most likely to be hit. For each color, find the probability of being hit.

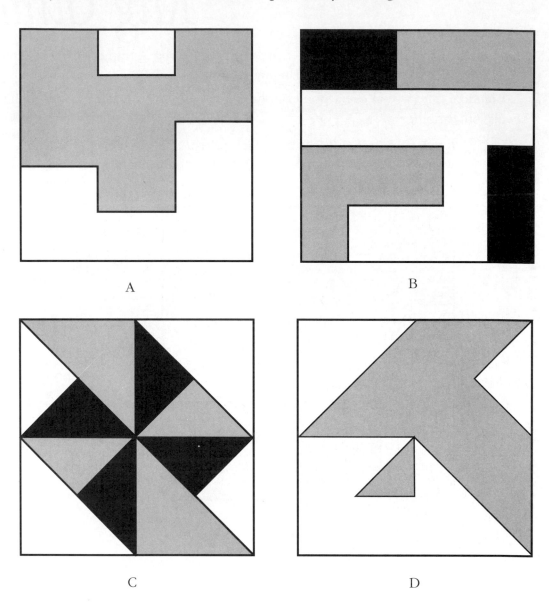

A

B

C

D

Homework 7   Portraits of Probabilities

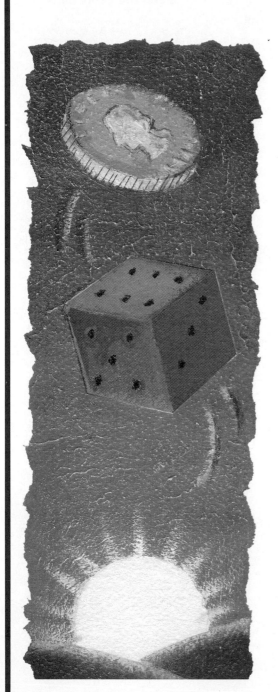

Part I: Rugs for Events

Do these three tasks for each of the events numbered 1 through 5 below.

- State the probability of the event happening.

- Write a short explanation of why you believe you are correct.

- Draw a rug with a shaded portion that represents this probability.

1. Rolling a 6 with one die.

2. Being chosen as one of three POW presenters out of a class of 30 students.

3. Flipping a coin twice and getting two heads.

4. The sun rising tomorrow.

5. Having no homework for the rest of the semester.

Continued on next page

Part II: Events for Rugs

For each of the rugs illustrated, describe an event that you believe has the probability of occurrence represented by the shaded part of the rug.

6.

7.

8.
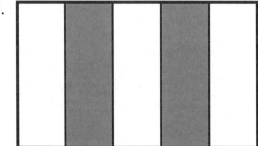

9.

POW 5   *What's on Back?*

In a certain game, there are three cards:

- One card has an **X** on both sides.
- One card has an **O** on both sides.
- One card has an **X** on one side and an **O** on the other side.

The three cards are placed in a bag, and the bag is shaken. You draw out one card and look at one side only. You cannot look at the other side or at the other cards. The goal is to predict whether there is an **X** or an **O** on the other side of the card you drew out.

There are many strategies for doing this, some good, some not as good. Here are two possible strategies.

- Predict that the mark on the other side will be different from the mark you see. (That is, if you see **X**, predict **O**; and if you see **O**, predict **X**.)

- Always predict that the mark will be an **X**.

No strategy will be successful all of the time, so you should try to find the probability of success for each strategy you consider.

Your ultimate goal is to find the strategy that has the highest possible probability of being right.

Continued on next page

For each strategy you consider, do these two tasks.

    a. Find an *experimental estimate* of the probability of success using that strategy. That is, devise an experimental method of testing your strategy. It will probably be useful to make a set of cards to do this.

       You will need to repeat your experiment quite a few times in order to get a good experimental estimate. You may want to keep repeating it until your overall results begin to stay roughly the same as you repeat the experiment.

    b. Analyze the probability of success for that strategy by using a *theoretical model*.

Begin with the two specific strategies described above, looking for both an experimental estimate and a theoretical analysis for the probability of predicting correctly with each of those strategies.

Then look at other strategies, trying to determine the strategy with the highest probability of success for correctly predicting "what's on back."

Write-up

Your write-up should contain these four parts.

1. *Problem Statement*

2. *Process:* Include a description of exactly what you did to carry out the experiments for part a.

3. *Results:* Describe each strategy you tried. For each strategy, tell what you found as the probability of predicting correctly. If you can, describe your results in terms of both

    a. your *experimental results*

    b. your *theoretical analysis*

    Also state what strategy you think gives the highest probability of predicting successfully, and justify this answer.

4. *Evaluation*

Homework 8

Mystery Rugs

In each of the following situations, you are given some information about the probabilities of certain outcomes.

Your task in each problem is to

- make up a situation with outcomes that fit the given probabilities

- draw and label a rug that shows the probabilities of each outcome

SEASONS OF THE YEAR

1. There are two possible outcomes for an experiment. One of the outcomes has a probability of $\frac{2}{7}$.

2. There are three possible outcomes for an experiment. One outcome has a probability of .4, and a second outcome has a probability of .25.

3. There are three possible outcomes for an experiment. One outcome has a probability of 50%, the second outcome has a probability of 30%, and the third outcome has a probability of 25%.

The Counters Game

The Game

Each player in this game needs a board, which consists of 11 boxes numbered from 2 through 12, as shown below.

2	3	4	5	6	7	8	9	10	11	12

At the start of the game, players each place 11 counters on their individual boards. The counters can be placed in the different boxes in any way the player chooses (including putting more than one counter in a single box).

During the game, a pair of dice is rolled repeatedly, and the numbers on the dice are added each time. Every player who has any counters in the square corresponding to the sum of the dice removes *one counter* from that square. (Even if a player has more than one counter in that square, only one counter is removed. If a player has no counters in that square, the player does nothing on that roll.)

The winner of the game is the first player whose counters are all removed.

The challenge of the game is to initially place the counters so that they will be removed as quickly as possible during the game.

The Activity

1. Play one or two practice games in your group. Just guess about where to place the counters.

2. Now, think about where to place the counters. Write a sentence or two explaining what you think would be a good way to place them and why.

3. Play some games in your group, with each member of the group using her or his own strategy for placing the counters.

4. Discuss the different strategies used in your group, in preparation for a competition between all the groups. Choose a single strategy to use in the competition, and state what this strategy is.

Homework 9   Rollin', Rollin', Rollin'

Roll a pair of dice 50 times and record the sums in an organized way.

1. Draw a graph of the data you gathered.

2. Write a paragraph about your results. You should summarize your observations about the data and discuss why the results come out the way they do.

3. What new thoughts does this experiment give you about how to play the counters game?

The Theory of Two-Dice Sums

You have played a game that involved two-dice sums, and you have done some experiments to get an idea of how two-dice sums are distributed.

Now it's time to look at the theory and to get more precise information about this distribution.

Work with your group to develop a rug diagram that will help you understand two-dice sums and provide a theoretical model for finding the probability of each possible sum.

Keep in mind that equal areas of your rug should represent equally likely events. You should assume that the dice are fair. That is, for a single die, the probability of getting each possible result is $\frac{1}{6}$.

You may find it useful to use two dice, preferably of different colors, as you work. Think about the portion of your rug that corresponds to a given result on the dice.

Homework 10 Coins, Coins, Coins

1. Binky was working on Question 3 from *Homework 7: Portraits of Probabilities*, which asks for the probability of getting two heads if you flip a coin twice.

   She said that if you flip twice, there are exactly three possible outcomes— two heads, one head and one tail, and two tails—and so the probability of getting two heads is $\frac{1}{3}$.

   Explain why she's wrong. Make your explanation as clear as you can, using diagrams as needed.

2. Imagine that you have two pockets and that each pocket contains a penny, a nickel, and a dime.

   You reach in and remove one coin from each pocket. Assume that, for each pocket, the penny, the nickel, and the dime are equally likely to be removed.

   a. What are the possible amounts you could get for the total of the two coins?

   b. What is the probability that your two coins will total exactly two cents?

   c. What is the probability for each of the other outcomes in Question 2a?

3. What do Questions 1 and 2 have in common, and how are they related to the problem of two-dice sums?

Homework 11

Two-Dice Sums and Products

Suppose you roll a pair of dice and add the numbers that you roll.

1. Which is more likely—that the sum is an odd number or that the sum is an even number? Explain why.

2. Make up two new probability questions about two-dice sums that can be answered from the rug diagram for two-dice sums. Answer your two questions if you can, and explain your answers.

Now suppose that instead of adding the numbers on the two dice, you *multiply* them. Let's call the result a **two-dice product**.

3. What are the possible two-dice products? What is the probability of getting each of the two-dice products?

4. Which is more likely—that the two-dice product is an odd number or that the two-dice product is an even number?

5. Make up two probability questions about two-dice products, and answer them if you can.

Days 12–21

In the Long Run

In recent activities, you have looked at ways to find the probability of a given event, such as flipping two heads in a row or getting a sum of 9 on a pair of dice. For example, you've flipped coins or rolled dice to determine the probability of a particular outcome. You've used "rug diagrams" to analyze probabilities and have confirmed some of your results with experimental evidence.

In the game of Pig, the probabilities are pretty simple, because each number on the die is equally likely to occur. But the situation is complicated by the fact that the payoff differs with each possible result and ranges from a gain of six points to a loss of all points.

Kristin Livingston, Katy Anderson, Emily White, and Megan Hall discuss strategies for "The Counters Game."

How do you use probability to analyze what will happen in the long run in a game like this? This unit looks first at simple situations involving the long run, then gradually works toward more complex problems. You're moving toward your goal of finding the best strategy for Pig!

Spinner Give and Take

Al and Betty are playing a game with the spinner shown at the left.

Each time the spinner comes up in the white area, Betty wins one dollar from Al.

Each time the spinner comes up in the gray area, Al wins four dollars from Betty.

Al wins
$4 from
Betty

Betty
wins $1
from Al

1. In the long run, which of the two players is more likely to be the winner in this game? Write down your prediction and explain your reasoning.

2. Now play the game for 25 spins and write down what happens.

3. If Al and Betty play 100 games, how far ahead is the expected winner likely to be?

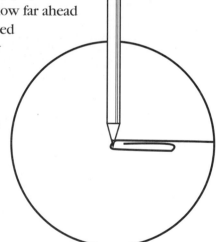

Suggestion: You can make a spinner using a pencil and a paper clip, as shown at the right, by bending open one end of the paper clip and then using the pencil to hold the other end in place as the paper clip spins.

Homework 12   Pointed Rugs

In *Rug Games,* you decided which color was most likely to be hit by a falling dart for each of the rugs below. In this homework you are asked to work again with these rugs. But in this assignment, points are awarded for each color. This means that your choice of color involves more than just finding probabilities—you must also take into account the number of points that are awarded each time that the dart lands on a certain color.

For each rug, decide which color is the best to bet on to maximize your points in the long run. (*Hint:* Imagine dropping a dart a large number of times, and decide which color would be likely to give the most points.)

Write clear explanations to support your answers.

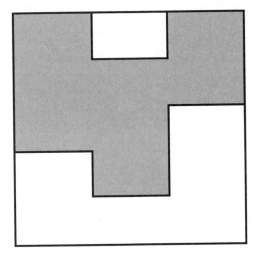

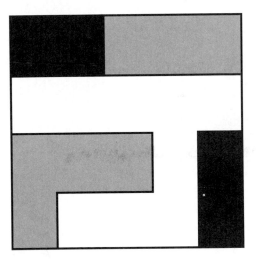

A

Gray   6 points

White   8 points

B

Gray   10 points

White   8 points

Black   16 points

Continued on next page

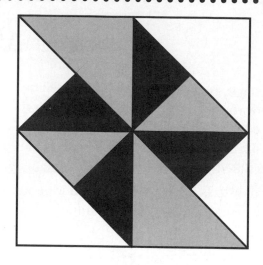

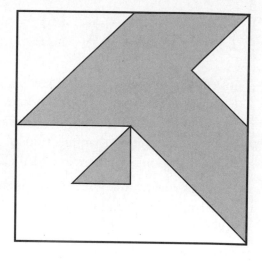

C

Gray   5 points

White   6 points

Black   10 points

D

Gray   15 points

White   13 points

Homework 13

Mia's Cards

1. Mia is playing a game that involves picking a card from a standard deck. A standard deck consists of 52 cards, with 13 cards in each of 4 suits. The suits are clubs, diamonds, hearts, and spades. The 13 cards in each suit are called the ace, 2, 3, 4, 5, 6, 7, 8, 9, 10, jack, queen, and king.

   In Mia's game, she mixes up the cards and then picks a card at random from the deck. She gets 10 points if it's a heart and 5 points if it's a club, spade, or diamond. Then she puts the card back in the deck.

   If she does this many times, what will be her average number of points for each time she picks a card? Explain your answer.

2. On February 14, Mia changes the game so that she gets 20 points for a heart, 15 points for a diamond, and no points for a club or a spade. If she plays this new game many times, what would you expect her average score per card to be?

3. a. Make up a game like Mia's, in which a person picks a card and receives a number of points that depends on the type of card picked.

   b. Calculate the average score per card in the long run for your game.

POW 6   *Linear Nim*

There are many strategy games in which two players take turns removing objects from one of several piles according to certain rules, with the winner being the person who removes the last object.

These games often go by the name Nim.

In one version of the game there is only one pile. In that case, you can represent the objects by a single row of marks on a piece of paper, and so we will call this game Linear Nim.

Here's how a particular form of Linear Nim works.

> At the beginning, there are 10 marks on a piece of paper, as shown below.
>
> | | | | | | | | | |
>
> Each player, in turn, crosses off 1, 2, or 3 of the marks.
>
> Play continues until all of the marks have been crossed out. The player crossing off the last mark is the winner.

Part I: Finding a Strategy

Your first task in this POW is to find a winning strategy for this particular game.

You might want to begin by finding a partner and playing the game together for a while.

Continued on next page

As you and your partner play, pay attention not only to who wins, but also to when you realize who is going to win and how you know.

The question of who wins may depend on which player goes first. So one element of your strategy might be deciding whether you want to go first or second.

Be sure that the strategy you develop is complete. That is, you should take into account every possible move that your opponent might make.

Part II: Variations

Once you have developed your strategy for this particular game, investigate how the strategy would have to change if the game were to vary in different ways.

The particular game above starts with 10 marks and allows a player to cross out up to 3 marks at a time. What if these numbers were changed? For instance, suppose you start with 15 marks instead of 10, or allow a player to cross out up to 4 marks at a time instead of 3? In other words, you can change the *initial number* of marks and you can also change the *maximum per turn* that a player can cross out.

How would your strategy change if you varied the game? Are there some cases where you should choose to go first and others where you should choose to go second? What does it depend on?

Consider a variety of examples and look for generalizations.

Write-up

1. *Process:* Describe how you went about understanding the original game and developing a strategy. Indicate the key insights you had that were important in your understanding.

2. *Strategies*

   a. Describe the strategy you developed for the original game.

   b. Describe some specific variations you looked at and what the strategy was for each.

3. *Generalizations:* State any general principles you developed about variations on Linear Nim. In particular, can you describe, in terms of the *initial number* and the *maximum per turn,* how to decide whether to go first or second?

4. *Evaluation*

Homework 14   A Fair Rug Game?

1. Tony and Crystal are sitting around a rug watching darts randomly fall from the ceiling.

   The rug they are using is pictured above.

   If the dart lands on the white part of the rug, Crystal wins $5 from Tony. If it lands on the black part, Tony wins $3 from Crystal.

   Do you think this is a fair game? What is Tony's expected value for each turn? What's Crystal's?

2. If you think the game is not fair to one of the players, change the amount of money they each win in order to make the game fair. (Don't change the rug.)

One-and-One

Sometimes in a basketball game, a player is presented with a situation known as a "one-and-one."

In a one-and-one situation, the player begins by taking a free throw. If the player misses, that's the end of it. But if the shot is successful, the player gets to take a second shot.

One point is scored for each successful shot. So the player can end up with 0 points (by missing the first shot), 1 point (by making the first shot, but then missing the second), or 2 points (by making both the first and the second shots).

Terry is a basketball player who has shown over a period of time that whenever she attempts a free throw, she has about a 60% probability of making it.

> In a one-and-one situation, how many points is Terry *most likely* to score: 0, 1, or 2?

Write down your intuitive guess about the answer to this question.

Adapted from *The Middle Grade Mathematics Project Series: Probability,* by Lappan et al., © 1986 Addison-Wesley Publishing Co., Inc.

Homework 15   A Sixty-Percent Solution

In this assignment, the situation is the same as the one described in the activity *One-and-One*.

> Terry is in a one-and-one free-throw situation, and she has a 60% probability of getting any given shot.

Devise some way to simulate the situation at home.

1. Do your simulation of Terry's one-and-one situation 40 times. Describe your method of doing the simulation and record your results.

2. What was the *most frequent outcome* in your simulation?

3. What was the *average score* per one-and-one situation?

The Theory of One-and-One

You've guessed about it and done simulations about it. Now it's time to work out the theory.

Once again, Terry has a 60% chance of making any given shot.

Develop a theoretical analysis, using a rug diagram, of her expected value for each one-and-one situation.

(A rug diagram is more formally called an **area model**.)

Homework 16   Streak-Shooting Shelly

When Streak-Shooting Shelly steps up for a one-and-one situation, her chances of making the first shot are 80%. However, if she makes her first free throw, then there is a 90% chance that she will make her second free throw.

1. In what percentage of the situations will Shelly score no points? One point? Two points?

2. What is Shelly's expected value per one-and-one situation?

Spins and Draws

1. Al and Betty are playing spinner games again. This time the spinner is divided up so that the arrow will land in Al's area $\frac{1}{5}$ of the time and in Betty's area the remaining $\frac{4}{5}$ of the time.

   Al pays Betty 30¢ when the arrow lands in her area. Betty pays Al $1.25 when it lands in his area.

   a. What is Al's expected value per spin? What is Betty's?

   b. How might the payments be changed so that the game is fair?

2. Archibald and Beatrice are playing a game that involves drawing a card from a standard deck. After each draw, the card is returned to the deck. (It doesn't matter which person draws the card—all that matters is which card is drawn.)

   If the card drawn from the deck is a jack, then Beatrice pays Archibald 20¢. If the card drawn is a heart, then Archibald pays Beatrice 8¢. If neither a jack nor a heart is drawn, then Archibald and Beatrice each give a penny to charity.

   What is the expected value per draw for Archibald, for Beatrice, and for the charity?

Homework 17   Aunt Zena at the Fair

Aunt Zena has gone to the weekend fair that her nephew's school is running. The school is trying to raise funds so they can offer some special classes.

One of the games that Aunt Zena likes is a ring toss. The goal is to toss a large ring so that it lands on a stick.

Each time Aunt Zena succeeds, she wins a coupon, donated by a local restaurant, for a free dinner. She figures that the coupon is worth about $12. It costs Aunt Zena $1 for each toss.

1. On Saturday when Aunt Zena played this game, she was only able to win about once every 20 tries. (She spent most of the afternoon at the ring toss booth.)

    If she continued like this, would she win or lose money in the long run? (You should consider each coupon she wins as the equivalent of $12.)

    What would be her expected value per toss?

2. Aunt Zena went home that night, determined to do better the next day. She practiced and practiced, and Sunday she went back to the fair. Now she was able to win about once every ten tries.

    If she continued like this, would she win or lose money in the long run? What would be her expected value per toss?

POW 7   *Make a Game*

Working with a partner, you are to invent a game that uses *probability* and *strategy*.

You will need to write very clear instructions so that other people can understand how to play your game. Test your instructions several times with someone at home to make sure that the instructions are easy to follow.

You will also have to turn in a written explanation of how you used ideas about probability and strategy in your game. Your grade on this POW will depend in part on how well you have used such ideas.

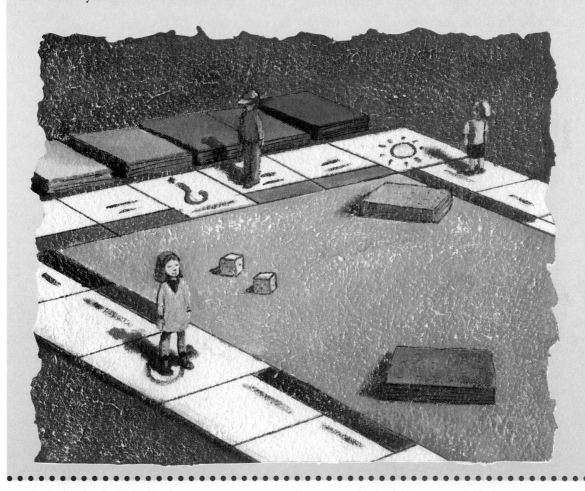

Homework 18

The Lottery and Insurance—Why Play?

This assignment looks at two real-life situations that involve probabilities to see if expected value tells the whole story.

1. *The Lottery*

Many states raise funds through various lottery games. (If your state has one, you may want to learn more about how it works and what happens to the proceeds.)

Assume that each lottery ticket costs $1. The number of tickets sold and the value of a winning ticket often vary from week to week. Suppose that, for a certain week, about 14 million tickets were sold and that the winning ticket is worth $6 million.

   a. Calculate the approximate expected value of a lottery ticket that week.

   b. Do you think buying a lottery ticket is a wise investment? Explain your answer.

2. *Insurance*

Buying insurance can be thought of as similar to playing a lottery game.

You pay a certain amount, called the *premium,* every month to the insurance company. Most of the time, the insurance company just gets to keep your money, and they pay you nothing.

Sometimes, however, you have a claim that is covered by insurance. When that happens, the insurance company has to pay your expenses (for a car crash, illness, fire, or whatever the incident is), and they generally have to pay you much more in that month than you paid as a premium. So, in a sense, you "win" whenever you collect on your insurance. This means that the "insurance game" is a game that you don't really want to win.

In the long run, insurance companies take in more money in premiums than they pay out in claims, or they wouldn't be in business. In other words, their expected value in the insurance "game" is positive, and yours is negative.

So why do people play?

Martian Basketball

In Martian basketball, instead of having one-and-one free throw situations, they have one-and-one-and-one situations.

In other words, if a player makes both the first and second shots, then the player can take a third one as well (so the player can get 0 points, 1 point, 2 points, or 3 points).

Suppose our friend Streak-Shooting Shelly moved to Mars and played basketball there.

Shelly still shoots better when she has just made a shot, but her overall quality is down because she is getting adjusted to the different gravity on Mars.

So now she has a 60% probability of making her first shot. If she gets the first one, she has an 80% probability of making the second one, and if she gets the first two, her probability of getting the third is 90%.

1. How many points is she most likely to score in a one-and-one-and-one situation?

2. What is her expected value for each one-and-one-and-one situation?

Homework 19

The Carrier's Payment Plan Quandary

In some places, newspapers are delivered by a newspaper carrier who has already paid for the papers. The carrier then collects from the customer, and keeps whatever he or she collects.

Suppose one day a customer says to the carrier, "Instead of collecting the usual $5 per week, how about if you just pick two bills at random out of this bag? You get to keep whatever you pick instead of the $5. If you choose to pick out of the bag, you'll do that every week from now on."

Continued on next page

The customer shows the newspaper carrier the bag, which contains one $10 bill and five $1 bills. Thus, two sums are possible: $11 and $2. (Of course, the customer will put in new bills each week to replace the ones that were taken the week before.)

You need to figure out if the carrier should take the customer's offer.

1. First, plan and carry out a simulation for a reasonable number of trials. Based on your simulation, decide which is the better choice for the carrier, and explain your decision.

2. Then use an area model or other method to compute the carrier's expected value from the alternative payment plan. That is, find the average the carrier would expect to get per week in the long run using this payment plan. Based on this theoretical analysis, decide which is the better choice, and explain your decision.

3. Which method do you trust more—the simulation or the theoretical analysis—and why?

Adapted from *The Middle Grade Mathematics Project Series: Probability,* by Lappan et al., © 1986 Addison-Wesley Publishing Co., Inc.

Homework 20 A Fair Deal for the Carrier?

This problem is a simpler version of the situation in *Homework 19: The Carrier's Payment Plan Quandary*.

As in that situation, the customer would ordinarily pay $5 per week for newspapers.

In this problem, though, the customer places a $20 bill and four $1 bills in a bag, and offers the carrier the option of drawing out just one bill at random.

1. Imagine that you are the paper carrier, and figure out whether this option would give you a better-than-fair deal in the long run. In other words, is the expected value for this option better than the usual $5 per week? Explain how you arrive at your decision.

2. Devise some way to simulate this alternate payment plan, and carry out 20 trials. Find the average result of your trials.

3. Think about how you might write a program for the graphing calculator to do a simulation of the alternate payment plan, and write down any ideas you have about this.

Using the Programmed Simulation

Now that you have a calculator program that simulates the situation of *Homework 20: A Fair Deal for the Carrier?*, it's time to see what you can learn from that program.

1. Run the program several times using the same number of trials. How do your answers for the expected value vary from one run to the next? How do they compare to the theoretical prediction?

2. Now do several runs with a larger number of trials, and again compare your answers to each other and to the theoretical prediction. How are these results different from the results in Question 1?

3. What conclusions can you draw about the influence of the number of trials on the results?

4. Does your calculator simulation give you more confidence in the theoretical analysis? Explain.

Homework 21

Another Carrier Dilemma

Here is one more variation on the newspaper carrier's situation. This time the customer places two $5 bills and three $1 bills in a bag, and allows you to draw out two of the bills at random.

If you use this method week after week, how much would you expect to get, on the average, in the long run?

Explain your reasoning for this problem using more than one method of analyzing the situation.

Days 22–25

Little Pig

In *One-and-One*, Terry took at most two shots at the basket in each one-and-one situation. In *Martian Basketball*, each "turn" involved at most three shots.

In the game of Pig, there is no limit to how long a turn can last. A person could roll 20, 50, even 100 times without getting a 1 on the die, continuing to accumulate more points. This is one reason why the game is so complicated to analyze.

You have one more task before you return to finding the best strategy for Pig, and that is to look at a simplified version of the game, called Little Pig. You'll play around for a little while to get used to this new game, and then you'll start analyzing strategies by using area diagrams.

Edward Rokos prepares his analysis of "Little Pig."

The Game of Little Pig

The game of Little Pig is similar to the game of Pig that you have already played.

To play Little Pig, you need a bag containing three cubes—one red, one blue, and one yellow.

Instead of rolling a die, as you did in the game of Pig, you will draw a cube out of the bag.

In each turn, you can draw as many times as you want (replacing the cube after each draw), until either you decide to stop or you draw a yellow cube. Each time you draw a red cube, you add one point to your score. Each time you draw a blue cube, you add four points to your score.

If you stop drawing before you draw a yellow cube, your score for that turn is the total number of points for all draws in that turn. But if you draw a yellow cube, the turn is over and your score for that turn is zero.

Your eventual goal will be to find a strategy for Little Pig that will give the highest possible average score per turn in the long run. In other words, you want the strategy with the highest possible expected value per turn.

For now, you will just be informally investigating the game.

1. Play the game several times in your group, noting different possible strategies.

2. Make a list of some possible strategies for playing Little Pig.

3. Choose a single group strategy that you think might give the best results. Be sure to write this strategy clearly.

Homework 22

Pig Tails

The game of Pig Tails is another variation on the game of Pig. Here's how you play.

Each turn consists of flipping a coin until either you decide to stop or you get tails. If you stop before getting tails, your score for the turn is the number of heads you got, that is, the number of times you flipped.

But if you get tails before deciding to stop, your score for the turn is zero.

1. What is your expected value per turn if your strategy is to flip just once and then stop (no matter what the result)?

2. Next, consider the strategy of always flipping twice (unless you get tails on the first flip) and then stopping. What is your expected value for this strategy?

3. What is the expected value per turn if you always flip three times (unless you get tails on the first or second flip)?

4. Generalize Questions 1 through 3. That is, find the expected value per turn if your strategy is to flip n times and then stop (unless you get tails on an earlier flip).

Little Pig Strategies

Now that you have gotten some experience playing Little Pig, it's time to analyze some strategies.

Two strategies are described below. For each strategy, use an area diagram to describe what might happen and to find the expected value per turn if you play using that strategy.

1. The 2-Point Strategy

In this strategy, you stop as soon as you have at least two points. (Of course, if you draw a yellow cube before getting two points, you'll have to stop sooner.)

2. The 2-Draw Strategy

In this strategy, you stop after drawing two cubes, no matter what the results of those two draws. (Of course, if the first cube is yellow, you'll have to stop after only one draw.)

Homework 23

Continued Little Pig Investigation

At this point, you have found the expected value for some Little Pig strategies.

Your task in this assignment is to continue this investigation. You will either use strategies of your own choice or you will be assigned specific strategies to investigate by your teacher.

Homework 24   Even More Little Pig Investigation

Again, your task in this assignment is to continue the investigation of different strategies for Little Pig.

As you work, keep in mind the ultimate goal of finding the strategy with the largest possible expected value per turn.

Homework 25   Should I Go On?

1. Suppose there are two classes with 30 students in each class.

   In both classes, the students are individually playing Little Pig. In both classes, every student has gotten exactly 10 points so far in the current turn.

   In one class, each student draws just one more cube. In the other class, they all decide to stop at 10 points.

   a. For the class in which students all draw once more, how many would you expect to end up with 0 points? With 11 points? With 14 points? What would you expect for the total number of points in the class? What would you expect for the class average?

   b. Compare the expected class average from part a to the average for the class where everyone stopped at 10 points. Which class would you expect to have a better average?

2. Now suppose the situation is the same except that every student has only 2 points. Again, the students in the first class each draw just once more, while the students in the second class all stop at 2 points.

   a. What would you expect for the average score in the class where all the students draw once more?

   b. Which class would you expect to have a better average?

**Days
26–29**

Back To Pig

Ta-da! You're about to find the best strategy for Little Pig.
Then all you will need to do is apply your new insights to
the original game of Pig. Once you've done so, you'll be ready
to wrap up this unit with portfolios, end-of-unit assessments,
and work on *POW 7: Make A Game*.

**Anthony Pace, Geneva Fiore, Amy Jones, and Oscar Sharp try out their own
created games from "POW 7: Make a Game."**

The Best Little Pig

You've seen that in the long run, a person with 2 points in Little Pig will do better by drawing again, while a person with 10 points should stop.

So what is the best strategy for Little Pig? For what scores does it pay to draw again and for what scores should you stop?

Based on your findings, what strategy will give the highest possible expected value per turn?

Homework 26 Big Pig Meets Little Pig

In *Homework 25: Should I Go On?,* you looked at the question of when a player should draw again in Little Pig.

Now, you will examine how to apply that approach to Big Pig (that is, to the original game of Pig).

Assume that there are two large classes of students, but this time all the students are playing Big Pig.

1. Suppose each student has a current score of 10 points. In one class, each student rolls one more time and then stops. In the other class, each student stops at 10 points.

   Which class would you expect to end up with the better average score?

2. Consider at least two other initial scores (instead of 10 points), and decide which class you would expect to be better off—the class where each student rolls once more, or the class in which all the students stop.

Homework 27

The Pig and I

You've worked through Little Pig strategies and then gone back to study the original game of Pig.

Based on your experiences with both of these games, summarize what you have learned about the best possible strategy for Pig.

Be sure to include what you think is the best strategy, how you found it, how you can justify that choice, and what you learned about "roll" strategies and "point" strategies.

Homework 28

Beginning Portfolio Selection

This unit involved two main approaches for finding probabilities:

- simulations and experiments
- theoretical analyses—using rugs, area models, or tree diagrams

Select an activity from the unit that represents each approach.

Explain what each activity was about and describe what you learned about probability from it.

(This selection and explanation is the first step toward compiling your portfolio for this unit.)

"The Game of Pig" Portfolio

As with *Patterns,* your portfolio for *The Game of Pig* has three parts.

- Writing a cover letter that summarizes the unit

- Choosing papers to include from your work in this unit

- Discussing your personal growth during the unit

Cover Letter for "The Game of Pig"

Look back over *The Game of Pig* and describe the central problem of the unit and the main mathematical ideas. This description should give an overview of how the key ideas were developed and how they were used to solve the central problem.

As part of the compilation of your portfolio, you will select some activities that you think were important in developing the key ideas of this unit. Your cover letter should include an explanation of why you are selecting each particular item.

Selecting Papers from "The Game of Pig"

Your portfolio for *The Game of Pig* should contain

- *Homework 27: The Pig and I*

- *Homework 28: Beginning Portfolio Selection*

  Include the two activities from the unit that you selected in *Homework 28: Beginning Portfolio Selection,* along with your written work about these activities that was part of the homework.

Continued on next page

- *POW 7: Make a Game*

  Include your written explanation of how you used ideas about probability and strategy in your game, and any other written work you turned in during the development process. If possible, include the game itself.

- Other key activities

  Include two or three other activities that you think were important in developing the key ideas of this unit.

- Another Problem of the Week

  Select one of the first three POWs you completed during this unit (*A Sticky Gum Problem, What's on Back?,* or *Linear Nim*).

- Other quality work

  Select one or two other pieces of work that demonstrate your best efforts. (These can be any work from the unit—Problem of the Week, homework, classwork, presentation, and so forth.)

Personal Growth

Your cover letter for *The Game of Pig* describes how the mathematical ideas develop in the unit. As part of your portfolio, write about your own personal development during this unit. You may want to address this question:

> *How do you think the ideas in this unit might affect your own behavior in situations that involve probability?*

You should include here any other thoughts you might like to share with a reader of your portfolio.

Appendix

Supplemental Problems

Probability, expected value, and the use of strategies are three of the important themes in *The Game of Pig*. The supplemental problems for this unit continue these themes. These are some examples:

• *Different Dice, Three-Dice Sums*, and *Heads or Tails?* ask you to find the probabilities for some events involving dice and coins.

• *Expected Conjectures* and *Squaring the Die* offer you a chance to get further insight into how expected value works.

• *Counters Revealed* and *Piling Up Apples* involve strategy for the counters game (from the activity of that name) and for a new game involving picking apples from piles.

Average Problems

1. Lucinda bought a dozen eggs on three different occasions. The average cost per dozen was $1.18.

   Give several different possible combinations for what the costs might have been for the different purchases.

Continued on next page

2. Two classes took an exam. In the first class, the average score was exactly 78%. In the second class, the average score was exactly 86%. But when the two classes were treated as one large group, the average was not 82%.

   a. How is this possible?

   b. What's the highest that the combined average could be? What's the lowest?

   c. Under what circumstances would the average of the two class averages be the same as the average you get when you treat the two classes as one large group? Explain your answer and be as complete as you can.

   Be sure to justify your answers.

3. Garrison Keillor describes Lake Wobegon as a place where "the children are all above average."

   Suppose someone measured all 85 ten-year-olds in the town and found that their average height was 4 feet 7 inches.

   a. Is it possible that all the ten-year-olds are taller than 4 feet 7 inches?

   b. If not, what is the largest number of ten-year-olds who could be taller than that? Explain your answer.

   c. Is it possible that Garrison Keillor is right, and all the ten-year-olds in Lake Wobegon are taller than average? What could that mean?

Mix and Match

Glenn likes to wear gloves. But he has some funny habits about his gloves. He keeps all of the left-hand gloves in one drawer and all of the right-hand gloves in another.

When he gets ready to go out on a cold day, he just pulls out one glove at random from each drawer and puts them on, without checking to see if they match.

Right now his left-hand glove drawer has two brown gloves and three gray gloves. His right-hand glove drawer has one brown glove, two gray gloves, and two red gloves. (Glenn also loses a lot of gloves.)

1. What is the probability that he will pull out a pair of gray gloves today?

2. What is the probability that he will pull out a matching pair of gloves today?

3. What is the probability that neither of his gloves will be brown?

Counters Revealed

Here is a simplified version of the counters game.

As in the regular version, your board consists of a rectangle with squares numbered from 2 through 12.

2	3	4	5	6	7	8	9	10	11	12

But instead of 11 counters to place on the board, you have only 2. You can place them in the same square if you want, or you can place them in two different squares.

As before, a pair of dice is rolled on each turn, and the numbers are added. If you have a counter in the square that matches the sum, you can remove that counter (but only one counter per roll). Your goal is to remove your counters as quickly as possible.

The challenge is to decide where to place the two counters to make your chances of winning quickly as good as possible.

1. Decide on at least three ways of placing the counters that you want to test out.

2. Set up a game board for one of your choices.

3. Play the game, and see how long it takes to win. Keep repeating until you think you have a good idea of how many rolls it would take, on average, to win with that placement of the counters.

4. Now repeat steps 2 and 3 for each of your other choices of initial position.

5. Write a report describing your work and summarizing your results. State any conclusions you reached, explaining your conclusions as well as you can.

Different Dice

Imagine a set of dice in which every 4 was replaced by a 7. So each die could roll 1, 2, 3, 5, 6, or 7, with each result equally likely.

Find the probability of each of the following results when rolling two of these dice.

1. The sum of the dice is 7.

2. The sum of the dice is less than 7.

3. The sum of the dice is greater than 7.

4. The product of the dice is even.

5. The product of the dice is odd.

6. Both dice are the same.

7. The sum of the dice is a multiple of 3.

8. The product of the dice is a multiple of 3.

Two-Spinner Sums

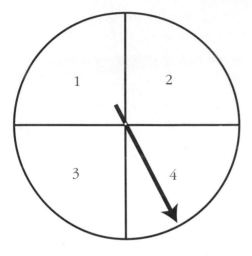 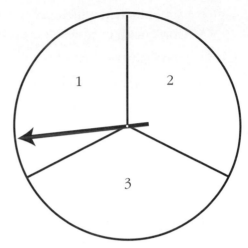

In some board games, you move your marker a certain number of spaces based on the result of a spinner.

Suppose you were playing a game using the two spinners above.

The rule is that you spin each spinner and move the same number of spaces as the sum of the two results.

1. Suppose you need a total of at least 5 from the two spinners to reach the winning position on the board. What is your probability of success?

2. Consider the various possible two-spin sums and the probabilities for each. How do these results compare to the results for two-dice sums? What are the similarities and what are the differences?

Three-Dice Sums

Suppose you roll three standard dice and add up the results. The lowest sum you can get is 3 (by rolling three 1's), and the highest is 18 (by rolling three 6's).

1. Without doing any analysis, what sums would you expect to be the most likely? Why?

2. Find the probability of getting each of the possible three-dice sums. Describe any patterns that you find, and explain them if you can.

3. Make up and answer some questions about three-dice sums.

Heads or Tails?

Coin #1

	H	T
H	Both heads	Tails on coin #1; heads on coin #2
T	Heads on coin #1; tails on coin #2	Both tails

Coin #2

You know that if you toss a balanced coin many times, you should get heads about half the time, and tails about half the time.

If you toss two balanced coins, the diagram at the left shows that the probability that they would both come out heads is $\frac{1}{4}$.

For example, if 100 people each tossed a pair of coins, about 25 of them would get two heads. Similarly, about 25 would get two tails, and about 50 would get one head and one tail.

1. Do a similar analysis for the case of three coins. That is, suppose three coins are all tossed at once, and find each of these probabilities.

    a. The probability of getting heads for all three coins

    b. The probability of getting two heads and one tail

    c. The probability of getting one head and two tails

    d. The probability of getting tails for all three coins

2. Now do the case of four coins. (*Hint:* Begin by making a list of the possible results.)

3. If there were ten coins, what would be the probability of getting

    a. all heads?

    b. nine heads and one tail?

4. What generalizations can you make about your results?

Expected Conjectures

Al and Betty were getting used to the idea of expected value, and they were making some conjectures.

Al wanted to find the expected value if you roll a die. He imagined rolling 600 times and figured that he would get about 100 one's, 100 two's, and so on.

So he did this computation:

$$100 \cdot 1 + 100 \cdot 2 + \cdots + 100 \cdot 6$$

This gave a total of 2100 points for the 600 rolls. He then divided by 600 to get the average per roll, which came out to 3.5.

1. Betty tried it with 6000 rolls and got the same average. Explain why their averages are the same. (Look for more than one explanation.)

2. When Al saw that the average was the same both ways, he decided he could find the average with only six rolls. Would he still get the same result? Explain.

3. Could you find the average with only one roll? Explain.

Squaring the Die

Here are some more conjectures that Al and Betty are making about expected value. What do you think of their ideas?

Use the definition of expected value based on "the long run" to justify your evaluation of their conjectures.

1. Al says: If you roll a die, the expected value is 3.5, since results of 1 through 6 are equally likely, and 3.5 is the average of the numbers 1, 2, 3, 4, 5, and 6.

   Does this give the right answer? Explain.

2. Betty says: If you roll two dice, the expected value should be twice as big as if you roll one die. Based on Al's idea in Question 1, she thinks the expected value for a two-dice sum is 7.

   What do you think? Explain.

Continued on next page

3. Al says: If the expected value for the *sum* of two dice is 3.5 + 3.5, then the expected value for the *product* of two dice should be 3.5 · 3.5, which is 12.25.

   Is Al right? Explain.

4. Finally, Betty says: If you roll a die and square the number that shows, the expected value for the result should be the square of the expected value for a single die, that is, 3.5^2, which is 12.25.

   Is Betty right? Explain.

Fair Spinners

1. Al and Betty are interested in changing their spinner game so that neither player has an advantage.

   They decide to use the same spinner that you saw in *Spinner Give and Take,* but they want to modify the game by changing the amount that Al wins when the spinner lands on the gray area.

   In other words, Betty still wins $1 from Al when the spinner lands in the white section. But Al wins some other amount when the spinner lands in the gray section.

   What should the new amount be so that the game is fair? Explain how you arrived at your answer.

2. Make up and solve a spinner problem of your own.

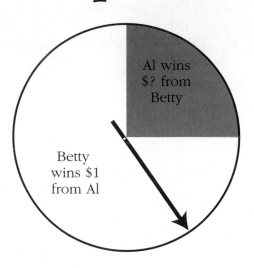

Al wins $? from Betty

Betty wins $1 from Al

A Fair Dice Game?

Here's a game to consider.

> We throw a pair of dice. If the sum is 2, 11, or 12, you win. If the sum is 7, I win. If the sum is anything else, no one wins, and we throw again. We keep throwing until one of us wins.

1. Do you think this game is fair? In other words, are we each equally likely to win? Explain why or why not. Use a rug (or rugs) in your explanation.

2. If you think it *is* a fair game, make up another dice game that you think *is not* fair. If you think the game *is not* fair, make up another dice game that you think *is* fair. Once again, use a rug in your explanation.

Free Throw Sammy

Sammy has a free throw success rate of 80%.

Construct an area model for the one-and-one situation with Sammy.

1. Using your area model, what is the probability that Sammy will get

   a. zero points?

   b. one point?

   c. two points?

2. Use your area model to find Sammy's expected value per one-and-one situation.

Get a Head!

At a school fund-raiser, students set up a booth with this game:

> You start flipping a regular coin. Each time you get heads, you get a payoff of $1. If you get tails, the game ends, and you get to keep the money you've won so far. (If you get tails on your first flip, you get nothing.)
>
> Also, if you get ten straight heads, you get your $10, but the game ends and you are given a $50 bonus.

For example, if you flip four heads and then tails, you win $4. If you flip ten heads, you win $60 altogether.

1. If the school charges $2 to play and each of the 1000 students at the school plays five times, how much profit should the school expect to make altogether?

2. The students are considering eliminating both the limit of ten heads and the bonus. How much profit should they expect to get if they make these changes? (*Note:* You may need to give an approximate answer to this problem, and you should definitely explain your reasoning.)

Piling Up Apples

Once upon a time, Al and Betty were collecting apples. They had collected two piles and were bored. So they decided to play a game.

They would take turns taking some apples from one of the piles. The one who took the last apple would win. They decided on these rules.

- On any turn, a player must take at least one apple.

- On any turn, a player can take apples from only one of the piles.

Continued on next page

At first, they decided to go alphabetically, so that Al would always choose first. At the end of each game, they would put the piles back the way they originally were.

There were 11 apples in Pile A and 8 apples in Pile B. After a few games, Al found a strategy so that he always won.

1. Figure out Al's strategy, and explain how he could always win.

The next day they played the same game, except the piles they played with were not the same size as the day before. Al still insisted on going first, but now, no matter what he did, Betty always won.

2. Figure out how many apples might have been in each pile, so that Betty could always beat Al, and explain how she won.

Each morning after that, they would decide what size piles they were going to use for that day. On each day, either Al won every game or Betty won every game. (Al still always went first.)

3. a. Find a rule, in terms of the sizes of the piles, that explains which player will always win.

   b. For the sizes where Al always wins, explain what his strategy is.

   c. For the sizes where Betty always wins, explain what her strategy is.

Eventually, they decided to switch to playing the game with three piles. Al still always went first, and they kept the same rules:

• On any turn, a player must take at least one apple.

• On any turn, a player can only take apples from one of the piles.

They found that with three piles, it was harder to tell who would win.

4. Find three piles so that Al can always win, and explain how he should play with these piles to insure a win.

5. Find three piles so that Betty can always win, and explain how she should play with those piles to insure a win.

Paying the Carrier

Now, you are the customer. Instead of paying $5 weekly, you decide to offer your newspaper carrier a different payment method.

The carrier will roll a pair of dice. If the sum is 4 or less, the carrier will get $20. If the sum is more than 4, the carrier will get some other fixed amount.

1. What should you choose for the other fixed amount (that is, the amount that the carrier gets for anything over 4) in order for this payment method to be equivalent, in the long run, to the $5 per week payment?

2. Describe in words how you found the answer in Question 1.

3. Now suppose that the normal weekly cost of the paper was Y but the carrier still gets $20 for a sum of 4 or less. What should you choose for the other fixed amount that the carrier gets (for any sum over 4) in order to make the payoff fair in the long run? (*Hint:* Work with some specific values for Y.)

More Martian Basketball

You may recall from the activity *Martian Basketball* that instead of having one-and-one free throw situations, Martians have one-and-one-and-one situations.

Here is information on three of the Martian Basketball Association All-Star players.

- Splurge Ripo: a 70% shooter in any situation

- Crago Dit: makes 70% of first shots, 60% of second shots, and 90% of third shots

- Lufy Boz: makes 80% of first shots, 50% of second shots, and 90% of third shots

Suppose the Martian All-Stars were playing the team from Venus, and for the last play of the game, the Martians got to choose one of their players for a one-and-one-and-one situation. Who would be the best person to have shooting? Who would be the worst? How might it depend on the score at that point?

Write an analysis of different cases and how you would decide each one.

Interruptions

Al and Betty are at the park flipping coins. Al gets a point if the coin is heads, and Betty gets a point if the coin is tails.

The first one to reach 10 points wins a prize of $15.

But with Al leading by a score of 8 to 7, Al's parents and Betty's parents interrupt the game, and Al and Betty are told that they each have to go home. They decide that, rather than hope to finish the game another time, they should just give out the prize now.

Al says, since he was leading, he should get the prize. Betty figures that each point should be worth $1, so Al should get $8 and she should get $7.

One of the parents suggests that they should figure out the probability each had of winning, and divide the money according to that.

1. How should they divide the money if they take this parent's advice? Explain your results carefully.

2. Pick two other possible incomplete games, and figure out how Al and Betty should divide the money using the parent's system.

Pig Strategies by Algebra

In *Homework 25: Should I Go On?* and in *Homework 26: Big Pig Meets Little Pig,* you looked at the question of when it pays for a player of Little Pig or Big Pig to draw or roll again.

In those assignments, you assumed that a group of students each had a particular score, and you found the expected value if they each drew or rolled once more.

In this assignment, you should work more generally.

1. Assume that a player has exactly S points in Little Pig. Find an algebraic expression in terms of S for that player's expected value if the player decides to draw one more cube and then stop.

2. a. For what values of S is your expression from Question 1 greater than S? In other words, when does the player gain in the long run by drawing again?

   b. For what values of S is your expression from Question 1 less than S?

3. Now do the analogous questions for Big Pig. That is, suppose a player has S points in Big Pig.

   a. Find an algebraic expression in terms of S for that player's expected value if the player decides to roll the die one more time and then stop.

   b. For what values of S is your expression from Question 3a greater than S? In other words, when does the player gain in the long run by rolling again?

   c. For what values of S is your expression from Question 3a less than S?

Fast Pig

Fast Pig is another variation of the game of Pig.

Instead of rolling one die again and again, you roll several dice at once, and you get only one roll per turn. (That's what makes it fast.)

If none of the dice comes up 1, your score is the sum of the dice. But if one or more of the dice comes up 1, your score for the turn is 0.

Although Fast Pig with just one die isn't very exciting, you may want to think about that game to get some ideas about the questions below.

1. Suppose you play Fast Pig with two dice.

   a. What is the probability that neither die will be a 1?

   b. If you consider only those turns with a non-zero score, what is your expected value for a turn of Fast Pig? (You might imagine dice with only five sides, labeled 2 through 6.)

   c. Taking into account your answers to parts a and b, what is the expected value altogether for a turn of two-dice Fast Pig?

2. Answer the same questions for three-dice Fast Pig.

3. Can you generalize the results? (You may want to think about one-die Fast Pig as well.)

4. What does the analysis of *n*-dice Fast Pig tell you about the expected value for certain strategies for Pig?

The Overland Trail

**Days
1-6**

A Journey Back in Time

This unit follows the nineteenth-century movement of
settlers from Missouri to California. You will see ways in
which these settlers may have used mathematics as they
undertook a trip that lasted several months and almost
two thousand miles.

You will encounter some very important mathematical
ideas—such as graphs, different uses of variables, lines of
best fit, and rate problems—as you travel across the continent.
You'll also learn interesting history as you and your fictional
family encounter some real-life participants in your travels.

Stanley Pinkston sets the stage for the long journey west.

The Overland Trail

from *Women's Diaries of the Westward Journey*

Between 1840 and 1870, a quarter of a million Americans crossed the continental United States, some twenty-four hundred miles of it, in one of the great migrations of modern times. They went West to claim free land* in the Oregon and California Territories, and they went West to strike it rich by mining gold and silver. Men and women knew they were engaged in nothing less than extending American possession of the continent from ocean to ocean. . . .

The westward movement was a major transplanting of young families. All the kinfolk who could be gathered assembled to make that hazardous passage together. . . .

The emigrants came from Missouri, Illinois, Iowa, and Indiana, and some all the way

*Note to students: While the land was offered "free" to these migrants, it was not land that was free for the taking. It was the home of the indigenous peoples who had been living there for thousands of years.

Continued on next page

Interactive Mathematics Program

from New York and New Hampshire. Most of them had moved to "free land" at least once before, and their parents and grandparents before them had similarly made several removals during their lifetime. These were a class of "peasant proprietors." They had owned land before and would own land again. They were young and consumed with boundless confidence, believing the better life tomorrow could be won by the hard work of today. . . .

The journey started in the towns along the Missouri River between St. Joseph and Council Bluffs. These settlements came to be known as the "jumping-off places." In the winter months emigrants gathered to join wagon parties and to wait for the arrival of kin. It was an audacious journey through territory that was virtually unknown. Guidebooks promised that the adventure would take no more than three to four months time—a mere summer's vacation. But the guidebooks were wrong. Often there was no one in a wagon train who really knew what the roads would bring, or if there were any roads at all. Starting when the mud of the roads began to harden in mid-April, the emigrants would discover that the overland passage took every ounce of ingenuity and tenacity they possessed. For many, it would mean six to eight months of grueling travel, in a wagon with no springs, under a canvas that heated up to 110° by midday, through drenching rains and summer storms. It would mean swimming cattle across river and living for months at a time in tents.

From *Women's Diaries of the Westward Journey* by Lillian Schlissel. Copyright © 1983 by Schocken Books Inc. Reprinted by permission of Schocken Books, published by Pantheon Books, a division of Random House, Inc.

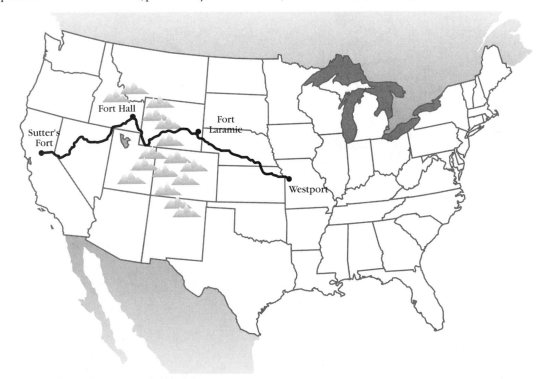

Homework 1   Just Like Today

Throughout history there has been movement of people from place to place.

In this assignment, consider a present-day movement of people and compare it to the movement of people along the Overland Trail.

There are many different levels on which you can consider this topic.

For instance, you can look at your own family and a move they made, or you can look at the movement of people from one country to another.

Write about how the two movements—Overland Trail and present-day—are similar and about how they are different. You might comment on why the people are moving in each case and how they get from one place to another.

Overland Trail Families

[From the diary of Catherine Haun]

Ada Millington was twelve when her family set out for California. It was a large family; her father, who had five children by his first marriage, was traveling with his second wife and their six children. The youngest was a year and a half old. In addition, there were five young hired hands. And there was Mrs. Millington's sister and brother-in-law, their children, and their hired hands. And there was the brother-in-law's sister, stepfather and mother. The party seemed large and secure. . . .

Our own party consisted of six men and two women. Mr. Haun, my brother Derrick, Mr. Bowen, three young men to act as drivers, a woman cook and myself. . . .

A regulation "prairie schooner" drawn by four oxen and well filled with suitable supplies, with two pack mules following on behind was the equipment of the Kenna family. There were two men, two women, a lad of fifteen years, a daughter thirteen and their half brother six weeks of age. This baby was our mascot and the youngest member of the company. . . .

One family by the name of Lemore consisted of man, wife and two little girls. They had only a large express wagon drawn by four mules and meager but well chosen, supply of food and feed. A tent was strapped to one side of the wagon, a roll of bedding to the other side, baggage, bundles, pots, pans and bags of horse feed hung on behind; the effect was really grotesque. . . .

Mr. West from Peoria, Ill. had another man, his wife, a son Clay about 20 years of age and his daughter, America, eighteen. Unfortunately Mr. West had gone to the extreme of providing himself with such a heavy wagon and load they were deemed objectionable as fellow argonauts. After disposing of some of their supplies they were allowed to join us. . . .

A mule team from Washington, D.C. was very insufficiently provisioned. . . [by] a Southern gentlemen "unused to work. . . ." They deserted the train at Salt Lake as they could not proceed with their equipment. . . .

Much in contrast to these men were four batchelors Messers Wilson, Goodall, Fifield and Martin, who had a wagon drawn by four oxen and two milch cows following behind. The latter gave milk all the way to the sink of the Humboldt where they died, having acted as draught animals for several weeks after the oxen had perished. Many a cup of milk was given to the children of the train and the mothers tried in every way possible to express their gratitude.

The Family

Your group is going to be responsible for the planning and travel of four family units on the wagon train. In this activity, you will decide on the composition of each of your families.

Here are some general conventions.

- Anyone more than 14 years old is considered an adult.

- A *young child* is anyone less than 6 years old.

- An *older child* is anyone from the age of 6 through the age of 14.

- Only adults have children.

- Hired hands are adults and are not related to the other members of the family unit. They are considered to be part of the family with which they travel.

- A wagon can accommodate at most 6 people. So a family unit of 6 or fewer people needs only one wagon, but a family unit of between 7 and 12 people needs two wagons, a family unit of between 13 and 18 people needs three wagons, and so on.

The information below and on the next two pages describes four types of family units that traveled on the trail. Your group should create one family of each type, and each group member will have final responsibility for one of the families.

Make up a complete list of all the people in each family. *Give each person a first and last name, an age, and a sex.* (Use names from the list in *Overland Trail Names*.)

Record how many adult men, adult women, older children, and young children there are in each family. (You will use this information in later assignments.)

The Minimal Family

Some family units were quite small, by the standards of the time. A *minimal family* fits the conditions listed on the facing page.

Continued on next page

- There are more adults than children.

- There is at least one child.

- There are at least as many adult men as adult women.

- There is at most one married couple.

- There is at least one pair of adult siblings.

- The number of people in the family unit is less than eight.

The Large Family

In a large family, one finds not only many children but many other adults in addition to the father and mother. A *large family* meets these criteria.

- The number of children is greater than the number of adults.

- There are between one and six hired hands.

- Four generations of family members are represented.

- At least two married couples are present in the group.

- There are more young children than there are older children.

- There are at most 25 family members.

Continued on next page

The Nonfamily

Some groups traveling on the trail were hardly families at all. A *nonfamily* is one that fits the conditions below.

- There are no married couples.

- Any adult women in the group are traveling with a brother or a father.

- There is at most one adult woman for each four adult men.

- The number of adult men in the group can range from two to eight.

- There is no more than one child for each five adults.

- There are at least as many older children as young children.

The Conglomerate Family

Sometimes small families banded together into a single unit for the trip. Such a *conglomerate family* meets these conditions.

- There are two or three "partial families" in the unit.

- Each partial family includes at least one adult.

- Each partial family has fewer than five people in it.

- The total number of children equals at least one-third the total number of adults.

- There are more young children than older children.

Overland Trail Names

The names in these lists are taken from sources contemporary to the period of the Overland Trail.

Last Names

Ackley	Cazneau	Frizzell	Kelsey	Smith
Adams	Clappe	Frost	Ketcham	Spencer
Agatz	Clarke	Fulkerth	Knight	Stewart
Allen	Collins	Geer	Mason	Stone
Ashley	Colt	Goltra	Millington	Tabor
Bailey	Cooke	Hall	Minto	Ward
Ballou	Cox	Hanna	Norton	Washburn
Behrins	Dalton	Haun	Parker	Waters
Bell	Deady	Helmick	Parrish	Welch
Belshaw	Duniway	Hines	Pengra	Whitman
Bennett	Findley	Hixon	Porter	Wilson
Bogart	Fish	Hockensmith	Powers	Wood
Brown	Foster	Hodder	Pringle	
Buck	Fowler	Hunt	Rudd	
Butler	French	Jones	Sanford	
Carpenter	Frink	Kellogg	Sawyer	

Female First Names

Abigail	Catherine	Esther	Louise	Nancy
Ada	Celinda	Hallie	Lucinda	Rebecca
Amelia	Charlotte	Helen	Lucy	Roxana
America	Clara	Jane	Lydia	Sarah
Ann	Elizabeth	Julia	Margaret	Susan
Caroline	Ellen	Lavinia	Mary	Velina

Male First Names

Addison	Evan	Henry	Lafayette	Robert
Alpheus	Ezra	Holmes	Lewis	Samuel
Charles	Francis	James	Moses	Solomon
Dexter	George	Jared	Perry	Thomas
Edward	Gilbert	Jay	Peter	Tosten
Enoch	Godfry	John	Richard	William

POW 8 *The Haybaler Problem*

The Situation

You have five bales of hay.

For some reason, instead of being weighed individually, they were weighed in all possible combinations of two: bales 1 and 2, bales 1 and 3, bales 1 and 4, bales 1 and 5, bales 2 and 3, bales 2 and 4, and so on.

The weights of each of these combinations were written down and arranged in numerical order, *without keeping track of which weight matched which pair of bales*. The weights in kilograms were 80, 82, 83, 84, 85, 86, 87, 88, 90, and 91.

Your Task

Your initial task is to find out how much each bale weighs. In particular, you should determine if there is more than one possible set of weights, and explain how you know.

Once you are done looking for solutions, look back over the problem to see if you can find some easier or more efficient way to find the weights.

Continued on next page

Write-up

1. *Problem Statement*

2. *Process:* This is especially important in this problem. Include a description of any materials you used. Be sure to discuss ways in which you tried to attack the problem but which didn't lead anywhere.

   Also discuss any insights you had after working on the problem about other ways you might have solved it.

3. *Solution:* Show both how you know your weights work and how you know that you have not missed some other possibilities.

4. *Extensions*

5. *Evaluation*

Adapted from *Problem of the Week* by Lyle Fisher and Bill Medigovich (Dale Seymour Publications, © 1981).

Homework 2   Hats for the Families

Everyone on the westward journey on the Overland Trail will be spending long hours in the hot sun. Before setting out on the road, each person will need to have one good hat to help keep the sun off.

1. What is the minimum and maximum number of hats that might be needed for each type of family unit?

2. What would be the minimum and maximum number of hats that might be needed for a wagon train consisting of one family unit of each type?

3. Estimate the number of hats that might be needed for all the family units in your class. Explain your reasoning.

Homework 3 The Search for Dry Trails

The Setting

Families used to arrive in the Westport area (near present-day Kansas City, Missouri) during the winter before they were to make their journey across the west. Around April, the muddy trails would begin to dry and the settlers would start their trip. But rainy weather could still make roads muddy and significantly slow a wagon train's progress.

Continued on next page

The three main trails to the eastern slope of the Rocky Mountains were

- the Smoky Hill Trail, which followed the Smoky Hill River to Denver, Colorado

- the Santa Fe Trail, which followed the Arkansas River to southern Colorado

- the Oregon Trail, which followed the North Platte River to Laramie, Wyoming

Note: These descriptions use the names given by settlers to places and geographical features.

Your Problem

Over the years, the owner of the Westport Trading Post has gotten word back from various friends concerning the rainfall that they encountered on their routes.

The owner has compiled the table below, in which each entry for a given trail represents a different year on that trail.

Santa Fe Trail		Smoky Hill Trail		Oregon Trail	
Name	Number of rainy days	Name	Number of rainy days	Name	Number of rainy days
William	24	Tosten	18	Enoch	42
Amelia	3	Roxana	16	Sarah	9
Ezra	21	Hallie	13	Godfry	11
Lavinia	5	Ada	14	Alpheus	10
Moses	23	Dexter	19	Ann	12
				Jared	13

A big argument occurs one evening. It seems that family members looking at the same data cannot agree on which trail would be the driest. (Of course, the dryness of a trail was not the only factor in choosing the route.)

1. If you were deciding for your Overland Trail family, which trail would you choose? Why?

2. Give good reasons why each of the two paths that you did not choose could have been chosen.

Homewok 4   Family Constraints

The families described in the following questions do not necessarily belong to an Overland Trail wagon train.

1. The Hickson household contains three people, of different generations. The total of the ages of the three family members is 90.

    a. Find reasonable ages for the three Hicksons.

    b. Find another reasonable set of ages for them.

Continued on next page

c. One student, in solving this problem, wrote

$$C + (C + 20) + (C + 40) = 90$$

i. What do you think C means here?

ii. How do you think the student got 20 and 40?

iii. What set of ages do you think the student came up with?

2. There are four members in the Jackson family, again representing three generations. As in the Hickson household, the total of the ages of these people is 90.

a. Find a possible set of ages in which there are two children, one parent, and one grandparent.

b. Find a possible set of ages in which there is one child, two parents, and one grandparent.

c. Find a possible set of ages in which there is one child, one parent, and two grandparents.

d. In solving Question 2a, one student wrote

$$C + C + (C + 18) + (C + 36) = 90$$

i. What does C represent here?

ii. What do 18 and 36 represent?

iii. Why do you think this student used 18 and 36 while the student in Question 1c used 20 and 40?

iv. What set of ages do you think this student came up with?

Planning for the Long Journey

Your group will be planning the Overland Trail trip for the four families you created.

The first leg of the journey takes you from Westport, Missouri, to Fort Laramie, Wyoming, some 600 miles away. Wagon trains traveled about 20 miles each day during this part of the journey.

In this activity, you will choose supplies for the first leg of the journey.

Continued on next page

Part I: Generating Ideas

1. The first task is to identify those supplies you think the four Overland Trail families will need. Brainstorm to create a list. Be specific. For example, don't just say *tools*—make a list of the tools that you think it would be important to take. Don't just say *food*—include in your list the different kinds of food the family will need.

2. As you brainstorm and compile this tentative list, questions may occur to you that you cannot answer. *Write these down* to share with the rest of the class.

Part II: Making Decisions

3. *Overland Trail Price List* gives the cost for certain items that you may wish to purchase. Assume that you have $10 for each Overland Trail person to spend on these supplies. Decide how much of each of these items you want to buy for each of your group's Overland Trail families.

   Your purchase list must include gunpowder, sugar, and beans. You may wish to save some money for use along the trail.

   Note: Whatever you purchase now, an identical amount will be ordered to be waiting for you in Fort Laramie when you arrive there. Unless you make changes when you get to Fort Laramie, those will be your supplies from Fort Laramie to the next major stop, Fort Hall. The supplies you purchase may affect the fate of your Overland Trail families on their trip across the country.

Overland Trail Price List

Item	Cost
flour	2¢/lb
biscuits	3¢/lb
bacon	5¢/lb
coffee	7¢/lb
tea	50¢/lb
sugar	10¢/lb
lard	6¢/lb
beans	8¢/lb
dried fruit	24¢/lb
salt	4¢/lb
pepper	4¢/lb
baking soda	4¢/lb
gunpowder	25¢/lb

Prices in the list are taken from
Women and Men on the Overland Trail
by John Mack Faragher (New Haven:
Yale University Press, 1979).
Copyright © 1979 by Yale University Press.

Homework 5   Lunchtime

Imagine that the students in your mathematics class are going to have lunch together. The meal will consist of four parts.

- Main dish

- Side dish

- Dessert

- Beverage

1. Make a list of the items that will have to be purchased.

2. How much of each item will be needed? Explain how you made your decision.

3. Find the cost of each item on the list either by asking a person in your house who shops and would know, or by going to the grocery store and getting the actual price.

4. Compute the total cost of the food for lunch.

5. How much should each student be charged in order for the class to be able to purchase the food? Explain your answer.

Homework 6   Shoelaces

Shoelaces are one small item that must be taken on the Overland Trail. In this assignment you will consider how much of this commodity is needed.

Assume that shoes already have laces, but that you want to be able to replace each lace once during the journey. (Also assume that each pair of shoes or boots needs its own laces.)

Here is some detailed information about shoelace requirements that you should use.

- Each man needs to bring two pairs of boots and one pair of shoes.

- Each woman needs to bring one pair of boots and two pairs of shoes.

- Each child needs to have three pairs of boots.

- A shoelace for each adult boot is 48 inches long.

- A shoelace for each adult shoe is 32 inches long.

- A shoelace for each child's boot is 24 inches long.

1. How many inches of shoelace does a woman need?

2. How many inches of shoelace does a man need?

3. How many inches of shoelace does a child need?

4. Find the total length of shoelace needed for the specific Overland Trail family for which you are responsible.

5. Describe in words how you used your answers from Questions 1, 2, and 3 to get your answer to Question 4.

Days 7-10

Setting Out with Variables

You've formed your Overland Trail families, packed up some supplies, and off you go from Westport, Missouri, toward Fort Laramie, Wyoming. You're about to see how equations and algebraic expressions may have helped the settlers plan their journey and meet its challenges.

The new POW coming up, *POW 9: Around the Horn,* involves a different journey, with some complicated comings and goings.

In order to focus on the meaning of variables, students are creating their own "ox expressions" to share with the class.

Homework 7   Laced Travelers

In *Homework 6: Shoelaces,* you used certain information to find out how much shoelace each man, woman, and child needs.

In this assignment, you are told how much they each need. These amounts are different from those in the previous assignment, and you should use these new amounts to answer the questions below. Suppose that the statements below were true in 1852.

- You could purchase shoelaces for about 2¢ per yard.
- An average wagon train consisted of 25 families.
- An average family had six people in it (counting unmarried relatives and hired hands): two men, one woman, and three children.
- Approximately 150 wagon trains went through Westport, Missouri, in the year 1852 on their way west.
- Each man needed 5 yards of shoelace.
- Each woman needed 4 yards of shoelace.
- Each child needed 3 yards of shoelace.

Continued on next page

Answer these questions.

1. How many yards of shoelace did the settlers who went through Westport in 1852 need altogether?

   Once you've found an answer, describe in words how you did the computation.

2. Write two more interesting questions related to the journey that you can answer from the given data.

3. Answer one of the questions you made up in Question 2.

4. Suppose that in 1853, smaller families were migrating west, so that the mean family size was only five people (one less child). Answer Question 1 for the year 1853 (assuming that the other information is unchanged).

POW 9   *Around the Horn*

Instead of going overland to reach California, some families migrated west by taking a ship that went around Cape Horn at the tip of South America.

Suppose a ship leaves New York for San Francisco on the first of every month at noon, and at the same instant a ship leaves San Francisco for New York.

Suppose also that each ship arrives exactly six months after it leaves.

If you were on a ship leaving from New York, how many ships from San Francisco would you meet?

Write-up

1. *Problem statement:* If there were any assumptions that you needed to make in order to do this problem, be sure to state them clearly.

2. *Process:* Include any diagrams or materials you used in working on this problem.

3. *Solution*

4. *Extensions*

5. *Evaluation:* Instead of evaluating the problem itself, write an evaluation of your own work on this problem. How well do you think you understood the problem and explained your thinking?

Homework 8   To Kearny by Equation

When the first emigrants went west, crossing rivers was dangerous and time consuming. Travelers were grateful and travel time was shortened when people started ferries to shuttle wagons across the rivers.

The first major stop along the way from Westport to Fort Laramie was at Fort Kearny (now Kearney, Nebraska).

1. Joseph and Lewis Papan, two brothers, were among the "mixed bloods" of the time—those who had one Native American parent and one parent of European origin. They operated a ferry over the Kansas River at Topeka, on the way from Westport to Fort Kearny.

   Make the following assumptions:

   - The fee for crossing the 230-yard-wide river was $1 for each wagon.

   - The ferry captain received pay of 40¢ per hour from the Papans for the time he spent going back and forth.

Continued on next page

The Papan brothers could then calculate the profit each of them made by using the equation

$$\text{profit} = \frac{W - 0.4H}{2}$$

in which W was the number of wagons that crossed the river and H was the number of hours that the ferry captain spent going back and forth. (This profit formula takes into account the captain's salary, but does not take into account the Papans' other expenses, such as upkccp of the boat.)

a. Explain why this formula makes sense.

Suppose further that a round trip on the ferry took 20 minutes and that the ferry carried only one family at a time.

b. How much profit would each of the Papan brothers make from the family unit for which you are responsible? (*Reminder:* A family unit of between 7 and 12 people requires two wagons, a family unit of between 13 and 18 people requires three wagons, and so on.)

c. How much profit would each of the Papan brothers make from your group's four family units?

2. Louis Vieux was a business manager, interpreter, and chief of the Potawatomi. He made many trips to Washington to consult with officials about the affairs of Native Americans.

Vieux was also a ferry operator. He operated a ferry and toll bridge over the Vermillion River, the third major river crossing in Kansas.

Suppose that he charged a certain amount for each wagon and then an additional amount for each person, with different amounts for men, women, and children. More specifically, suppose that the amount Louis Vieux charged was given by the equation

$$\text{price to cross (in dollars)} = 0.5W + 0.25M + 0.1F + 0.05C$$

in which W was the number of wagons, M the number of men, F the number of women, and C the number of children.

a. Use this formula to explain what Vieux charged in each of the individual cost categories (that is, for each wagon, for each man, and so forth).

b. What would be the crossing cost for the family unit for which you are responsible?

c. What would be the total cost for your group's four family units?

Ox Expressions

The table below defines some symbols as variables to represent certain quantities. For example, *F* stands for "the number of **F**amilies in a wagon train." (The **boldface** letters in the table will help to remind you of what each symbol represents.)

A specific numerical value is provided for each variable. You should treat this value as constant for all cases. For example, assume that *every* wagon train contains 25 families. (Of course, these values will probably not be the actual numbers in your class wagon train.)

Symbol	Meaning	Numerical value
F	the number of **F**amilies in a wagon train	25 families per train
M	the number of **M**en in a family	2 men per family
W	the number of **W**omen in a family	1 woman per family
C	the number of **C**hildren in a family	3 children per family
V	the number of wagons (**V**ehicles) per family	1 wagon per family
T	the number of wagon **T**rains in one year	150 trains per year
Y	the number of pairs (**Y**okes) of oxen per wagon	3 yokes per wagon
A	the number of oxen (**A**nimals) per yoke	2 oxen per yoke
P	the weight of one ox (in **P**ounds)	1200 pounds per ox
L	the **L**oad for one wagon (in pounds)	2500 pounds per wagon
G	the amount of **G**rass eaten by one ox in one day (in pounds)	40 pounds of grass per ox per day
H	the amount of water (**H**$_2$O) consumed by one ox in one day (in gallons)	2 gallons of water per ox per day
B	the amount of water (**B**everage) consumed by one person in one day (in gallons)	0.5 gallons of water per person per day
D	the number of **D**ays on the trail	169 days

Using the given letters, it is possible to write many different algebraic expressions. Although you can always substitute numbers for the letters and do the arithmetic, most of the expressions you create will have no real meaning.

Continued on next page

For example, for the expression *MG*, you can multiply the number of men per family by the amount of grass an ox can eat in a day, but the product you get doesn't have any useful application. In other words, *MG* doesn't really mean anything.

But some expressions *do* have a meaning. For example, *FC*, the number of families in a wagon train times the number of children in a family, represents the total number of children traveling in a wagon train. So the expression *FC* has meaning.

The phrase "the number of children traveling in the train" is a concise way to describe the number represented by *FC*. We will call this the **summary phrase.**

The table tells you that there are 25 families in a wagon train, so $F = 25$, and that there are 3 children in a family, so $C = 3$. Therefore, $FC = 25 \cdot 3 = 75$, and there are 75 children in a wagon train. Even if the numbers were different, *FC* would still represent the number of children in a wagon train.

Your Task

Your task is to come up with as many meaningful algebraic expressions as you can, using the symbols above. For each expression, go through the steps listed below.

- Write the expression.

- Explain what the expression means, using a summary phrase.

- Give the numerical value of the expression, based on the values of the individual variables given in the table.

Homework 9 Ox Expressions at Home

In this assignment you continue to work with algebraic expressions and summary phrases.

You will be given specific algebraic expressions and asked to write summary phrases for them; you also will be given specific summary phrases and asked to write algebraic expressions for them.

Reminder: The summary phrase for *FC* is "the number of children on the wagon train" and not "the number of families in a wagon train times the number of children in a family."

The symbols below are the same as those used in *Ox Expressions*. Though no specific numerical values are assigned here, you should assume that each symbol represents a single number.

Symbol	Meaning
F	the number of **Families** in a wagon train
M	the number of **Men** in a family
W	the number of **Women** in a family
C	the number of **Children** in a family
V	the number of wagons (**Vehicles**) per family
T	the number of wagon **Trains** in one year
Y	the number of pairs (**Yokes**) of oxen per wagon
A	the number of oxen (**Animals**) per yoke
P	the weight of one ox (in **Pounds**)
L	the **Load** for one wagon (in pounds)
G	the amount of **Grass** eaten by one ox in one day (in pounds)
H	the amount of water (**H₂O**) consumed by one ox in one day (in gallons)
B	the amount of water (**Beverage**) consumed by one person in one day (in gallons)
D	the number of **Days** on the trail

1. Write a summary phrase for the expression $W + M + C$.

2. Write an algebraic expression for the water consumed in a day by a family.

3. Write a summary phrase for the expression $D(H + B)$.

Continued on next page

4. Write an algebraic expression for the number of people in a wagon train.

5. Write a summary phrase for the expression *FM*.

6. Write an algebraic expression for the amount of water consumed by an ox on the trip.

7. Does the expression *WL* have a meaning? If so, what is it?

8. Make up a meaningful algebraic expression of your own and give a summary phrase for it.

Homework 10 If I Could See This Thing

No nation was safe from the ravages of smallpox, cholera, measles, scarlet fever, influenza, and tuberculosis. These diseases, which were imported from Europe, took a great toll on Native Americans, bringing death, destruction, and untold misery, killing more people than warfare, slavery, or starvation.

The passage below is taken from a description by George Bent of the Southern Cheyenne nation.

> In '49, the emigrants brought cholera up the Platte Valley, and from the emigrant trains it spread to the Indian camps. "Cramps" the Indians called it....On the Platte whole camps could be seen deserted with tepees full of dead bodies...Our Tribe suffered very heavy loss; half of the tribe died, some old people say.
>
> My Grandmother took the children that summer...to the Canadian [to get] medicine. During the medicine dance an Osage visitor fell down in the crowd with cholera cramps. The Indians broke camp at once and fled in every

Continued on next page

direction. Here a brave man…mounted his horse…and rode through camp shouting, "If I could see this thing, if I knew where it was, I would go there and kill it." He was taken with cramps as he rode.

From *Life of George Bent* by Savoie Lotinville (Norman, OK: University of Oklahoma Press, 1968).

1. It has been estimated that between 1492 and 1900 the Native American population decreased by about 90%.

   Use variables and an equation to show how you would find the population of Native Americans at the end of this time period if you knew the population of Native Americans at the beginning of this period.

   Suggestion: Pick a number that you think might represent the population in 1492, and figure out what the 1900 population would have been. Then describe your computation in words, before putting the relationship into equation form using variables.

2. Death occurred among travelers on the Overland Trail as well.

   The fatality rate differed from one wagon train to the next. Assume that in your wagon train, five percent of the adults and ten percent of the children will die of cholera on the road from Fort Kearny, Nebraska, to Fort Laramie, Wyoming.

   a. Figure out how this will change the size of your total class wagon train.

   b. Put the result from Question 2a into an In-Out table in which there are two inputs—the number of adults and the number of children—and the output is the total number of people who will be left in a wagon train after this leg of the journey.

      Add two more rows to this table, using your own choice of values for the two inputs in each row. That is, make up two possible combinations for the number of adults and number of children, and then find the output in your table for each combination.

   c. Introduce variables and write a rule for the In-Out table in Question 2b.

Days 11-14

The Graph Tells a Story

They say that a picture is worth a thousand words. While you rest in Fort Laramie and prepare for the next leg of your journey, you look at some posters describing certain aspects of the journey. These posters contain graphs, which depict how two quantities are related. As you will see, graphs are closely related to equations and In-Out tables.

By the way, your next POW involves a different kind of adventure. In *POW 10: On Your Own,* you will imagine you have finished high school and are living on your own. Are you ready for that?

Teachers preparing to teach "The Overland Trail" get their own presentations ready on "Wagon Train Sketches and Situations."

Wagon Train Sketches and Situations

Number of pairs
of shoes needed

Number of people
in a wagon train family

A graph sketch can be used to describe a
real situation.

For example, the graph sketch at the left
shows that the number of pairs of shoes
needed for a wagon train family unit
depends on the number of people in the
family unit.

In this activity, you will look at such sketches and say what you think is happening, and
you will also create sketches to express information presented about situations.

Part I: From Sketch to Situation

When you arrive in Fort Laramie, you see posters promoting the journey westward.
These posters contain the graph sketches below, and describe relationships concerning
the trip on the Overland Trail.

For each graph, describe a situation that the graph could represent. In addition, answer
any questions next to the graph.

1. According to the graph sketch at the
   right, do people on the trail drink the
   same amount of coffee each day?

   Explain your answer.

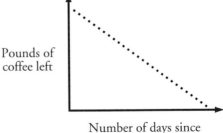

Pounds of
coffee left

Number of days since
leaving Fort Laramie

Continued on next page

2. What do you think is happening at the points on the graph sketch labeled *A*, *B*, and *C*?

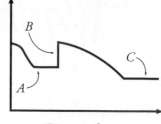

Amount of water in storage on the wagon

Distance from Fort Laramie

3. At what part of this graph sketch was the wagon train moving fastest? (You can trace the graph and mark your answer.)

Distance from Fort Laramie

Time elapsed since leaving Fort Laramie

4. Why does the graph sketch at the right consist of individual dots instead of a line?

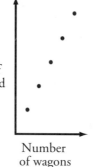

Number of oxen needed

Number of wagons

Part II: From Situation to Sketch

Below you will find descriptions of relationships concerning the trip on the Overland Trail. For each description, sketch a graph that illustrates the relationship.

5. Wagons of the same size and type can accommodate a fixed number of people. Make a graph sketch that shows the relationship between the number of wagons (of a fixed size and type) and the number of people those wagons can carry.

6. As the number of settlers on the trail increased, the buffalo population declined. Make a graph sketch that shows the relationship between the number of settlers and the buffalo population.

Homewcrk 11   Graph Sketches

Part I: Sketches to Situations

Each of the graph sketches below illustrates a relationship between two quantities. In each case, describe a situation that is illustrated by the graph.

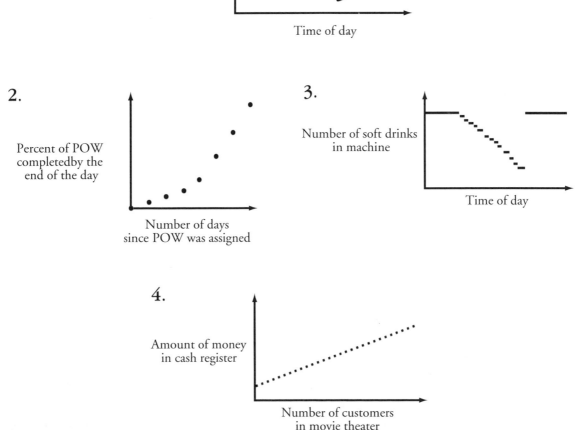

1.

Hunger level

Time of day

2.

Percent of POW completedby the end of the day

Number of days since POW was assigned

3.

Number of soft drinks in machine

Time of day

4.

Amount of money in cash register

Number of customers in movie theater

Continued on next page

Part II: Situations and Sketches

Begin with a situation in which you describe a possible relationship between two quantities.

Put this description on a separate piece of paper, and on the back, sketch the appropriate graph for that relationship. Remember to label the axes.

In Need of Numbers

Graph sketches describe a situation, but the description would be more complete if the graph included numerical information.

You can do this by putting a scale on each axis, showing the numerical values that the points on each axis represent.

To scale an axis, you have to decide what range of values is appropriate for the particular situation and for the quantities involved. You also have to decide how to display the scale on each axis.

For each of the sketches illustrated on the next page, go through the three steps listed below.

• Make a copy of the sketch on graph paper.

• On your copy, scale the axes with appropriate values.

• Write down why your scales are reasonable and what assumptions you had to make.

Continued on next page

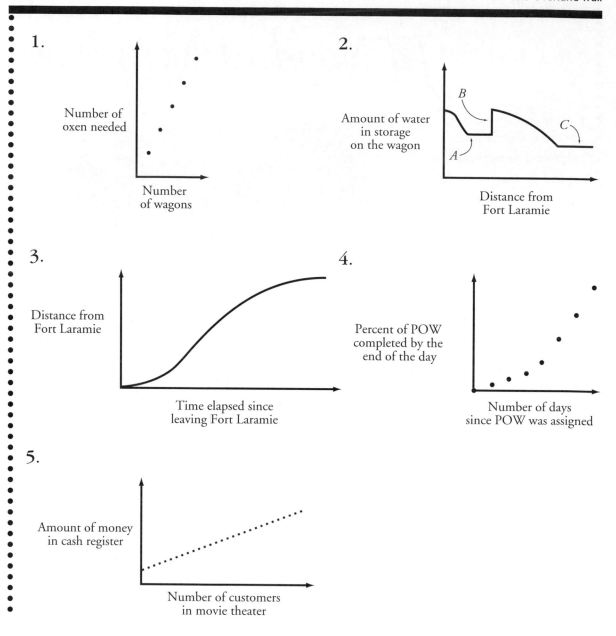

1.

Number of
oxen needed

Number
of wagons

2.

B

Amount of water
in storage
on the wagon

A

C

Distance from
Fort Laramie

3.

Distance from
Fort Laramie

Time elapsed since
leaving Fort Laramie

4.

Percent of POW
completed by the
end of the day

Number of days
since POW was assigned

5.

Amount of money
in cash register

Number of customers
in movie theater

Homework 12   The Issues Involved

1. In *In Need of Numbers,* you put appropriate scales on the axes of different graphs.

   Make a list of difficulties you had and questions you would like answered that are related to scaling the axes of a graph.

The following questions will help you think in more detail about graphs and scaling. Use examples to explain your thinking and be detailed in your explanations.

2. Should the vertical axis always begin at zero? What is the effect if the axis does not begin at zero? What about the horizontal axis?

3. How do you decide what numbers to write along the axes?

4. The graph at the right shows the average height of boys in the United States at different ages.

   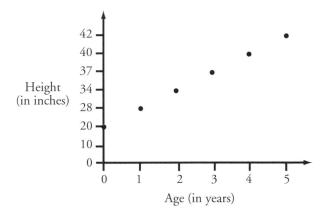

   The graph appears to suggest that boys grow at a constant rate through age five.

   a. Why might someone make this conclusion from a quick glance at the graph?

   b. Why is this an incorrect conclusion?

   c. Redraw the graph so it is not misleading.

5. Suppose you wanted to sketch a graph showing the number of livestock deaths during the Overland Trail trip. Would you use a continuous or a discrete graph to represent this situation? Why?

Out Numbered

The scaled graphs in this activity are similar to examples you have seen before. Base your answers to the questions *on the scales shown in these graphs*.

1. This graph shows the number of people that can be carried in a given number of wagons.

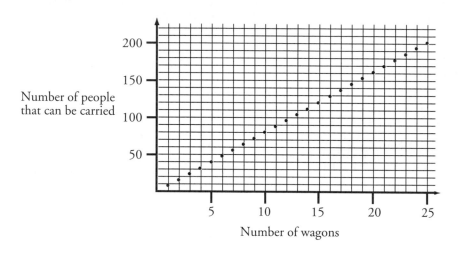

Number of people that can be carried

Number of wagons

a. How many people can three wagons carry?

b. How many people can five wagons carry?

c. How many people can ten wagons carry?

d. Make an In-Out table with the information from Questions 1a through 1c (In = number of wagons; Out = number of people that can be carried).

e. Find a rule for the number of people that *x* wagons can carry. (Use the graph to generate additional rows for the In-Out table if you need more information.)

2. The next graph shows the amount of coffee left in terms of the number of days since leaving Fort Laramie.

a. How much coffee was left 10 days after leaving Fort Laramie?

b. How much coffee was left 15 days after leaving Fort Laramie?

c. How much coffee was left 35 days after leaving Fort Laramie?

Continued on next page

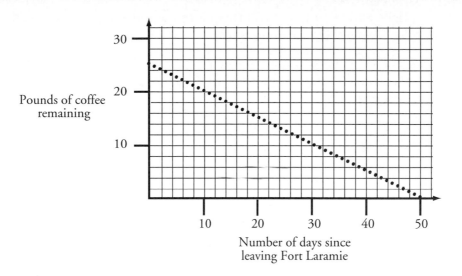

d. Make an In-Out table with the information from Questions 2a through 2c (*In* = number of days since leaving Fort Laramie; *Out* = number of pounds of coffee left).

e. Find a rule for the amount of coffee left *x* days after leaving Fort Laramie. (Generate additional rows for the In-Out table if you need more information.)

3. The next graph shows the amount of money in a movie theater cash register as a function of the number of customers in the theater.

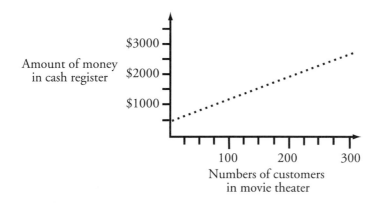

a. How much money would be in the cash register if there are 25 customers?

b. How much money would be in the cash register if there are 75 customers?

c. How much money would be in the cash register if there are 250 customers?

Continued on next page

d. Make an In-Out table with the information from Questions 3a through 3c (*In* = number of customers; *Out* = amount of money in cash register).

e. Find a rule for the amount of money in the cash register if there are *x* customers. (Add more rows to the In-Out table if you need more information.)

Homework 13

Situations, Graphs, Tables, and Rules

In *Out Numbered,* you used three different ways to represent a situation.

- A graph

- An In-Out table

- A rule for the table

The relationships between these three forms of representation, and the relationship of each to the original situation, are among the most fundamental ideas in mathematics.

In *Patterns* you expressed real-world situations by using In-Out tables and found rules for the tables. In this unit you have been using *graphs* to represent situations.

Explain how the four ideas—situations, graphs, In-Out tables, and rules—relate to one another. Use examples from this unit and examples of your own to show how you can go from one form of representation to another.

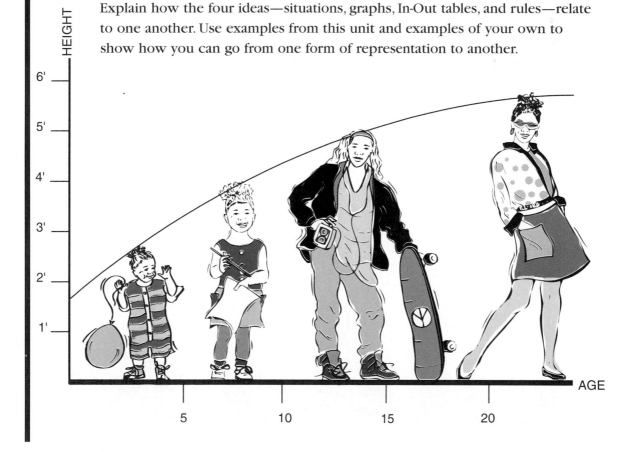

Homework 14

Rules, Tables, and Graphs

In *Out Numbered,* you started from graphs, made In-Out tables, and then found rules for those tables.

This process can be reversed. You can start from a rule, make an In-Out table by finding pairs of numbers that fit the rule, and then create a graph from the table.

By convention, we find the *In* on the horizontal axis and the *Out* on the vertical axis. So each pair of numbers that fits the rule corresponds to a point on the graph.

Continued on next page

Interactive Mathematics Program

The *In* and *Out* values are called the **first** and **second coordinates** of the point on the graph. The graph consists of all the points that correspond to number pairs that fit the rule.

In these problems, do not restrict yourself to whole numbers. Consider all numbers, including negative and noninteger values.

1. You came across many different In-Out rules in *Patterns*. Sometimes the rules came from problem situations. Sometimes you looked at rules that had no particular context.

   For each of the rules below, find as many points on the graph as you think you need to get an idea of what the whole graph looks like. Then draw the graph.

   a. *Out* = 4 · *In* – 4 (this rule occurred in *Homework 21: The Garden Border* in *Patterns*)

   b. *Out* = *In*² (this rule relates to area, among other things)

   c. *Out* = 550 – 20 · *In*

2. The concept of a graph can also be applied to an equation that does not directly express an *Out* in terms of an *In*.

   For each of the equations shown below,

   • find some number pairs that fit the equation

   • make a graph from your number pairs, using the *x*-value as the first coordinate and the *y*-value as the second coordinate

   a. $3x + 2y = 9$

   b. $y^2 = x$

POW 10

On Your Own

One of the key themes of this unit is that of planning. You have planned a lunch and you have planned what supplies your wagon train needs to bring.

One reason for doing such assignments is so that you can get better at organizing details. Another is so you can get better at asking yourself questions like "What will I need?" and at developing responses to such questions.

This is a research POW. You are to go out and find information. Your topic? Living on your own.

Imagine that you have just completed high school. There may have been adults who took care of many things for you before, but now you want to move out on your own.

Continued on next page

For the purpose of this assignment, assume that you need to provide your own financial support. What sorts of things do you need to plan for?

Be very detailed and accurate in your plan. If you are going to get your own apartment, then find an example of one in the classified section of a newspaper and find the cost. You will need a job—a job that you can enter with a high school education. You will need to know what you would get paid and how much of that is "take-home pay."

It will probably be helpful to you to interview people for this POW. There is nothing like experience. What bills are you going to have to pay? Does your apartment rent include the cost of electricity? People already living on their own will be able to share with you how they manage the bills.

Your report should include a budget, which is a plan for how your money is going to be spent on a month-to-month basis.

Good luck!

Write-up

Since this is not a standard POW, you can't use the standard POW write-up. Use the categories listed below instead.

1. *Description of the Task:* Explain in your own words what you are trying to do in this POW.

2. *Your Job:* You can consider such questions as

   • What is the job?

   • How do you find it?

   • What are your hours and salary?

3. *Your Living Arrangement:* Would you live with roommates? By yourself? What about furniture?

4. *A Monthly Budget:* Include more than just numbers. Discuss how and why you decided on your budget and where you got your information.

5. *Evaluation:* Did you enjoy doing this POW? In what ways do you think it will be helpful to you in the future?

Days 15-18

Making Predictions with Graphs

Graphs don't just tell stories; they can also be very useful in making predictions. The lives of travelers on the Overland Trail often depended on their ability to accurately foresee what could happen to them. The data they worked with didn't fit formulas as neatly as data in textbook problems, so they had to make approximations.

As travelers set out from Fort Laramie toward Fort Hall, Idaho, one of the decisions they made involved a shortcut called Sublette's Cutoff. When you get there, think about what choice you might have made.

Mariela Miranda, Erica Chavez, and Roxanne Farler present their graph to the class.

Previous Travelers

The first settlers had to make the long journey west without any help from previous travelers. However, subsequent wagon trains used information from the early travelers to decide on the quantity of supplies appropriate for their journey.

The Letter

While in Fort Laramie, Wyoming, you get the letter below from friends describing the supplies they and others used on the leg of the trip from Fort Laramie to Fort Hall, Idaho.

Continued on next page

Dear friends:

We've arrived in Fort Hall after many adventures, both good and bad. It would take me forever to describe all that happened, so we can talk about all of that when we meet up again in California.

I know that you're anxious for some practical information for your own trip. Several of the families on our wagon train kept track of the quantities of various goods they actually needed on the journey. The families were of different sizes, so this information should help you and your friends decide how the amounts vary from group to group. I know this won't answer all your questions, but it's a start.

Number of people	Pounds of gunpowder	Pounds of sugar	Pounds of beans
5	3	20	61
8	4	50	95
6	2.5	30	56
7	4.1	23	75
11	5	60	125
10	5.8	40	135
5	1.8	39	80
7	3.8	44	100
10	4.3	53	103
6	3.6	35	75
8	3.2	35	100
7	3.1	36	105
9	4.7	45	125
12	6.1	55	150
10	5.2	31	125

Well, good luck to you all!

The Helmicks

Continued on next page

Part I: The Analysis

1. Make a separate graph for each of the supply items needed, using appropriate scales for the axes.

2. Do the following tasks for each of the graphs in Question 1.

   a. Sketch the **line of best fit** for the graph; that is, find the straight line that you think best fits the data.

   b. Make an In-Out table *from your line* and determine the rule for the In-Out table.

   c. Use either the In-Out table or your graph to find the quantity of each item needed for each of your group's four family units.

Part II: More Planning

3. In *Planning for the Long Journey,* you decided on supply amounts of gunpowder, sugar, and beans for the trip from Westport to Fort Laramie. Through good fortune or the generosity of others, you made it successfully so far, but you have used up those initial supplies.

   The same supplies, in the same quantities, were ordered in advance to be ready for you here at Fort Laramie, and you picked up those supplies on your arrival yesterday. Now that you have analyzed the information from the Helmicks, you need to rethink your provisions.

   Compare the supply amounts found in Question 2c for gunpowder, sugar, and beans to the amounts you decided on in *Planning for the Long Journey* and which you now have again for the next leg of the trip, from Fort Laramie to Fort Hall.

   If your supply of a certain item is not what it should be, then you will need to trade for more of that item with another group. (The trading post has run out of supplies, so you can't buy more there.)

   Warning: If you fail to get sufficient supplies, then some members of your Overland Trail family might perish before you get to Fort Hall.

Homework 15

Broken Promises

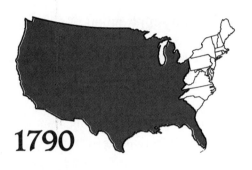

1492

Over the years, Native Americans were forced onto smaller and smaller parcels of land. Though the United States government signed treaties with the native peoples, the government repeatedly broke those treaties.

The maps at the left and below show the outline of the contiguous 48 states of the United States. The colored portion represents the extent of Native American land within this area at different times.

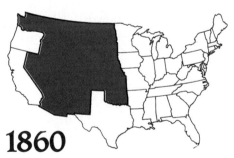

1790

1830

1860

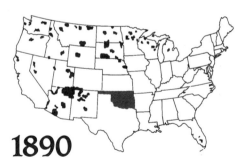

1890

Maps reproduced by permission of Thunderbird Enterprises, Phoenix, Arizona.

Continued on next page

1. Approximate the area of Native American land at each of the given times. The total area shown for 1492 is approximately 3,000,000 square miles. (*Suggestion:* You may want to trace each map onto grid paper and use one square as the unit of area.)

2. Make a graph showing the relationship between the passage of time and the area of Native American land. (Be careful to use appropriate spacing on your time interval.)

3. If it were 1861 and you were only looking at the maps of what had happened so far, what would you predict as the area of Native American land in the year 2020?

4. What prediction might you have made in 1900 about Native American land in the year 2020?

Homework 16   Sublette's Cutoff

The Shortcut

As more and more emigrants made the journey west, scouts found shortcuts to lessen the travel time. Help provided by Native Americans in the area was also important in facilitating the journey.

The Shoshone, Assiniboin, and Crow nations were prominent in the area of what is now Wyoming and Idaho.

One such shortcut, along the way between Fort Laramie and Fort Hall, was known as Sublette's Cutoff. The cutoff began just past South Pass in Wyoming, about 250 miles west of Fort Laramie, and ended near the Wyoming-Idaho border.

Continued on next page

This shortcut saved 50 miles and a week of travel, but crossed a dry and barren stretch of land. It was a grueling route of 15 days with little grass and no water.

Your Problem

Three families decide to attempt to cross Sublette's Cutoff. The table below shows how much water each of these families has left at the end of the first, second, fourth, and sixth days.

Gallons of Water Remaining

Family	Day 1	Day 2	Day 4	Day 6
Jones	52	49	41	34
Sanford	76	64	48	36
Minto	34	32	26	24

1. Graph the water supply data for all three families on the same set of axes. (Colored pens or pencils might help.)

2. Based on this information, who do you think will make it and who will not? Explain your reasoning.

3. Is there a time when all three families will have about the same amount of water left? If so, when?

Note: If any member of one of your group's families has a last name from this assignment, then that family took Sublette's Cutoff and may have saved some time. More to come on this!

Who Will Make It?

Dagny Appel bought an almanac at the trading post in Fort Laramie. The almanac included predictions about the weather, crops, and livestock.

Dagny was a tireless planner. She shared the predictions with almost everyone in her wagon train. Other wagon trains also became concerned.

One particular prediction worried Dagny: The Green River, some 330 miles away, was expected to flood in 30 days, which was about how long it might take to get there.

Three wagon trains kept track of their distances remaining from the Green River. The table on the next page shows how far each wagon train still was from the river at the end of three different days.

Continued on next page

Distance to the River (in miles)

Wagon train	Day 4	Day 7	Day 11
Fowler	270	235	185
Belshaw	285	260	230
Clappe	280	245	200

Graph the data for all three wagon trains *on the same set of axes.* (Colored pens or pencils might help.)

Then answer these questions.

1. If the almanac is correct about when the flood will take place, who will make it to the Green River before the flood and who will not? Explain your reasoning.

2. If the almanac is wrong and all three groups make it past the river, which wagon train do you think will arrive at the river first? Last? Explain your reasoning.

3. When the first of these wagon trains gets to the Green River, how far back is the next wagon train? What about the last wagon train? Explain how you found your answer.

Note: If any member of one of your group's families had a last name from this assignment, then you should use the data above to figure out how long it took them to get from Fort Laramie to the Green River, and record this time.

Homework 17 The Basic Student Budget

Cal, Bernie, and Doc are college students on basic student budgets.

Sometimes the three have a little difficulty keeping to their budgets. Their biggest problem is the rent.

The total rent for their apartment is $450, which is split evenly among the three roommates. The rent is due on the last day of each month, and the guys don't get paid until the first day of the next month.

Their landlord has no tolerance for late payments.

Continued on next page

Each of the three students had a different amount of money after being paid on April 1. At the end of that day, Cal had $550, Bernie had $400, and Doc had $300. As the month goes by, they each make note occasionally of how much they have left at the end of the day.

The table shows their records so far.

Amount of Money Remaining (in dollars)

Date	Cal	Bernie	Doc
April 3	498	383	285
April 10	352	349	245
April 17	220	313	215

1. Sketch and label a graph that accurately represents this situation. (Show all three students *on the same graph*.)

2. Who will be able to pay his rent on time and who will not? How do you know?

3. It's April 21, and there's a great concert on campus. This would be an extra cost, beyond the three students' normal expenses. How much, if anything, can each one spend and still have enough for rent money on April 30?

4. Suppose each of them starts May with the same amount with which he started April.

   Find an approximate rule for each roommate that will tell him how much money he should expect to have at the end of the *x*th day of May if his spending habits don't change.

Homework 18   Out of Action

The general manager of the Slamajamas basketball team has a difficult decision to make.

A key player, Marcus Dunkalot, suffered a sprained knee on March 20, about one month prior to the beginning of the playoffs, and was put on the disabled list.

It is now just over two weeks later, April 6. The general manager needs to decide immediately whether or not to keep Marcus on the disabled list. If he keeps Marcus on the disabled list, it will be for the remainder of the regular season, which means that Marcus will be disqualified for the playoffs.

Here are the advantages and disadvantages of each choice.

- If he takes Marcus off the disabled list now, he can hope that Marcus will be well in time for the playoffs. But if Marcus is not ready in time, then the Slamajamas will have one less player available for the rest of the season, including the playoffs.

- If he keeps Marcus on the disabled list, he can sign another player (of lesser ability) to take his place. But then he gives up all hope of having Marcus for the playoffs.

The playoffs begin on April 18.

On the next page is a copy of the physical therapist's report, on which the general manager must base his immediate decision.

Continued on next page

• •

PROFESSIONAL PHYSICAL THERAPY

Patient's name: Marcus Dunkalot

Sex: male   Height: 6′8″

Age: 24   Weight: 225 lbs.

Diagnosis: sprained knee

Prescribed treatment: strengthen and stretch

3/20   Mr. Dunkalot was administered a Cybex strength test upon arrival. Quadriceps of the injured leg measured 55 foot-pounds in extension. Normal measurement for a player to return to play without reinjury is 250 foot-pounds.

3/25   Daily regimen is contributing to patient's progress. Cybex test measures 90 foot-pounds.

4/1   Some swelling earlier in the week. General reports of less pain. Cybex test measures 140 foot-pounds.

4/6   Less swelling. Range of motion has shown marked increase. Cybex test measures 185 foot-pounds.

1. Graph Marcus Dunkalot's progress.

2. Imagine that you are the general manager. The team owners want a complete report on why and how you made your decision. What will you decide? Write the report.

Calculators on the Trail?

You've got a big advantage over the folks on the Overland Trail—you get to use a graphing calculator in your work. As you reach Fort Hall and then move on toward California, you'll see how to use the calculator to make graphs and you'll use calculator graphs to look back at some problems you've already worked on.

Brian Jones explains his work from "Fair Share on Chores" to Judy Kodotan, parent of a prospective student.

You've already seen that every equation has a graph. In one new type of problem, you'll look at how graphs can help you find a solution when you have two equations in a single situation.

Graphing Calculator In-Outs

Some of the things you have been doing with pencil-and-paper graphs can also be done on a graphing calculator.

You will probably decide that some problems are easier to do on the graphing calculator than on paper, and others are easier to do on paper. This activity will help you get used to the new method.

Continued on next page

Keep in mind that you may often have to adjust the viewing window for your graphing screen. You may find this easiest to do by using the zoom feature of the graphing calculator.

1. In the activity *Previous Travelers,* you found a rule for estimating the number of pounds of beans needed for different numbers of people making the trip from Fort Laramie to Fort Hall.

   Although you may have found a different rule in that activity, you should now use the function listed here.

   Number of pounds of beans = 12 · (number of people)

   a. Enter and graph this function on a graphing calculator.

   Now use the trace feature on your graphing calculator to answer the questions below.

   b. How many pounds of beans are needed for 20 people?

   c. A certain family brought 155 pounds of beans. According to the function above, how many people can they feed?

2. In *Homework 8: To Kearny by Equation*, you were given an equation for the profit that Joseph and Lewis Papan each made from their ferry service. That equation depended in part on how many hours the captain worked.

   But suppose the Papans decide to pay the captain for ten hours of work each day, regardless of the amount of business.

   In that case, the profit each gets for a given day could be determined by the equation below (in which W is the number of wagons that the ferry captain takes across the river).

   $$\text{profit} = \frac{W - 4}{2}$$

   a. Enter and graph this function on your graphing calculator.

   Now use the trace feature on your graphing calculator to answer the questions below.

   b. How much profit will the Papans each make if 25 wagons use their ferry?

   c. How many wagons will have to use the Papans' ferry for the Papans to make $15 each?

Continued on next page

3. The In-Out table shown here is for the function

$$Y = 3X^2 - 7X + 2$$

Graph this function on your graphing calculator and use the zoom and trace features to find the missing entries.

Where the *Out* value is given, find all possible *In* values that will give the desired *Out*. If there aren't any, write "none."

Give your answers to the nearest tenth.

In	Out
1.31	?
−3.02	?
?	−1.04
?	−2.12
?	−2.05
8.57	?

Homework 19

What We Needed

Part I: Traveling Time

In the first part of this assignment, you will figure out how long it took for your group's families to travel the entire distance from Fort Laramie to Fort Hall.

1. You should already know how many days it took for your group's families to go from Fort Laramie to the end of Sublette's Cutoff.

   Write down this time.

2. Next, you need to find out how long it took your group's families to go from the end of Sublette's Cutoff to Fort Hall.

   You should have rolled a pair of dice, found the sum, and added that to 8. Use this result to represent the average rate (in miles per day) at which your

Continued on next page

families traveled for this portion of the trip, which is a distance of 120 miles. (You should have a rate between 10 miles per day and 20 miles per day.)

Based on this rate, find out how many days it took from the end of Sublette's Cutoff to Fort Hall.

3. Add the results from Questions 1 and 2 to get the total number of days it took for your families to get from Fort Laramie to Fort Hall.

Part II: Supplies Needed

4. It turns out that each person in your group's families ate an average of 0.22 pounds of beans per day between Fort Laramie and Fort Hall. Calculate the amount of beans each of your group's four families needed to bring on the trip.

5. It also turns out that each person used an average of 0.08 pounds of sugar per day. Find the amount of sugar that each of your group's families needed to bring.

Homework 20   More Graph Sketches

Do you remember graph sketches? For each of the situations below, sketch a graph that might represent what is happening.

Include an appropriate scale on each of your axes.

1. The length of a burning candle as a function of the amount of time the candle has been burning.

2. The weight of a person as a function of that person's age, over the course of a lifetime.

3. The distance left to California as a function of the length of time since the wagon train left Westport.

4. The height off the ground of a buffalo chip stuck to a wagon wheel as a function of time (over three revolutions of the wheel).

5. Make up a situation of your own and sketch a graph.

"Out of Action" and "Sublette's Cutoff" Revisited

In both *Homework 18: Out of Action* and *Homework 16: Sublette's Cutoff,* you were given certain data about a situation, and asked to make a prediction.

In both problems, you plotted the data and based your prediction on a pencil-and-paper graph.

Now, you are to reexamine those two situations, answering a slightly different question for each and using a different technique.

Here is the technique you will use.

- Plot the data on a graphing calculator.

- Leave the data on the screen and graph a function that you think might approximate the data well.

- Examine how closely your function's graph approximates the data, and adjust the function until you think it approximates the data as well as possible.

- Use your final choice of function to make a prediction.

Continued on next page

1. *"Out of Action" Revisited*

In *Homework 18: Out of Action,* you were given data about a basketball player's leg strength. The information from that problem is given below.

- March 20   55 foot-pounds

- March 25   90 foot-pounds

- April 1   40 foot-pounds

- April 6   185 foot-pounds

Use the technique described above to predict what Marcus Dunkalot's leg strength will be on April 18.

2. *"Sublette's Cutoff" Revisited*

In *Homework 16: Sublette's Cutoff,* you were given data showing the amount of water each of three families had at the end of certain days. The information from that problem is reproduced in this table.

Gallons of Water Remaining

Family	Day 1	Day 2	Day 4	Day 6
Jones	52	49	41	34
Sanford	76	64	48	36
Minto	34	32	26	24

Use the technique described above to predict how much water each family would have at the end of Day 15. You will probably want to do one family at a time.

(If you think a family would run out of water before Day 15, then you will give a negative prediction here.)

Homework 21   Biddy Mason

Hundreds of thousands of people traveled to California in the middle of the nineteenth century.

Some came across the Pacific Ocean from China. Some sailed from the Atlantic coast to Panama, crossed land there, and then sailed again to California.

Still others, as you know, came by boat around Cape Horn or came by wagon or by horse on the Overland Trail.

Biddy Mason walked.

About Biddy Mason

Biddy Mason walked to California behind her master's 300-wagon train. Her job was to watch the cattle, but her master would not give her a horse, so she had to walk. She was one of the uncounted number of enslaved African Americans brought to California by southern slave owners to work in the gold fields.

Continued on next page

Biddy Mason broke away from her slave master and had the courage to sue for and win her freedom. She settled in California, where she became known for her generosity and great charity, taking in homeless children and supporting schools, churches, and hospitals.

Most enslaved people, however, were not able to win their freedom as Biddy Mason did.

Your Problem

Suppose that shortly after you leave Fort Hall, your Overland Trail family encounters a family that has escaped from slavery.

You need to think about whether to let them join your group. Since they have no supplies of their own, you would need to share what you have with them.

1. Pick one of your supply items, and decide how much of that item you have at the time you meet this family. (Pick an amount that seems reasonable as a total for about 20 days.)

    a. Write down your total amount of this supply item and the number of people in your Overland Trail family.

    b. Figure out how much of the supply item there is per person (for your Overland Trail family).

2. a. Suppose that the family you meet consists of four people. If you let them join you, how much of the supply item will there be per person? (Assume that everyone gets an equal share.)

    b. What if the family you meet has six people?

3. Find an equation that gives the amount you will have for each person as a function of the number of people in the family you meet.

4. Graph the function from Question 3. Choose scales for your axes that are appropriate to the information you are considering.

Fair Share on Chores

About 50 miles past Fort Hall, the California Trail splits from the Oregon Trail and heads into Nevada.

Two families, the Murphys and the Bensons, have decided to continue on the Oregon Trail, and you say good-bye to them as you head for California.

Wagon trains often put their wagons in a circle to make a corral for the livestock. (It was only in the movies that wagon trains created a circle to protect themselves from Native Americans.)

Now that the Murphys and the Bensons have split from the wagon train, you have fewer wagons available.

Continued on next page

The Washburn family decides that someone needs to keep an eye on their animals during the night, and that their children will take shifts each night, with one child at a time guarding the animals. Altogether, the animals need to be watched for ten hours. This family has two girls and three boys.

This sounds simple—two hours each. But the girls have other chores, and so do the boys. In order to balance out other assigned chores, the Washburn family decides that there should be one length of time for each girl's shift and another length of time for each boy's shift.

1. How long would you suggest that *each type* of shift be? Provide at least three different pairs of answers.

2. Using G to represent the length of each girl's shift and B to represent the length of each boy's shift, write an equation expressing the fact that the total of all their shifts is ten hours.

3. Now suppose you know how long each girl's shift is. Describe *in words* how you could find the length of each boy's shift.

4. Write your sentence from Question 3 as a function expressing B in terms of G. That is, write an equation that begins "$B = \ldots$," and has an expression using G on the right of the equal sign.

5. Graph the function from Question 4 on your calculator, and check to see if your answers from Question 1 are on the graph.

6. Use the trace feature on your calculator to find three more pairs of possible shift lengths from your graph.

Homework 22 Fair Share for Hired Hands

The Fulkerth family is a large one, and they have seven hired hands.

The family has a total of about $20 per week available for salaries.

Four of the hired hands are experienced at working on the trail, and the other three are on their first trip.

It seems fair that the experienced hired hands should get more pay than those without experience. So the Fulkerths decide that there will be two weekly pay rates—one rate for each of the four experienced workers and another rate for each of the three without experience.

1. What should each of the weekly pay rates be? Suggest three possible combinations. (The salary total can be a few cents more or less than $20 if that helps you avoid fractions of a penny.)

2. Plot your three combinations from Question 1, using X for the pay rate of an inexperienced hired hand and Y for the pay rate of an experienced hired hand.

3. Connect the points with a straight line and use this graph to find two more possible pairs.

4. Describe *in words* how you could compute the weekly pay rate for an experienced hired hand if you knew the rate for an inexperienced hired hand.

5. Express your sentence from Question 4 as an equation giving Y in terms of X.

6. Check to see if the two new pairs from Question 3 fit the equation from Question 5.

More Fair Share on Chores

As you saw in *Fair Share for Chores,* the Washburn family's two girls and three boys are responsible for watching the animals in shifts during the night.

After some experience, the family has decided that in order to balance out other chores, the shift for each boy should be half an hour longer than that for each girl.

They have realized, however, that as the season gradually changes, the total amount of time needed for the shifts is not always ten hours. Therefore, they want to know about combinations of shift lengths with different totals.

Continued on next page

1. a. What are some possible combinations of shift lengths in which the shift for each boy is half an hour longer than that for each girl? Give four possibilities. (Remember that the total time does not need to be ten hours.)

   b. Describe *in words* how you could find the length of each boy's shift if you knew the length of a girl's shift.

   c. Use your answer to Question 1b to write an equation in which *G* represents the length of each girl's shift and *B* represents the length of each boy's shift.

   d. Graph your equation on the calculator.

   e. For each combination that you gave in Question 1a, state how much *total time* will be covered by all the children combined.

2. On a particular evening, it turns out that ten hours of animal watching is required after all.

   Find a pair of shift lengths that would total ten hours and still have the shift for each boy be half an hour longer than the shift for each girl.
   (*Reminder:* There are two girls and three boys. You may want to use your earlier work from *Fair Share on Chores*.)

Water Conservation

Nevada seemed like a desert to the emigrants, who had been following large rivers most of the way from Westport. As you have seen, water was a very precious commodity on the Overland Trail, and travelers had to be careful not to run out.

They kept track of their water use, planning for the next opportunity to refill their water containers.

1. The Stevens family had a 50-gallon water container. In an effort to conserve water, they reduced their daily consumption to three gallons per day.

   If they began with a full container, how many gallons of water would they have left after three days? Eight days? Twelve days? X days?

2. The Muster family was larger. They had a 100-gallon water container. Their daily consumption was eight gallons per day.

   If they began with a full container, how many gallons of water would they have left after three days? Eight days? Twelve days? X days?

3. Use your answers to the last part of Questions 1 and 2 to graph each family's water supply. Use *number of days* for the horizontal axis and *amount of water left* for the vertical axis. Graph both functions on the same set of axes.

4. Is there a time when both families would have the same amount of water left? If so, when would it happen and how much water would both families have at that time?

5. In how many days would each family run out of water?

Homework 25

The Big Buy

Seve and Jillian Vicaro want to make some money over the spring break from school. They ask their parents to let them work around the house to earn the money. Their parents agree, since Jillian and Seve are saving to buy graphing calculators.

Dad tells Jillian that he will give her a starting bonus of $10, and then pay her $5 an hour for the work she does around the house. Mom offers Seve a slightly different deal. She will give him $40 to start, but only $3 an hour.

1. Write two separate equations, one for Jillian and one for Seve, expressing how much money each has earned (including their starting money) in terms of time worked. (Use x for the number of hours worked and y for the amount earned.)

2. Graph both equations on the same set of axes. (Be sure you know which graph is for which person.)

3. If the graphing calculator costs $72, who will be able to buy one with the least work time? Explain your answer.

4. If the graphing calculator costs $100, who will be able to buy one with the least work time? Explain your answer.

5. For what price must the calculator sell in order for Jillian and Seve to earn that amount with the same number of hours of work? Explain your answer.

**Days
26-27**

How Fast Should You Go?

You can probably *walk* faster than the Overland Trail wagons sometimes traveled. Imagine what the settlers would think of today's automobiles and speed limits! Whatever the speed at which a vehicle travels, it has to fit the situation. Not unlike today's travelers, settlers on the trail had to think about the rate at which they traveled in order to compensate for poor weather and to keep up with one another.

Don't lose heart—you're almost to California.

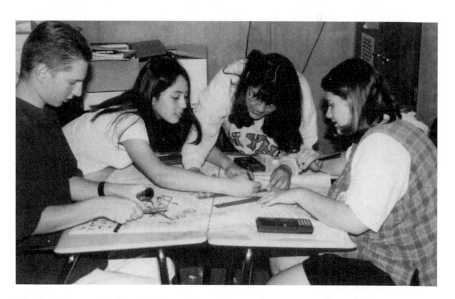

Mark Hansen, Robin LeFevre, Jennifer Rodriguez, and Karla Viaramontes make a group graph.

Catching up

1. *By a Specific Date*

Your family has arrived a little late in Winnemucca, Nevada. (Roll one die to find the exact date in September when you arrive there.) You find the following note from your cousin's family:

> It is early on the morning of September 1, and we are leaving Winnemucca today with the wagon train. We hope you can catch up with us. We plan to make 15 miles a day. We hope to see you in a few days.

Continued on next page

Assume that you will need the rest of today (the day you arrive) and all of tomorrow to get ready, and that you will leave the day after tomorrow.

How fast will you have to travel (in miles per day) to catch up by the end of September 12?

2. *By a Specific Place*

It is 10 A.M. on September 19. Your wagon has just broken a wheel outside of Lovelock, Nevada, and you have to stop to fix it. (Roll two dice and add the numbers to find out how many hours of traveling time you will lose.)

The rest of the wagon train proceeds without you. They are traveling at a rate of 2 miles per hour.

You want to catch up with them by the time they get to Reno, Nevada, which is 80 miles away. Assume that once you get going again, you'll be traveling the same hours as the wagon train.

How fast will you have to travel to catch up by Reno? Give your answer to the nearest tenth of a mile per hour.

Homework 26   Water for One More

It is September 23, and you are stopping for the night in what is now Reno, Nevada. (The town got that name in 1868.)

While you are stopped, a straggler comes by who fell off his horse and got left behind by his wagon train. You have decided to let him ride with you for a while and to share your supplies with him.

With an extra person, you need to ration your water more carefully. You expect to reach a river by the end of the day on September 29, where you can replenish your water, and where he will probably be able to rejoin his group. Had the straggler not joined you, you would have had three gallons per day for each person.

1. Give the size of the Overland Trail family for which you are responsible.

2. Based on that family size, how much water can you now allow per day for each person (that is, with the addition of one more person)?

3. Suppose instead that your Overland Trail family contained ten people (with three gallons per day for each person). How much water would you have per person with the straggler included?

4. Answer Question 3 for the case where the Overland Trail family contains 20 people.

5. Generalize Question 3 to the case where the Overland Trail family contains x people.

Catching Up by Saturday Night

It is Wednesday morning, October 1, and you are in the mountains the settlers call the Sierra Nevada. Your daughter has given birth during the night to a healthy baby girl.

You decide your wagon should stop for a day to allow her to rest briefly. You will start moving again Thursday morning, but the rest of the wagon train is going to continue traveling this morning.

You want to be able to catch up with the rest of the wagon train by the end of Saturday, so that you will be able to celebrate the birth of your new granddaughter with your fellow travelers that night.

You confer with the wagon train leader Wednesday morning before the wagon train leaves. Together, you want to agree on the rates at which you and the wagon train will each travel so that you can catch up with them late Saturday. (The wagon train will travel the same amount of time each day and you will travel the same amount of time each day, although your rate will differ from the wagon train's. The leader is willing to let you propose the two rates.)

1. Figure out a possible pair of rates—one for the main part of the wagon train and one for you—so that you will catch up with the main group at the end of Saturday. Express your rates in *miles per day*.

2. Using these rates, figure out how far down the trail you and the wagon train will be when you catch up to them.

3. Find three more pairs of rates that satisfy Question 1, and then answer Question 2 for each of them.

Homework 27   Catching Up at Auburn

You are now northwest of Reno, Nevada. You are intrigued by the man who runs an inn and trading post, and you decide to spend two days visiting.

The innkeeper is James P. Beckwourth.

About James Beckwourth

James Beckwourth, born around 1798 in Virginia, was the son of an African American woman and her master, a white man. At 19, during a fight with one of his bosses, he

Continued on next page

slugged his way to freedom and subsequently traveled from one end of the continent to the other.

On the trail, he fought with and against several Native American nations, and also served as a scout for the United States Army in the war against the Seminole. A contemporary of Kit Carson and Davy Crockett, Beckwourth was part of the brutal frontier tradition. He was said to have "fought and killed with ease and pleasure."

He also married often. After marrying a Crow woman, he was adopted into the Crow Nation and led the Crow in battle.

In 1850, Beckwourth located a pass through the Sierra Nevada into the American Valley that became a gateway to California during the gold rush. The mountain peak, the town, and the pass still bear his name. For a number of years, a Denver street and church also carried his name.

Your Problem

Since you are going to spend time with Beckwourth, you will need to make arrangements with the rest of the wagon train. You want to catch up with them as they reach Auburn, California, which is 140 miles away.

You confer with the wagon train leader, to arrange to meet at the river. The leader tells you the rate at which the wagon train will move. You then have to find a compatible rate so that you and the wagon train will arrive in Auburn at the same time.

1. Roll a die four times and use the sum as the wagon train's rate (in *miles per day*). Based on this rate, find the rate at which you will have to travel in order to catch up at Auburn.

2. Do Question 1 twice more, with different wagon train rates. (The leader is unpredictable.)

3. Make an In-Out table that shows the relationship between the wagon train's rate and your rate.

4. Graph the relationship in Question 3.

5. For each of your results in Questions 1 and 2, figure out how many days you will have to travel after you leave Beckwourth.

6. Suppose the wagon train travels x miles per day.

   a. Describe how to figure out what your rate should be.

   b. Find an algebraic expression for this rate in terms of x.

**Days
28-30**

California at Last!

You've finally arrived in California. As you'll see, life in this state wasn't all golden. You'll also see how the mathematics of expenses and profits played a role in people's everyday decisions.

Perhaps the portfolio for this unit ought to be called a scrapbook. Did you bring your camera along on your trip?

Ken Weaver writes the cover letter for his portfolio.

The California Experience

Who were the people in California in the 1850s?

Of course, Native Americans were there, probably for millennia. Some 300 different nations, including the Modoc, Washo, Maidu, Pomo, Cahuilla, and Miwok, held territory, in what is now known as California.

Continued on next page

Then came the Spanish. Out of their conquest and mixture with the Native Americans came a new culture and a new nation called Mexico, which became politically independent of Spain in 1821.

Indeed, that new Mexican nation claimed all of what is now the state of California, as well as all of Nevada and Utah and parts of Arizona, New Mexico, Colorado, and Wyoming. But in 1846, the United States provoked a war with Mexico in an attempt to gain territory. The United States won the war, which ended in 1848 with the Treaty of Guadalupe Hidalgo. In this treaty, Mexico was forced to cede much of what is now the southwestern United States.

Although the first wagon trains left Missouri for California in 1841, the great migration of the mid-nineteenth century was spurred by the discovery of gold in 1848, just nine days before the signing of the Treaty of Guadalupe Hidalgo.

The arrival of hundreds of thousands, many in search of gold, permanently changed the lives of the people who had been there before and led to the destruction of whole nations of native peoples.

The gold rush also led to thousands of people being brought from China to work as menial laborers. Though in 1850 there were only a few hundred Chinese in California, by 1852 about 10 percent of the population was Chinese, many of whom lived in slave-like conditions.

Those who traveled on the California Trail in search of gold often ended up destitute, and a number of women resorted to prostitution to survive.

So the California experience was a mixture of many things. Just a very few became rich from the mining of gold.

Getting the Gold

Many of those who made the long trek to California were in search of gold. Though few were able to get rich, many tried.

One of the most common ways to get gold was to pan for it in streams.

To pan for gold, all a person needed was a $9 shovel, a $50 burro, and a $1 pan. A person could get an ounce of gold each day, on the average, by panning.

One ingenious person discovered a way to get gold from a stream by using a trough. The trough was a long chute that miners set in the stream and rocked back and forth to separate the gold from the silt of the stream.

Although it was more expensive to get started with the trough method, that technique produced about twice as much gold each day as the pan method. To use a trough, a person needed a team of two burros, a shovel, and a trough. The trough cost $311.

At that time, gold was worth $15 an ounce. The following questions involve the amount of profit (income minus expenses) from each method after a certain number of days. (A loss of money is considered a negative profit.)

1. How much profit will each method yield after 16 days?

2. How much profit will each method yield after 30 days?

3. How much profit will each method yield after 5 days?

4. Make two graphs on the same set of axes: one graph should show the profit from panning; the other should show the profit from using a trough. (The horizontal axis is the number of days.)

5. How many days will it take for a miner using each method to break even?

6. After how many days will the two methods yield the same amount of money?

Homework 28   California Reflections

The California Experience outlines some of the historical and social background of the period of the gold rush.

Write about your own feelings concerning this period of American history.

You may want to talk about the group or groups you identify with, about issues of justice or injustice, or about the process of social change.

You may also want to comment on how your ideas about the period have changed over the course of this unit.

Homework 29

Beginning Portfolio Selection

The meaning and use of graphs played an important role in this unit.

Select one assignment from the unit that illustrates how graphs can describe a problem situation.

Select another assignment that illustrates how graphs can be used to make a decision about a problem situation.

Explain how each of these assignments helped you to understand the meaning and use of graphs.

(Making these selections and explaining them are the first steps toward compiling your portfolio for this unit.)

"The Overland Trail" Portfolio

Now that *The Overland Trail* is completed, it is time to put together your portfolio for the unit. Compiling this portfolio has three parts.

- Writing a cover letter that summarizes the unit

- Choosing papers to include from your work in the unit

- Writing about your reactions to using a graphing calculator

Cover Letter for "The Overland Trail"

Look back over *The Overland Trail* and describe the main mathematical ideas of the unit. This description should give an overview of how the key ideas were developed.

As part of the compilation of your portfolio, you will select activities that you think were important in developing the key ideas of this unit. In your cover letter, you should include an explanation of why you selected the particular items you did.

Selecting Papers from "The Overland Trail"

Your portfolio for *The Overland Trail* should contain the items on this list.

- *Homework 29: Beginning Portfolio Selection*

  Include the two activities about graphs that you selected in *Homework 29: Beginning Portfolio* Selection, along with the explanation you wrote about how these assignments helped you to understand the meaning and use of graphs.

- *Homework 28: California Reflections*

  This assignment should be included in order to reflect the historical elements of the unit and your reaction to them.

- *Homework 13: Situations, Graphs, Tables, and Rules*

  This assignment is included because it summarizes the connections between situations, graphs, tables, and rules—four different ways of representing functions.

Continued on next page

- An activity about the use of variables

  Select an item from the unit that illustrates or helped you to understand the meaning or use of variables, and explain your selection.

- An activity about rates

  The unit included problems about rates in several different contexts. Select an activity that illustrates important points about rates or that helped you to understand how to work with rates. Explain your selection.

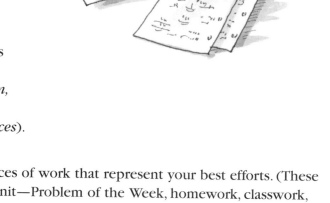

- A Problem of the Week

  Select one of the four POWs you completed during this unit (*The Haybaler Problem, Around the Horn, On Your Own,* or *High-Low Differences*).

- Other quality work

  Select one or two other pieces of work that represent your best efforts. (These can be any work from the unit—Problem of the Week, homework, classwork, presentation, and so forth.)

Graphing With and Without Calculators

Many of the problems in this unit involved graphs, and you learned how to use a graphing calculator to make graphs. Write about your reactions to using this tool. You may want to address the questions below.

- What are the advantages of using the calculator to make graphs?

- What are the advantages of doing graphs by hand?

- How does each approach help in your understanding of graphs and in your ability to use them to solve problems?

Appendix

Supplemental Problems

Some of the supplemental problems for *The Overland Trail* extend POWs from this unit. Others continue your work with variables or build on the theme of the western migration. These are some examples.

- *More Bales of Hay* and *High-Low Proofs* pose some questions related to *POW 8: The Haybaler Problem* and *POW 11: High-Low Differences.*

- *Classroom Expressions* and *Variables of Your Own* ask you to form meaningful expressions with variables.

- *Movin' West* and *The Perils of Pauline* pose problems that relate to the movement of people and goods across the country.

Pick Any Answer

Lai Yee has a new trick. He tells someone:

- Pick any number.

- Multiply by 2.

- Now add 8.

- Divide by 2.

- Subtract the number you started with.

- Your answer is 4.

1. Try out Lai Yee's trick. Is the answer always 4? If you think it always is, explain why. If not, explain why it sometimes will be something else.

2. Make up a trick whose answer will always be 5.

3. Pretend that someone gives you a number that he or she wants to be the answer. Using the variable A to stand for that number, make up a trick whose answer will always be A.

From Numbers to Algebra and Back Again

1. *One-and-One Generalization*

In *The Game of Pig*, you found the expected value in the one-and-one situation for a player who gets 60 percent of all shots.

You may have done similar problems using different percentages.

Continued on next page

Now consider the general case. Suppose the variable p represents the probability that a player succeeds with a given shot, and assume that this value is the same for every shot.

a. Explain, using the example of $p = 60\%$ as a model, why the expected value for this player is $2p^2 + p(1 - p)$.

b. Use the formula from Question 1a to find the player's expected value for the case in which $p = .9$.

c. What value of p would give an expected value of 1.5 points per one-and-one situation?

2. *Lots of Diagonals*

A quadrilateral has two diagonals. The diagram at the right shows a five-sided polygon with five diagonals.

It turns out (as you may already know) that a polygon with N sides has

$$\frac{N(N-3)}{2}$$

diagonals.

a. Based on this formula, how many diagonals does a 50-sided polygon have?

b. How many sides would a polygon need to have in order to have at least 1000 diagonals?

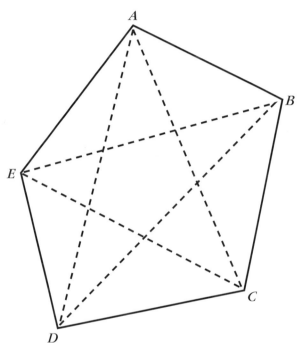

Painting the General Cube

Here is a problem you may have already worked on.

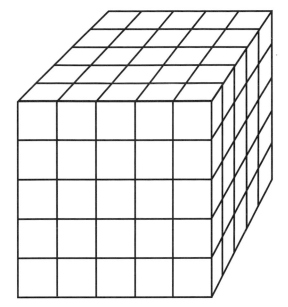

> A cube is 5 inches long in each direction, and is made up of smaller cubes, each of which is 1 inch on every side.
>
> Someone comes along and paints the large cube on all of its faces, including the bottom. None of the paint leaks to the inside.
>
> How many of the smaller cubes have just one face painted? How many have two faces painted? Answer the same question for three, four, five, and six faces.

Now answer the same questions for the situation where the large cube is *N* inches long on each side (still consisting of smaller cubes, each of which is 1 inch on every side).

More Bales of Hay

In *POW 8: The Haybaler Problem*, you were told that there were five bales of hay, which had been weighed two at a time in all possible combinations. You were given the weights for each of the ten possible pairs of bales and asked to find the weights of the five bales.

That problem had a unique solution.

You might wonder whether there would have been a unique solution, or any solution at all, if the ten weights given for the pairs had been different. That is, are there ten numbers that could not possibly stand for the weights of five bales of hay weighed two at a time in the different combinations?

Note: You may know that a typical bale of hay weighs about 100 pounds. In this problem, however, we want you to focus on the mathematical issues rather than on facts about hay. Therefore, you should think of "bales of hay"

Continued on next page

in the problem as representing arbitrary objects, whose weight could be much less or much more than that of a real bale of hay.

1. Before tackling the problem just described, consider the problem below, which involves only three bales of hay.

   > Three bales of hay were weighed two at a time in all three possible combinations. One combination weighed 12 pounds, one combination weighed 15 pounds, and one combination weighed 23 pounds.

   > What were the weights of the three different bales?

   Does this problem have a solution? If so, is the solution unique? Explain your results and how you got them.

2. Now suppose that instead of 12 pounds, 15 pounds, and 23 pounds, the weights given in Question 1 for the three different pairs had been different.

   a. Are there any sets of weights for the three pairs which would have made it impossible to solve Question 1? If so, for which sets of numbers is there a solution and for which sets is there no solution? Explain your answer.

   b. Which sets of weights for the three different pairs give *whole number* solutions for the weights of the individual bales?

3. Now think about a five-bale problem, where there are ten combinations in which to weigh the bales in pairs. Could there be ten numbers that could not be the weights for the ten different pairs of the five bales? Justify your answer.

Classroom Expressions

Variables and summary phrases are useful in many situations other than those involving wagon trains.

In this activity, you will work with a set of variables that relate to a classroom setting.

Subscripts and Superscripts

Mathematicians often use **subscripts** so that they can use similar symbols to represent related quantities. You can think of a subscripted symbol as a two-letter variable for a single quantity.

For example, the combined symbols P_B and P_G are used in this activity to represent the number of pencils that each boy in the classroom has and the number of pencils that each girl in the classroom has.

The subscript, such as B, is written below and to the right of the main symbol, P. The combined symbol P_B is usually read *P sub B*.

You need to exercise care in writing subscripted variables so that they don't look like the product of two separate variables.

Note: A symbol written *above* and to the right of the main symbol, the way we write exponents, is called a **superscript.**

Continued on next page

Variables for the Classroom

The list of variables for the classroom setting is shown below. As in *Ox Expressions,* you should assume that the values of the variables are constant in all cases. For example, assume that every boy has the same number of pencils.

Symbol	Meaning
B	the number of **B**oys in the classroom
G	the number of **G**irls in the classroom
P_B	the number of **P**encils each **B**oy has
P_G	the number of **P**encils each **G**irl has
L	the cost of **L**unch for each student (in cents)
S	the cost of a **S**nack for each student (in cents)
M	the amount of time each student spends in **M**ath class per day (in minutes)
E	the amount of time each student spends in **E**nglish class per day (in minutes)
H_M	the amount of time that each student spends on **H**omework for **M**ath per day (in minutes)
H_E	the amount of time that each student spends on **H**omework for **E**nglish per day (in minutes)

1. What, if anything, does each of the following algebraic expressions represent? (Use a summary phrase, if possible.)

   a. $B + G$

   b. GP_G

   c. $BM + BH_M$

   d. LS

2. Write an algebraic expression for each of the phrases below.

   a. The total number of pencils for the students in the class

   b. The cost of lunch for the whole class

   c. The total amount of time that the students in the class spend on English each day (both in class and on homework)

3. Make up some other meaningful expressions using the list of variables above.

Variables of Your Own

1. Make up a set of between five and ten variables for a situation, the way you did in *Ox Expressions.*

You might choose something like Marching Band Expressions, Baseball Game Expressions, Dating Expressions, or Clothing Store Expressions, or you might prefer to make up a situation of your own.

On the front of a sheet of paper, write down your variables and what they stand for.

2. Below your list of variables, write three algebraic expressions using your variables for which someone can write a summary phrase.

On the back of the same sheet of paper, write a summary phrase for each of your algebraic expressions.

3. On the front side of the paper, write three summary phrases for which someone can write an algebraic expression using your variables.

On the back side, write an algebraic expression for each of your summary phrases.

When you are ready, you will exchange papers with other students. Your task will then be to find summary phrases for each other's algebraic expressions and algebraic expressions for each other's summary phrases.

Integers Only

In *Homework 10: If I Could See This Thing,* you developed a formula for the number of people who would die on the trail between Fort Kearny and Fort Laramie.

You may have wondered about the fact that this formula perhaps showed 1.7 people dying, or a number like that which didn't make any sense.

Continued on next page

There are many problems where the function involved should only give whole number outputs or only give integer outputs. Mathematicians have invented a special function and notation for dealing with such situations.

The function is called the **greatest integer function**. If the input to this function is represented by the letter N, the output is represented by the notation $[N]$.

This function is defined by "rounding down" the input, which means choosing the integer that is as large as possible without being larger than the input. If the input is already an integer, no rounding is needed. For example:

$$[7.2] = 7$$

$$[3] = 3$$

$$[-3.3] = -4 \text{ (Remember that } -3 \text{ is bigger than } -3.3.)$$

1. Which of the statements below are true? If you think a statement is false, give a specific counterexample. If you think a statement is true, prove it as best you can.

    a. $[x + y] = [x] + [y]$

    b. $[x + 5] = [x] + 5$

    c. $[-x] = -[x]$

2. Draw the graph of the function defined by the rule $Out = [In]$.

Movin' West

The westward movement of people across the continent began well before the Overland Trail era.

In fact, the United States population has been moving westward since the earliest years of the country.

The "population center of gravity" of the United States is the point at which the country would balance if it were looked at as a flat plate with no weight of its own and every person on it had equal weight.

In 1790, this center of gravity was near Baltimore, Maryland. In 1990, it crossed the Mississippi River to Steelville, Missouri (southwest of St. Louis).

1. From 1950 until today, the population center of gravity has moved about 50 miles west for every 10 years.

   Suppose this pattern continues for a while. Find a rule that expresses approximately how many miles west of Steelville the population center of gravity would be when it is x years after 1990.

2. Steelville is about 700 miles west of Baltimore. (It is also slightly south, but ignore that.)

   How does the rate of westward movement of the center of gravity between 1790 and 1950 compare to its rate from 1950 to 1990? Explain your answer carefully.

3. How long do you think the rule you found in Question 1 could continue to hold true? How do you think it might change?

Spilling the Beans

Three travelers met one night along the Overland Trail, and decided to have dinner together.

Sam had seven cans of beans to contribute and Kara contributed five cans of beans. Jock didn't have any beans, but the three cooked up what they had, and each ate the same amount.

After dinner, Jock offered the 84¢ in his pocket and said that the other two could divide it up in an appropriate way. They all agreed that in this way everyone would have contributed a fair share to the dinner.

Jock thought that Kara's share of the money should be 35¢, but Sam and Kara convinced him that this was wrong.

1. Explain why Jock might have thought that Kara's share was 35¢.

2. Then explain what Kara's correct share should be.

From *Mathematics: Problem Solving Through Recreational Mathematics* by Averbach and Chein. Copyright © 1980 by W.H. Freeman and Company. Adapted with permission.

The Perils of Pauline

In 1869, the transcontinental railroad was completed. People could then travel westward by train instead of by covered wagon. But trains could also be dangerous.

One day, for example, Pauline was walking through a train tunnel on her way to town. Suddenly, she heard the whistle of a train approaching from behind her!

Pauline knew that the train always traveled at an even 60 miles per hour. She also knew that she was exactly three-eighths of the way through the tunnel, and she could tell from the train whistle how far the train was from the tunnel.

Pauline wasn't sure if she should run forward as fast as she could, or run back to the near end of the tunnel.

Well, she did some lightning-fast calculations, based on how fast she could run and the length of the tunnel. She figured out that whichever way she ran, she would just barely make it out of the tunnel before the train reached her. Whew!!!

How fast could Pauline run? (Carefully explain how you found the answer.)

High-Low Proofs

You may have come up with some interesting observations as you investigated *POW 11: High-Low Differences*.

But perhaps it's still a mystery to you why high-low differences work the way they do.

In this activity, you are to *prove* as many observations about high-low differences as you can.

Although you may want to use specific examples to illustrate your thinking, try to make your arguments as general as possible.

The Pit and the Pendulum

Days 1-6

Edgar Allan Poe—Master of Suspense

The title of this unit comes from a short story by Edgar Allan Poe, who wrote poetry and fiction in the first half of the nineteenth century. (Probably some of the folks on the Overland Trail were readers of Poe.)

Many of his stories involve mystery, suspense, and the bizarre, and *The Pit and the Pendulum* is no exception.

Lindsay Crawford and Catherine Bartz work on their group's initial experiments.

The Pit and the Pendulum

Excerpts from
"The Pit and the Pendulum"
by Edgar Allan Poe (1809-1849)

. . . Looking upward, I surveyed the ceiling of my prison. It was some thirty or forty feet overhead, and constructed much as the side walls. In one of its panels a very singular figure riveted my whole attention. It was the painted picture of Time as he is commonly represented, save that, in lieu of a scythe, he held what, at a casual glance, I supposed to be the pictured image of a huge pendulum such as we see on antique clocks. There was something, however, in the appearance of this machine which caused me to regard it more attentively. While I gazed directly upward at it (for its position was immediately over my own) I fancied that I saw it in motion. In an instant afterward the fancy was confirmed. Its sweep was brief, and of course slow. I watched it for some minutes, somewhat in fear, but more in wonder. Wearied at length with observing its dull movement, I turned my eyes upon the other objects in the cell. . . .

It might have been half an hour, perhaps even an hour, (for I could take but imperfect note of time) before I again cast my eyes upward. What I then saw confounded and amazed me. The sweep of the pendulum had increased in extent by nearly a yard. As a natural consequence its velocity was also much greater. But what mainly disturbed me was the idea that it had perceptibly *descended*. I now observed—with what horror it is needless to say—that its nether extremity was formed of a crescent of glittering steel, about a foot in length from horn to horn; the horns upward, and the under edge evidently as keen as that of a razor. Like a razor also, it seemed massy and heavy, tapering from the edge into a solid and broad structure above. It was appended to a weighty rod of brass, and the whole *hissed* as it swung through the air. . . .

What boots it to tell of the long, long hours of horror more than mortal, during which I counted the rushing oscillations of the steel! Inch by inch—line by line—with a descent only appreciable at intervals that seemed ages—down and still down it came! . . .

Continued on next page

The vibration of the pendulum was at right angles to my length. I saw that the crescent was designed to cross the region of the heart. It would fray the serge of my robe—it would return and repeat its operation—again—and again. . . .

Down—steadily down it crept. . . .

Down—certainly, relentlessly down! It vibrated within three inches of my bosom! . . .

I saw that some ten or twelve vibrations would bring the steel in actual contact with my robe, and with this observation there suddenly came over my spirit all the keen, collected calmness of despair. For the first time during many hours—or perhaps days— I *thought*. It now occurred to me, that the bandage, or surcingle, which enveloped me, was *unique*. I was tied by no separate cord. The first stroke of the razor-like crescent athwart any portion of the band, would so detach it that it might be unwound from my person by means of my left hand. But how fearful, in that case, the proximity of the steel! The result of the slightest struggle how deadly! Was it likely, moreover, that the minions of the torturer had not foreseen and provided for this possibility? Was it probable that the bandage crossed my bosom in the track of the pendulum? Dreading to find my faint, and, as it seemed, my last hope frustrated, I so far elevated my head as to obtain a distinct view of my breast. The surcingle enveloped my limbs and body close in all directions—*save in the path of the destroying crescent.*

Scarcely had I dropped my head back into its original position, when there flashed upon my mind what I cannot better describe than as the unformed half of that idea of deliverance to which I have previously alluded, and of which a moiety only floated indeterminately through my brain when I raised food to my burning lips. The whole thought was now present—feeble, scarcely sane, scarcely definite,—but still entire. I proceeded at once, with the nervous energy of despair, to attempt its execution.

Continued on next page

For many hours the immediate vicinity of the low framework upon which I lay, had been literally swarming with rats. They were wild, bold, ravenous; their red eyes glaring upon me as if they waited but for motionlessness on my part to make me their prey. "To what food," I thought, "have they been accustomed in the well?"

They had devoured, in spite of all my efforts to prevent them, all but a small remnant of the contents of the dish. I had fallen into an habitual see-saw, or wave of the hand about the platter; and, at length, the unconscious uniformity of the movement deprived it of effect. In their voracity the vermin frequently fastened their sharp fangs in my fingers. With the particles of the oily and spicy viand which now remained, I thoroughly rubbed the bandage wherever I could reach it; then, raising my hand from the floor, I lay breathlessly still.

At first the ravenous animals were startled and terrified at the change—at the cessation of movement. They shrank alarmedly back; many sought the well. But this was only for a moment. I had not counted in vain upon their voracity. Observing that I remained without motion, one or two of the boldest leaped upon the framework, and smelt at the surcingle. This seemed the signal for a general rush. Forth from the well they hurried in fresh troops. They clung to the wood—they overran it, and leaped in hundreds upon my person. The measured movement of the pendulum disturbed them not at all. Avoiding its strokes they busied themselves with the anointed bandage. They pressed—they swarmed upon me in ever accumulating heaps. They writhed upon my throat; their cold lips sought my own; I was half stifled by their thronging pressure; disgust, for which the world has no name, swelled my bosom, and chilled, with a heavy clamminess, my heart. Yet one minute, and I felt that the struggle would be over. Plainly I perceived the loosening of the bandage. I knew that in more than one place it must be already severed. With a more than human resolution I lay *still*.

Nor had I erred in my calculations—nor had I endured in vain. I at length felt that I was *free*. The surcingle hung in ribands from my body. But the stroke of the pendulum already pressed upon my bosom. It had divided the serge of the robe. It had cut through the linen beneath. Twice again it swung, and a sharp sense of pain shot through every nerve. But the moment of escape had arrived. At a wave of my hand my deliverers hurried tumultuously away. With a steady movement—cautious, sidelong, shrinking, and slow—I slid from the embrace of the bandage and beyond the reach of the scimitar. For the moment, at least, *I was free.*

The Question

The initial question of this unit is

Does the story's hero really have time to carry out his escape plan?

1. Based on the information you have, draw your own sketch of the prisoner's situation.

2. Next, go back through the story and carefully search for any additional information about the pendulum and the time for the prisoner's escape. Compile a group list of any information you find. If you are uncertain about the importance or relevance of a piece of information, write it down—you may need it later. Also write down any questions you have and identify any information you wish you had.

3. In your group, share your initial opinions about the question stated above.

Homework 1   Building a Pendulum

1. Tell the story of "The Pit and the Pendulum" to a family member, friend, or neighbor. Ask the listener if the time for the prisoner's escape plan seems realistic and how you could find out if it is.

2. Write about these topics.

   a. What were the reactions of your listener?

   b. Did the listener think the amount of time in the story seemed realistic? What was the listener's reasoning?

   c. How did the listener think you could find out how realistic this time estimate was?

3. Make a pendulum from materials that you find around your house.

4. Figure out a way to measure the period of your pendulum as accurately as you can. (Working with the family member, friend, or neighbor on this may be helpful.) *Remember:* The period is the time it takes for your pendulum to swing back *and* forth once.

5. Write about how you measured the period.

6. Bring your pendulum to class with you tomorrow.

POW 12   *The Big Knight Switch*

Strict rules determine how knight pieces may move on a chessboard. Each "move" consists of two squares in one direction and then one square in a perpendicular direction.

For example, knights may move forward (or backward) two squares and then to the right (or left) one square, as shown in A below; similarly, they may move to the left (or right) two squares and then down (or up) one square, as shown in B below.

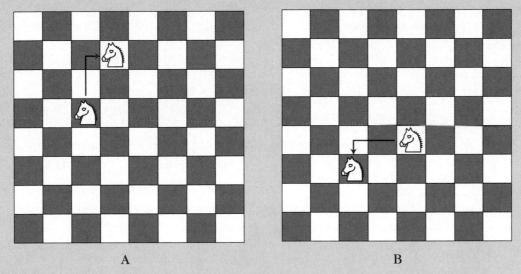

A   B

The rules also state that no two chess pieces may occupy the same square at the same time, although knights may pass or jump over other pieces on the way to an empty square.

That's it—there are no other choices. So knights can get pretty bored spending their days on the chessboard.

One day two black knights and two white knights were sitting around on a 3-by-3 chessboard, just as you see below, feeling restless.

Continued on next page

To liven things up, they decided to try to switch places, so that the white knights would end up where the black knights started out, and vice versa. Unfortunately, they could move only one at a time, according to the rules described above, and they had to stay within the nine squares of their board.

The big questions (to keep you from being bored) are:

1. Can they do it?

2. If so, what is the least number of moves it will take them to switch, and how do you know this number is the least?

3. If it is not possible, explain why not.

Reminder: Save your notes as you work on the problem. You will need them to do your write-up.

Write-up

1. *Problem statement*

2. *Process:* Be sure to include a description of how you kept track of the various moves. Also describe the different approaches you used to working on the problem.

3. *Solution:* Be sure to explain why you think your answer represents the least possible number of moves or why you think the task is impossible.

4. *Extensions*

5. *Evaluation*

Adapted from *aha! Insight,* by Martin Gardner, Scientific American, Inc./W. H. Freeman and Company, San Francisco, © 1978.

Initial Experiments

You know that *something* determines the period of a pendulum, but it may not be clear to you exactly what that something is. Maybe there are several things.

In this activity, you will do some preliminary experiments to get an idea about what affects a pendulum's period.

1. Your teacher will assign you a variable from the list made in class. Do some experiments to see if that variable affects the period of a pendulum.

2. Prepare a written report, describing what you did, what observations you made, and what questions you still have.

Homework 2

Close to the Law

Zoe was doing a report on crime. Some people she interviewed believed that building more police stations would result in less crime. These people claimed that the closer one gets to a police station, the less crime there is.

Others thought that nearness to a police station was not an important factor in the level of crime in a neighborhood.

Zoe wanted to check out these competing claims. She called her local police station and got data on crimes in her area in the past year. She focused on robberies and how far each of the robberies had been from the station. She made this chart.

Number of Blocks from Police Station	Number of Crimes per Block
0–5	13
5–10	14
More than 10	16

1. Given this information, what relationship do you think there is between nearness to a police station and amount of crime? Explain your reasoning.

2. Zoe's brother Max thinks there might be other factors affecting crime rate besides distance from the police station. List at least three other factors that might account for the differences in crime rates in the table.

Homework 3

If I Could Do It Over Again

The process of experimentation often requires a person to test, refine the experiment, and then test again.

Even if an experiment does not yield the expected results, important knowledge often emerges from it, such as information about what not to do.

What advice would you give someone who is doing your group's pendulum experiment for the first time? Address these issues.

- Problems encountered in setting up the experiment

- Problems encountered in doing the experiment

- Materials you would have liked to have

- Unexpected results

Time Is Relative

Nobody is a perfect timer. In this experiment you will explore how accurately people can time things. Members of your group will take turns timing five seconds.

Here is how the experiment works.

- One person watches the second hand of the clock on the wall or on a group member's watch. A second person holds a stopwatch.

- The first person says, "Start," and then says, "Stop" after five seconds. The second person tries to make the stopwatch start and stop on command so that it reads five seconds at the end of the experiment.

You will naturally be off a little bit each time you try it. Record your results to the nearest tenth of a second. Take turns timing and recording the results.

Homework 4   What's Your Stride?

Your **stride** is the length of a typical step when you are walking normally at a steady rate. For this assignment, you should measure a stride from the front of one foot to the front of the other foot.

Give all measurements to the nearest inch.

1. Take a guess at the length of your stride, and write it down.

2. Measuring your own stride may not be easy.

   a. Think of a method for measuring the length of your own stride, and describe it clearly.

   b. Use your method to find the length of your stride.

3. Using the same method, find the length of a stride of each of two people not in your class. (You can work with family members, neighbors, friends, and so on. In order to avoid too wide a variation, you should work only with people who are teenagers or older.)

4. What do you think a frequency bar graph of the stride lengths of 50 people might look like? Based on your best guess, make such a graph.

5. Why might people want to know the lengths of their strides?

Pulse Gathering

If you repeatedly measure the same thing very carefully in the same way, will you get the same answer every time?

This activity provides a setting in which to look at this question.

1. Begin with your body at rest. Then count the pulse beats at your wrist for a 15-second interval. Record your result as a whole number of pulse beats.

2. Repeat step 1, again recording your result. Continue to repeat step 1 until you have ten results. (Some of these results may be identical.)

3. In preparation for *Homework 5: Pulse Analysis,* share your data with everyone else in your group, and record each other's results. In other words, you should have ten results for each person in the group (including yourself).

Homework 5   Pulse Analysis

You should have a collection of data on the number of pulse beats in a 15-second interval—ten results for yourself and ten for each of your fellow group members.

1. Did you get the same result each time you counted your pulse beats for a 15-second interval? Why or why not?

2. a. Find the mean (average) of your own pulse data.

   b. Find the mean of the pulse data for your whole group.

   c. Was the whole group's mean the same as your own? Why or why not?

3. For the following frequency bar graphs, do not group your measurements.

   a. Make a frequency bar graph of your own pulse data.

   b. Make a frequency bar graph for the pulse data of the whole group.

Homework 6   Return to the Pit

This unit is complex and includes some investigations that are not directly concerned with the main problem.

Therefore, from time to time in this unit, we will ask you to reflect on where you are with respect to solving the unit problem.

Write answers to these questions so that someone who knows nothing about the story and knows little about mathematics could understand what you are saying.

1. Write about the problem that the class is trying to solve, stating the goal as clearly as you can.

2. Write about what you have done so far in the unit and how that work will help to solve the unit problem. Be sure to explain clearly how measurement variation is involved.

3. Finally, write down some questions you have about the unit and some points you don't yet clearly understand.

POW 13

Corey Camel

Consider the case of Corey Camel—the enterprising but eccentric owner of a small banana grove in a remote desert oasis.

Corey's harvest, which is worth its weight in gold, consists of 3000 bananas. The marketplace where the harvest can be sold is 1000 miles away. However, Corey must walk to the market, and she can carry at most 1000 bananas at a time. Furthermore, being a camel, Corey eats one banana during each and every mile she walks (so Corey can never walk anywhere without bananas).

The question is this:

How many bananas can Corey get to the market?

Write-up

1. *Problem statement*

2. *Process:* You will also work on a mini-POW that relates to this POW. In discussing your process on this POW, note how your work on that mini-POW helped you. Also, be sure to discuss all of the methods you tried in order to solve the POW itself.

3. *Solution:*

   a. State your solution (or solutions) as clearly as you can.

   b. Do you think your solution is the best possible one? Explain.

   c. Explain how and why the answer to this POW is related to the answer to the mini-POW.

4. *Evaluation*

Days 7–15

Statistics and the Pendulum

So now you've got an idea of what this unit problem is all about. You probably have a list of variables that might affect the period of a pendulum, but you've also seen that you can measure the exact same pendulum twice and get different periods. That makes things pretty unpredictable!

Actually, scientists are used to uncertainty in their experiments. You might say that this uncertainty is "normal." In the part of mathematics called statistics, people have a very special meaning for the word *normal,* and they've come up with ways to describe how *abnormal* a particular measurement might be.

Lindsey Carvalho prepares a bar graph as an aid in analyzing the results from her experiment.

Homework 7   What's Normal?

You've now seen some examples of normal curves. But when does the normal distribution apply to real life?

This assignment describes several situations. You may not know what the real information is, so just do your best. You might just make up a set of data that seems reasonable to you.

For each situation, follow these steps.

   a. Draw a frequency bar graph of the situation based on your idea of what the data might look like. Your graph should show labeled axes and units of measurement, and you will need to decide on intervals that are suitable to the situation.

   b. Explain how you decided what the graph should look like. If you guessed, explain what made you guess the way you did.

   c. State whether or not your graph appears to be approximately a normal distribution.

1. The number of people in your school who wear hightop tennis shoes, lowtop tennis shoes, dress shoes, or sandals to school on a given day.

2. The frequency with which a 100-meter sprinter achieves certain times, running 200 races over the course of one year. (Assume that the sprinter's average time is 12 seconds.)

3. The number of people in the United States who earn certain amounts of money. (Use 250,000,000 as the total population of the United States. You might use categories such as "income from $0 to $20,000," "income from $20,000 to $40,000," "income from $40,000 to $60,000," and so on.)

4. The number of people in the state of Hawaii who are of certain ages. (Use 1,100,000 as the total population of Hawaii.)

A Mini-POW About Mini-Camel

Like Corey Camel, Mini-Camel also owns a banana grove.

But Mini-Camel's harvest consists of only 45 bananas, and Mini-Camel can carry at most 15 bananas at a time.

The marketplace where Mini-Camel's harvest can be sold is only 15 miles away. Like Corey, however, Mini-Camel also eats one banana during each and every mile he walks.

1. How many bananas can Mini-Camel get to market?

2. Explain how Mini-Camel achieves this result.

3. Discuss how the Mini-Camel problem is related to *POW 13: Corey Camel,* and explain how the mini-POW could help you solve the POW.

Note: Your POW write-up asks you to refer to your work on this assignment, so you'll need to keep a copy of your notes from this mini-POW.

Homework 8

Flip, Flip

Do the results of coin flips give a bell-shaped distribution? You can get an idea by performing some experiments.

1. Shake 10 coins together and let them fall, and then record the number of heads. Do this experiment 15 times, recording the result each time, so that you get a total of 15 results, each of which is a number from 0 to 10.

2. Make a frequency bar graph showing the results of your experiments.

3. Do you think anyone in the class will have an experiment with a result of 0 (*no heads*)? with a result of 10 (*all heads*)? Explain your reasoning.

4. Predict what the class results will look like. That is, draw a frequency bar graph that you think will resemble the combined results from your class. Explain your reasoning.

5. Suppose you are given two coins and are told that *one of them* is unbalanced (but you don't know which one). You flip one of the coins 50 times, and it gives 28 heads and 22 tails. How confident would you be in deciding whether or not the coin you flipped is the unbalanced one? Explain your reasoning.

What's Rare?

Part I: Stride Lengths

Use the frequency bar graph of
stride lengths to answer these
questions.

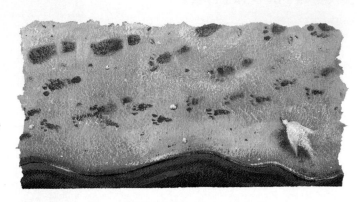

1. Name a single stride
   length that you would
   categorize as *ordinary*,
   and name a single
   stride length that you
   would categorize
   as *rare*.

2. Where would you put the boundaries for each category? In other words,
   complete these sentences.

   a. An ordinary stride length is from –?– to –?–.

   b. A rare stride length is less than –?– or greater than –?–.

3. Based on your answers to Question 2, estimate the answer to the following
   questions.

   a. What percentage of all the data is in the "ordinary" category?

   b. What percentage of all the data is in the "rare" category?

Part II: Pulse Rates

Use the frequency bar graph of pulse rates to categorize these measurements as ordinary
or rare for the pulse rate of a person at rest.

1. 20 beats for 15 seconds

2. 17 beats for 15 seconds

3. 12 beats for 15 seconds

4. 28 beats for 15 seconds

Continued on next page

5. Where would you place the borderline for each of the categories, ordinary and rare?

   a. An ordinary pulse rate is from –?– to –?–.

   b. A rare pulse rate is less than –?– or greater than –?–.

6. Based on your answers to Question 5, estimate the answers to the following questions.

   a. What percentage of all the data is in the "ordinary" category?

   b. What percentage of all the data is in the "rare" category?

Part III: Timing of Five Seconds

Use the frequency bar graph of the timing of five seconds to answer these questions.

1. Where would you place the borderline for each of the categories, ordinary and rare?

   a. An ordinary result is from –?– to –?–.

   b. A rare result is less than –?– or greater than –?–.

2. Based on your answers to Question 1, estimate the answers to the following questions.

   a. What percentage of all the data is in the "ordinary" category?

   b. What percentage of all the data is in the "rare" category?

Part IV: Comparing and Using Rarities

1. Compare the percentages you got in Question 2 of Part III with those you chose in Question 3 of Part I and Question 6 of Part II.

2. Suppose you got a new stopwatch, and used it to repeat the "timing of five seconds" experiments. If you found that you had an average of 5.7 seconds after 10 timings, would you think the new stopwatch was defective? What if your average after 10 timings with the new stopwatch was 4.9 seconds? Explain your reasoning.

Homework 9 Penny Weight

Sarah's and Tom's mom is a chemist, and one day she brought home a very sensitive scale. Sarah and Tom enjoyed learning how to use the scale.

One of the things they did was measure the weight of some pennies, one at a time. Here is a list of the results they got, arranged from lightest to heaviest (weights are in milligrams).

2600	2604	2607	2610	2612	2615	2616
2617	2618	2619	2623	2623	2624	2625
2626	2627	2630	2631	2636	2637	

1. Given this information, what do you think is the best estimate for the weight of a penny, and why?

2. Sarah's and Tom's Uncle Jack claimed that he had a counterfeit penny. Sarah and Tom didn't believe it was counterfeit, because it looked real and felt real and because their uncle was always trying to fool them. They asked him if they could borrow the penny, and they weighed it. They got 2641 milligrams.

Tom said the coin must be counterfeit because they never got a weight that high with their other pennies. Sarah isn't sure. She thinks that if they weighed it again, its weight might be closer to that of the weight of the others. Or, if they measured more pennies, then Uncle Jack's coin might not seem so weird. What do you think, and why? If you don't think Uncle Jack's penny is counterfeit, then how heavy or light would a penny need to be before you believed it was counterfeit?

Mean School Data

Students at Kennedy and King High Schools were trying to determine what would affect the period of a pendulum.

At each school, students decided on standard pendulum characteristics for their initial experiments, including the length, weight, and amplitude.

Then five groups in each school took a fixed number of measurements of the period of this standard pendulum and calculated the mean for those measurements. The tables below give the mean pendulum periods found at each school.

Kennedy High

Group	Mean Pendulum Period (in seconds)
1	1.21
2	1.25
3	1.22
4	1.19
5	1.23

King High

Group	Mean Pendulum Period (in seconds)
1	1.16
2	1.22
3	1.31
4	1.11
5	1.30

Continued on next page

1. Find the overall mean for each school's data.

2. One group from each school decided to test whether changing the weight of the bob would change the period of a pendulum, so they conducted the set of experiments again with a different weight. Both groups now got a mean pendulum period of 1.29 seconds.

   If you were at Kennedy High, what would you conclude? If you were at King High, what would you conclude? In each case, explain your reasoning.

Homework 10   An (AB)Normal Rug

One day, Al and Betty got bored playing spinner games and decided to try rug and dart games.

Betty thought that playing on square or rectangular rugs would not be challenging enough, so she made some rugs that looked like normal distributions. As usual, each point in the rug had an equally likely chance of receiving a dart.

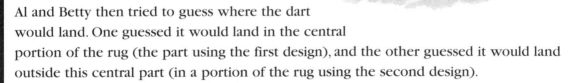

As shown in the diagram at the right, each rug consisted of three parts, with a central portion placed symmetrically between the other two. The central part of each rug resembled the area under the normal curve between two vertical lines symmetric around the mean. This part of the rug used one design. The two outer portions of the rug used a second design, and resembled the area under the normal curve to the left or right of such vertical lines.

Al and Betty then tried to guess where the dart would land. One guessed it would land in the central portion of the rug (the part using the first design), and the other guessed it would land outside this central part (in a portion of the rug using the second design).

1. The diagrams below are like the rugs used by Al and Betty, with the shaded area representing one design and the unshaded area representing the second design. In each case, estimate what percentage of the area is shaded.

    a.

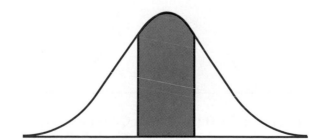

Continued on next page

---

b.

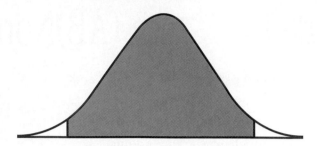

2. Trace each of the three rugs below. Then use two vertical lines to create regions like those above, to fit the condition in the next paragraph, and shade the region in the center. (Your shaded areas should each be centered around the vertical line of symmetry of the rug.)

   Your task is to estimate where to put the vertical lines so that a player who guesses that the dart will land in the shaded area wins twice as often as a player who guesses it will land in the unshaded area. Also, explain how you determined that one area is approximately twice as large as the other.

   a.

   b.

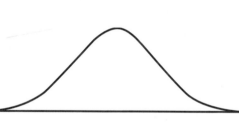

   c.

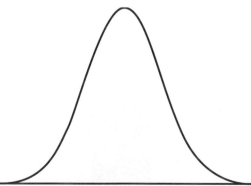

3. Make another copy of the three rugs in Question 2, and repeat the process described there, except this time make the player with the shaded region win 95% of the time. Again, explain how you estimated the areas.

Data Spread

Rinky, Dinky, and Minky understood how to find the mean of any set of data.
But they also knew that one set of data could have the same mean as another but
look quite different.

Continued on next page

On one occasion, they looked at these four sets of data, each of which has a mean of 20.

> Set *A*   19, 19, 20, 20, 21, 21
>
> Set *B*   10, 10, 20, 20, 30, 30
>
> Set *C*   12, 13, 13, 27, 27, 28
>
> Set *D*   9, 20, 20, 20, 20, 31

1. Based on your own intuition, arrange the four sets of data from the set that is "least spread out from the mean" to the set that is "most spread out from the mean." Explain your reasons for the order you choose. (You and your group members may want to discuss this together, but each of you should make your own decision.)

Rinky, Dinky, and Minky were looking for a way to assign a number to measure how spread out from the mean a set of data was. They wanted a method in which the bigger the number, the more spread out the data set would be from its mean.

2. Rinky liked the idea of using the **range** of the data to measure data spread. To find the range, you just subtract the smallest number in the list from the largest one. For example, you find the range for set *D* by taking the difference 31 – 9, which is 22.

   a. Find the range for each of the other sets of data.

   b. Based on Rinky's method, arrange the four sets of data from the set that is "least spread out from the mean" to the set that is "most spread out from the mean."

   c. Does your result from Question 2b change your mind about your answer to Question 1? Explain.

Note: You will learn about Dinky's and Minky's ideas in *Homework 11: Dinky and Minky Spread Data.*

Homework 11

Dinky and Minky Spread Data

In *Data Spread,* you saw Rinky's idea for measuring data spread. His two friends had other suggestions.

For your convenience, here are the sets of data from that activity:

$$\text{Set } A \quad 19, 19, 20, 20, 21, 21$$

$$\text{Set } B \quad 10, 10, 20, 20, 30, 30$$

$$\text{Set } C \quad 12, 13, 13, 27, 27, 28$$

$$\text{Set } D \quad 9, 20, 20, 20, 20, 31$$

1. Dinky proposed finding the distance of each number in the list from the mean and then just adding those distances to get a measure for data spread.

Continued on next page

For example, in set *C*, because the mean is 20, the number 12 is 8 away from the mean. Similarly, each number 13 is 7 from the mean, and so on. So Dinky would assign the number $8 + 7 + 7 + 7 + 7 + 8$, which is 44, to set *C*.

a. Find the number that Dinky would assign to each of the other sets of data.

b. Based on Dinky's method, arrange the four sets of data from the set that is "least spread out from the mean" to the set that is "most spread out from the mean."

2. Minky's idea was to ignore the highest and lowest data items, removing just one item at each end even if there were ties. Then, he said, one should find the remaining data item that's farthest from the original mean and use that distance to measure data spread.

For instance, with set *B*, Minky would drop the lowest number (one of the 10's) and the highest number (one of the 30's), leaving just 10, 20, 20, and 30.

Because the mean of set *B* is 20, the maximum distance from any of these numbers to the mean is 10. So Minky would assign the number 10 to set *B*.

a. Find the number that Minky would assign to each of the other sets of data.

b. Based on Minky's method, arrange the four sets of data from the set that is "least spread out from the mean" to the set that is "most spread out from the mean."

3. Examine your answers to Questions 1b and 2b, as well as the answer to Question 2b of *Data Spread*. Whose measure of data spread—Rinky's, Dinky's, or Minky's—is closest to the answer you gave in Question 1 of *Data Spread*? Explain your decision.

4. Invent a way to measure data spread that is different from these three. Describe how it works, and explain whether or not you think it is better or not.

Standard Deviation Basics

What Is Standard Deviation?

The **standard deviation** of a set of data measures how "spread out" the data set is. In other words, it tells you whether all the data items bunch around close to the mean or if they are "all over the place."

The superimposed graphs below show two normal distributions with the same mean, but the taller graph is less "spread out." Therefore, the data represented by the taller graph has a smaller standard deviation.

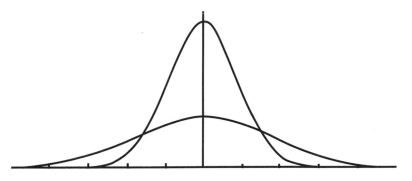

Calculation of Standard Deviation

Here is a list of the steps for calculating standard deviation.

1. Find the mean.

2. Find the difference between each data item and the mean.

3. Square each of the differences.

4. Find the average (mean) of these squared differences.

5. Take the square root of this average.

Organizing the computation of standard deviation into a table like the one on the next page can be very helpful. This table is based on a data set of five items: 5, 8, 10, 14, and 18. The mean for this data set is 11. The mean of a set of data is often represented by the symbol $\bar{x}$, which is read as "x bar."

Continued on next page

The computation of the mean is shown below the table to the left. On the right below the table, step 4 of the computation of the standard deviation is broken down into two substeps: (a) adding the squares of the differences and (b) dividing by the number of data items.

The symbol usually used for standard deviation is the lower case form of the Greek letter *sigma*, written σ.

x	$x - \bar{x}$	$(x - \bar{x})^2$
5	–6	36
8	–3	9
10	–1	1
14	3	9
18	7	49

sum of the data items = 55   sum of the squared differences = 104

number of data items = 5   mean of the squared differences = 20.8

$\bar{x}$ (mean of the data items) = 11   σ (standard deviation) = $\sqrt{20.8} \approx 4.6$

Suppose you represent the mean as $\bar{x}$, use n for the number of data items, and represent the data items as x_1, x_2, and so on. Then the standard deviation can be defined by the equation

$$\sigma = \sqrt{\frac{\sum_{i=1}^{n}(x_i - \bar{x})^2}{n}}$$

Standard Deviation and the Normal Distribution

The normal distribution was identified and studied initially by a French mathematician, Abraham de Moivre (1667–1754). De Moivre used the concept of normal distribution to make calculations for wealthy gamblers. That was how he supported himself while he worked as a mathematician.

But the normal distribution applies to many situations besides those that are of interest to gamblers. (Measurement variation is one important example.) Therefore mathematicians have studied this distribution extensively.

Continued on next page

When we use standard deviation to study the variation among measurements of a pendulum's period, we make this assumption:

> Normality Assumption
>
> If you make many measurements of the period of any given pendulum, the data will closely fit a normal distribution.

One of the reasons why standard deviation is so important for normal distributions is that there are some principles about standard deviation that hold true for any normal distribution. Specifically, whenever a set of data is normally distributed, these statements hold true.

• Approximately 68% of all results are within one standard deviation of the mean.

• Approximately 95% of all results are within two standard deviations of the mean.

These facts can be explained in terms of area, using the diagram "The Normal Distribution."

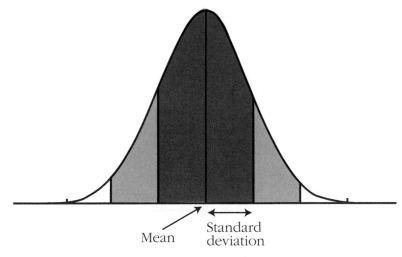

The Normal Distribution

In this diagram, the darkly shaded area stretches from one standard deviation below the mean to one standard deviation above the mean; it is approximately 68% of the total area under the curve.

The light and dark shaded areas together stretch from two standard deviations below the mean to two standard deviations above the mean, and constitute approximately 95% of the total area under the curve.

Continued on next page

So standard deviation provides a good rule of thumb for deciding whether something is "rare."

Note: In order to understand exactly where the specific numbers "68%" and "95%" come from, you would need to have a precise definition of *normal distribution,* a definition that is stated using concepts from calculus.

Geometric Interpretation of Standard Deviation

Geometrically, the standard deviation for a normal distribution turns out to be the horizontal distance from the mean to the place on the curve where the curve changes from being concave down to concave up.

In the diagram "Visualizing the Standard Deviation," the center section of the curve, near the mean, is concave down, and the two "tails" (that is, the portions farther from the mean) are concave up.

The two places where the curve changes its concavity, marked by the vertical lines, are exactly one standard deviation from the mean, measured horizontally.

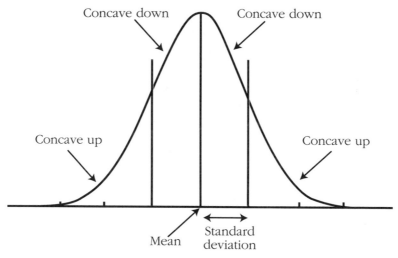

Visualizing the Standard Deviation

Homework 12   The Best Spread

Here are the four sets of data from
Data Spread.

Set *A*   19, 19, 20, 20, 21, 21

Set *B*   10, 10, 20, 20, 30, 30

Set *C*   12, 13, 13, 27, 27, 28

Set *D*   9, 20, 20, 20, 20, 31

1. Write down the way you arranged the four sets of data in that assignment, from the set that is *least spread out from the mean* to the set that is *most spread out from the mean*.

2. a. Calculate the standard deviation of each set of data.

   b. Use your answers from Question 2a to arrange the four sets of data from the set with the smallest standard deviation to the set with the largest standard deviation.

3. a. Are the two arrangements, from Questions 1 and 2b, the same?

   b. If the arrangements are not the same, explain the reasoning you used in your arrangement from Question 1.

4. Recall that Rinky thought that *range* was a good method for measuring data spread. Make up two new sets of data, set *X* and set *Y*, in which set *X* has a larger standard deviation than set *Y* but set *Y* has a larger range than set *X*.

Making Friends with Standard Deviation

You will be working with the concept of standard deviation in connection with the unit problem throughout the rest of the unit. Before you begin that work, it will be helpful for you to gain some more familiarity with the concept.

1. First, explore what happens to the mean and the standard deviation of a set of data when you add the same number to each member in the set.

   a. As a group, make up a set of five numbers that are all different. Find the mean and the standard deviation of your set.

   b. Now choose a nonzero number and add it to each member of your set. Find the mean and the standard deviation of your new set.

Continued on next page

c. Repeat Question 1b, using a different nonzero number. Add this number to each member of your original set of data, and find the mean and standard deviation of the new set. Keep repeating this process until you see a pattern, and then describe that pattern.

d. Explain why your pattern should occur.

   • Explain why the mean changes as it does when you add the same thing to each member of the set.

   • Explain why the standard deviation changes as it does when you add the same thing to each member of the set.

2. Now explore what happens to the mean and the standard deviation of a set of data when you multiply each member in the set by the same number.

   a. Begin with the same set of data as in Question 1a. Then choose a nonzero number other than 1. Multiply each member of your set by that number and find the mean and the standard deviation of the new set.

   b. Choose another nonzero number other than 1, and repeat what you did in part a.

   c. Keep choosing new nonzero numbers to use as multipliers for each member in your set. Find the mean and the standard deviation of each new set, until you see a pattern. Describe that pattern.

   d. Explain why your pattern occurs.

3. Make up a set of data for each of these pairs of conditions.

   a. Mean, 6; standard deviation, 1

   b. Mean, 10; standard deviation, 1

   c. Mean, 7; standard deviation, 2

Homework 13

Deviations

1. Find the mean and the standard deviation of this set of data.

24, 25, 15, 19, 17

Your task in the rest of this assignment is to make up new sets of data items, each having either the same mean or the same standard deviation as the data set in Question 1.

If you can, do these problems without actually calculating the mean or the standard deviation of each new set of data, and explain how you know without calculating that the data set fits the conditions.

2. Make up a set of five data items that has the *same mean* as the data set in Question 1 but has a *smaller standard deviation*.

3. Make up a set of five data items that has the *same mean* as the data set in Question 1 but has a *larger standard deviation*.

4. Make up a set of five data items that has the *same standard deviation* as the data set in Question 1 but has a *different mean*.

Homework 14 Penny Weight Revisited

In *Homework 9: Penny Weight,* you saw that Sarah and Tom had been weighing a bunch of pennies on a sensitive scale. For your convenience, here again are the results that they got (in milligrams).

2600	2604	2607	2610	2612	2615	2616
2617	2618	2619	2623	2623	2624	2625
2626	2627	2630	2631	2636	2637	

1. Compute the mean and standard deviation of these weights. Record all your computations clearly so you can compare results with others in your group.

    Remember the steps in finding the standard deviation.

    a. Find the mean.

    b. Find the difference between each data item and the mean.

    c. Square each of the differences.

    d. Find the average (mean) of these squared differences.

    e. Take the square root of this average.

2. Now reconsider the problem of the penny that Sarah's and Tom's Uncle Jack claimed was counterfeit. When Sarah and Tom weighed that penny, they got a weight of 2641 milligrams.

    a. Based on your results in Question 1, what can you say about the probability that a real penny would have a weight so far from the mean?

    b. Do you think that Uncle Jack's penny is real or counterfeit?

POW 14   *Eight Bags of Gold*

Once upon a time there was a very economical king who gathered up all the gold in his land and put it into eight bags. He made sure that each bag weighed exactly the same amount.

The king then chose the eight people in his country whom he trusted the most, and gave a bag of gold to each of them to keep safe for him. On special occasions he asked them to bring the bags back so he could look at them. (He liked looking at his gold, even though he didn't like spending it.)

One day the king heard from a foreign trader that someone from the king's country had given the trader some gold in exchange for some merchandise. The trader couldn't describe the person who had given her the gold, but she knew that it was someone from the king's country. Since the king owned all of the gold in his country, it was obvious that one of the eight people he trusted was cheating him.

The only scale in the country was a pan balance. This scale wouldn't tell how much something weighed, but it could compare two things and indicate which was heavier and which was lighter. The person whose bag was lighter than the others would clearly be the cheat. So the king asked the eight trusted people to bring their bags of gold to him.

Being very economical, the king wanted to use the pan balance as few times as possible. He thought he might have to use it three times in order to be sure which bag was lighter than the rest. His court mathematician thought that it could be done in fewer weighings. What do you think?

Continued on next page

To answer this question, follow these steps.

1. Develop a scheme for comparing bags that will always find the light one.

2. Explain how you can be sure that your scheme will always work.

3. Explain how you know that there is no scheme with fewer weighings that will work.

Note: Each comparison counts as a new weighing, even if some of the bags are the same as on the previous comparison.

Write-up

1. *Problem statement*

2. *Process:* Describe how you found your answer and how you convinced yourself that your method works in all situations. If you think your answer is the best possible, describe how you came to that conclusion.

3. *Solution:* Describe your solution to the king's problem as clearly as possible. Then write a proof that your method will work in every situation. If you think that the king cannot find the lighter bag in fewer than three weighings, prove it.

4. *Extensions*

5. *Evaluation*

Homework 15   Can Your Calculator Pass This Soft Drink Test?

1. A soft drink company sells its beverage in one-liter bottles. (*Reminder:* A liter is equal to 1000 milliliters. The abbreviation for millileter is mL.)

The machine that fills the bottles is not perfect. The amount of soft drink it puts into the bottles fits a normal distribution, with a mean of 1000 mL (fortunately) and a standard deviation of 5 mL.

Continued on next page

If the filling machine puts more than 1005 mL into a bottle, the bottle will very likely spill when opened, causing customers to complain. If the machine puts less than 995 mL into a bottle, the amount in the bottle will be visibly less than it should be, causing customers to feel cheated.

A quality-control worker checks the bottles after they are filled and before they are sealed to see if they fit within the bounds of these conditions. If a bottle is either too full or not full enough, the worker removes the bottle from the assembly line to be corrected.

Approximately what percentage of bottles get removed from the assembly line?

2. A manufacturer of graphing calculators keeps track of the length of time it takes before the product is returned for repair. She finds that the mean is 985 days and the standard deviation is 83 days.

   She wants to set a time period during which her company will warranty the calculators—that is, a period in which they will replace them at no cost to the customer if the products do not function properly. She does not want to have to replace more than 2.5% of those sold.

   Assume that the number of days before calculators need repair is normally distributed. How many days' warranty would you advise her to give her customers? Explain your reasoning.

3. Students' scores on a certain college entrance examination follow a normal distribution, with a mean of 490 and a standard deviation of 120. The college of your choice, Big State University, accepts only students whose scores on this test are 600 or higher.

   Estimate the percentage of students who are eligible for admission to Big State on the basis of their test scores, and explain your reasoning.

Days 16-20

A Standard Pendulum

It's been a while since you actually measured the period of a pendulum, but now you have some statistical tools—normal distribution and standard deviation—to understand the variation in measurements that can occur even if you don't change the pendulum.

Over the next few days, you will get back to measurements, and use these tools to decide "what matters?" In other words, you will figure out, statistically, what variable or variables really affect the period of a pendulum.

Carrell Cabacungan and Aaron Gago try out the experiment from the supplemental problem "Are You Ambidextrous?"

The Standard Pendulum

The pendulum that is illustrated below will be called the *standard pendulum* for the rest of the unit.

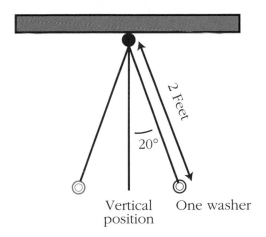

As you study whether changing a pendulum affects its period, you will be looking at pendulums that differ in some respect from this standard pendulum.

You will compare the periods of these other pendulums to the period of this one.

Here are the specifications for the standard pendulum.

- Weight of bob   1 washer

- Length of string   2 feet

- Amplitude   20°

Find the period of this standard pendulum using the procedure agreed upon by your class, and record your result.

Then repeat the experiment, again recording the period. Continue gathering more data as time allows.

Homework 16

Standard Pendulum Data and Decisions

You should have a large collection of measurements made for the period of the standard pendulum.

Although all groups worked with the same specifications for the pendulum, their results for the period probably were not all alike. In fact, each group probably came up with slightly different values each time they did the experiment to measure the period, even though the pendulum itself didn't change.

1. Why should different experiments using the exact same pendulum give different values for the period?

2. Make a frequency bar graph of the data you have, choosing intervals that you think are appropriate for grouping the data.

3. Draw a normal curve that approximates the graph you made in Question 2. Your curve should go approximately through the tops of the bars of your frequency bar graph.

4. Based on either your frequency bar graph from Question 2 or the curve from Question 3 (or both), estimate the mean and the standard deviation for the data.

5. Suppose you built a pendulum using different specifications, measured its period using the same procedure as in *The Standard Pendulum,* and got a result different from the mean you found in Question 4. How far from the mean would you need that new period to be before you were confident that the difference was not simply due to measurement variation? Explain your answer.

Pendulum Variations

You have seen that you may get slightly different results each time you measure the period of the standard pendulum.

As noted in *Standard Deviation Basics,* you are making this assumption about these measurement variations:

> Normality Assumption
>
> If you make many measurements of the period of any given pendulum, the data will closely fit a normal distribution.

In *Homework 16: Standard Pendulum Data and Decisions,* you estimated both the mean and the standard deviation of this normal distribution.

In this activity, you will look at what happens to the period if the pendulum is changed in certain ways. You will then use the results from this activity to decide what factor or factors seem to determine the period of the pendulum.

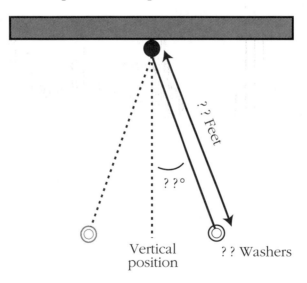

In conducting your experiments for this activity, you should measure the period in exactly the same way as you did in *The Standard Pendulum.* For example, if in that activity you measured the time for 10 swings and then divided by 10 to get the period, you should do the same thing here.

Continued on next page

Make each measurement *twice*, but treat each as a separate result. *Do not average your two measurements!*

In each experiment, your pendulum should be the same as the standard pendulum except for the characteristic being studied in that case. Here again are the specifications of the standard pendulum.

- Weight of bob   1 washer
- Length of string   2 feet
- Amplitude   20°

1. *Changing the Weight*

Measure the period of a pendulum that is the same as the standard pendulum except that it has a weight of 5 washers.

2. *Changing the Length*

Measure the period of a pendulum that is the same as the standard pendulum except that it is 4 feet long.

3. *Changing the Amplitude*

Measure the period of a pendulum that is the same as the standard pendulum except that it has an amplitude of 30°.

Homework 17

A Picture Is Worth a Thousand Words

It is said that "a picture is worth a thousand words." However, pictures, like words, can sometimes be misleading. This can be the case when people use graphs to make a point.

Graphs are pictures that convey information to people. And, just as there are people who forget to read the fine print in text, there are also people who don't look carefully at graphs to see what the numbers are really telling them. These people can be tricked into reaching false conclusions.

Here is an example. A television station wants to convince its advertisers that viewers are changing over to that channel in huge numbers. The station has experienced slow but fairly steady growth over the past year. If the station made a simple month-by-month graph of its ratings, this is what the graph might look like.

The Math Channel Makes Steady Progress!

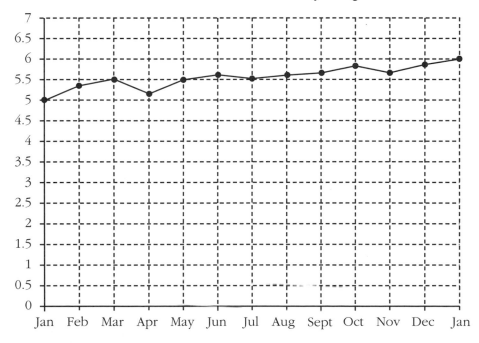

As you can see, the station has increased its viewers by one ratings point, from 5.0 last January to 6.0 this January.

Continued on next page

But there are many ways the graph can be changed to give the impression that the station is doing even better than it actually is.

One way is to show only part of the graph. The version below depicts only the changing part of the graph. It gives the appearance of a larger increase than does the graph above because the reader cannot see what the change relates to. The reader sees the graph starting at the bottom of the picture and ending at the top.

The Math Channel Adds Many Viewers!

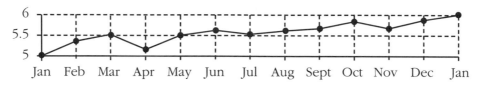

The graph can be made even more dramatic by changing the scales of the axes so that the distance between 5.0 and 6.0 is greater. For instance, if you change the vertical scale so that each interval is worth 0.1 instead of 0.5, here is what the graph will look like.

The Math Channel Is Hot!

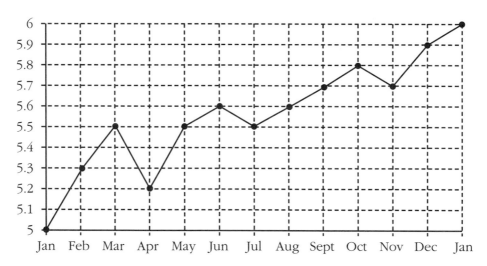

Continued on next page

Changing the horizontal axis can help too. In the next graph, the change is reported only every three months, so there are no "downs," only "ups." Making the graph line bolder also adds to the effect.

The Math Channel Is on Fire!

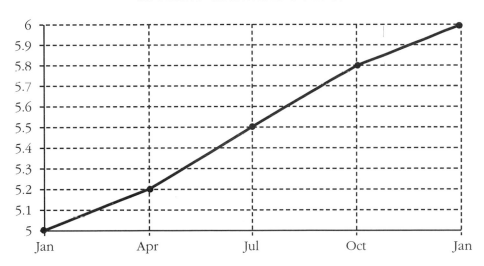

Your assignment

1. Create a misleading graph of your own. This actually requires that you make two graphs:

   a. an original graph

   b. a misleading graph

2. Describe the impact you were trying to create in Question 1. Explain how your graph is misleading.

3. Cut out a graph from a newspaper or magazine and write about why you think it is fair or why you think it may be misleading.

Homework 18 Pendulum Conclusions

1. In *Pendulum Variations,* you looked at what happened to the period of a pendulum when you changed from the standard pendulum. Based on those experiments, you have probably reached some conclusions about what factor or factors determine the period of a pendulum.

Summarize your conclusions clearly, and support them using the concepts of normal distribution and standard deviation.

2. In the experiments from both *The Standard Pendulum* and *Pendulum Variations,* you had to work closely with your fellow group members.

Decide what grade each member of your group deserves for the work he or she did in the last few days. Be sure to include yourself in this grading process.

In assigning a grade to each person, you may want to consider these factors.

- What suggestions the person made

- How well the person listened to others

- How supportive the person was to others

- Whether the person helped the group stay on task

- Whether the person helped the group when it got stuck

- Whether the person helped to settle disagreements in the group

- Whether the person ever helped the group reach a consensus

Homework 19

POW Revision

Tonight you will revise your write-up of *POW 14: Eight Bags of Gold,* based on the feedback given to you by your classmates.

Your revision should be on paper *separate from your original*, and it can take many forms, depending on the feedback you received.

- You can redo your entire write-up.

- You can rewrite certain sections that need refinement.

- You can add additional comments and diagrams that would improve or clarify parts of your write-up.

After revising your write-up, write a paragraph on the value of reading other students' papers and getting feedback on your own paper.

In summary, you should bring four items to the next class:

- Your original write-up

- The reviews you received from your classmates

- Your revisions

- Your evaluation of the experience of reading other students' write-ups and receiving feedback on your own write-up

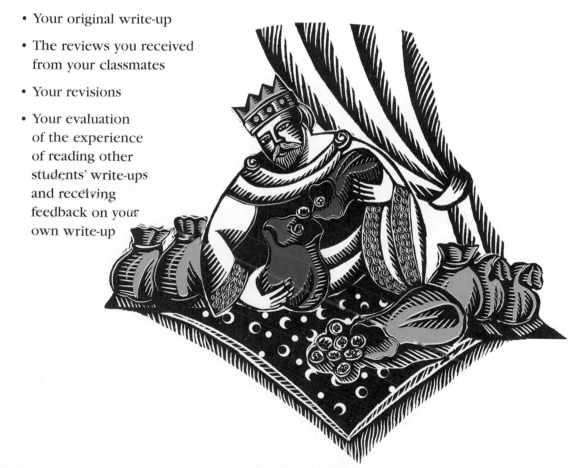

Homework 20

Mehrdad the Market Analyst

Mehrdad is a market analyst. He studies the relationship among an item's price, the number of items sold, and the amount of profit.

High price does not necessarily mean high profit. If a company sells a great product, but charges too much for it, the company will not sell very many units and therefore won't make very much profit.

On the other hand, low price does not necessarily mean high profit either. If the company sells the product for too low a price, it will sell a lot of units but will not be making much profit.

You can see the complexity. The ideal price is somewhere in the middle—not too low and not too high. Mehrdad studies the market and finds the most profitable price at which to sell an item.

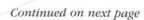

Continued on next page

You have hired Mehrdad to analyze the market and suggest prices to charge in your music store. In particular, you have asked him to provide information about the price to charge for compact discs and compact disc players. Mehrdad comes back with this information.

Compact Discs

Price Charged (in dollars)	Expected Profit (in dollars per month)
11	−1100 (loss of $1100)
14	1800
17	1600
18	0

Portable Compact Disc Players

Price Charged (in dollars)	Expected Profit (in dollars per month)
100	0
115	1250
130	2000
150	−4000 (loss of $4000)

1. For each item, sketch a graph showing the relationship between different prices and the expected profit. (*Warning:* Be careful how you set up the scales on the axes.)

2. Sketch a line or curve that you believe represents the relationship between price and profit.

3. What price do you think will maximize the profit for each item? Explain your answers.

POW 15 · *Twelve Bags of Gold*

Here we are back with our economical king. Thanks to your class's work on the *Eight Bags of Gold* POW, he found the thief in a very economical manner. Now, since he has been so economical, he has even more gold.

The eight bags got too heavy to carry, so he had to switch to 12 bags. Of course, each of his 12 bags holds exactly the same amount of gold as each of the others, and they all weigh the same. Well, . . . maybe not.

Rumor has it that one of his 12 trusted caretakers is not so trustworthy. Someone, it is rumored, is making counterfeit gold. So the king sent his assistants to find the counterfeiter. They did find her, but she wouldn't tell them who had the counterfeit gold she had made, no matter how persuasive they were.

Continued on next page

All the assistants learned from her was that one of the 12 bags had counterfeit gold and that this bag's weight was different from the others. They could not find out from her whether the different bag was heavier or lighter.

So the king needed to know two things.

- Which bag weighed a different amount from the rest?

- Was that bag heavier or lighter?

And, of course, he wanted the answer found economically. He still had only the old balance scale. He wanted the solution in two weighings, as in the other problem, but his court mathematician said it would take three weighings. No one else could see how it could be done in so few weighings. Can you figure it out?

Find a way to determine which bag is counterfeit and whether it weighs more or less than the others. Try to do so using the balance scale as few times as possible. Keep in mind that what you do after the first weighing may depend on what happens in that weighing. For example, if the scale balances on the first weighing, you might choose bags for the second weighing different from the bags you would choose if the scale does not balance on the first weighing.

Note: The problem can be solved with only three weighings, without any tricks, but it is very hard to cover every case.

Write-up

1. *Problem statement*

2. *Process:* Based on your notes, describe what you did in attempting to solve this problem.

   - How did you get started?

   - What approaches did you try?

   - Where did you get stuck?

   - What drawings did you use?

3. *Solution:* Since this problem is much more difficult than *Eight Bags of Gold,* you shouldn't be too disappointed if you don't get a solution using just three weighings. Your task is to give the best solution that you found. Explain fully which cases your solution works for and which cases it doesn't work for.

4. *Evaluation*

Days 21–24

Graphs and Equations

You're closing in on the unit problem. Now you know *what* determines the period of a pendulum, but you still need to figure out the relationship between the period and the controlling variable.

Pretty soon you'll gather some more data and look for a formula. In preparation for that, you're going to do a graphing "free-for-all"—an open-ended investigation of equations and their graphs—so you'll have an idea what kind of formula to try.

The discoveries by Cody Boling, Ethan Fitzhenry, Lindsay Crawford, Catherine Bartz, Melyssa Brixner, and Nikki Robinson are fast and furious during "Graphing Free-for-All."

Bird Houses

Mia and her classmates in carpentry class had spent the semester constructing bird houses. Today Mia was in charge of painting. Her group had painted two of the bird houses after one hour of work, and six of them after three hours.

1. How many bird houses do you think they will have painted at the end of eight hours?

2. How can you generalize this answer?

Homework 21

So Little Data, So Many Rules

1. Consider an In-Out table with just one pair:

$$In = 2, Out = 5$$

a. Find three rules that fit this pair.

b. For each of the rules you find, find three pairs of numbers that fit that rule.

c. Graph each of the rules that you made up.

2. Now repeat the steps in Question 1 for an In-Out table that has just this pair:

$$In = 4, Out = 2$$

Graphing Free-for-All

In this activity you will use a graphing calculator to explore the graphs of a variety of functions and equations. The understanding of graphs and their equations that you gain in this activity will help you to find the period of the 30-foot pendulum.

Take careful notes on the graphs you examine. You will be learning about other functions during presentations by classmates on this activity, and you will need to take notes on their presentations also.

You will summarize your own conclusions, as well as information from other students' presentations, in *Homework 24: Graphing Summary.*

For each of the equations you look at, your notes should include four kinds of information.

- The equation

- A sketch of the graph

- The viewing window you used on the graphing calculator

- A partial In-Out table, found both by using the trace feature on the graphing calculator and by substituting into the equation

You may find it helpful to put each example on a separate sheet of paper.

Homework 22

Graphs in Search of Equations I

The coordinate system below shows three graphs, labeled a, b, and c.

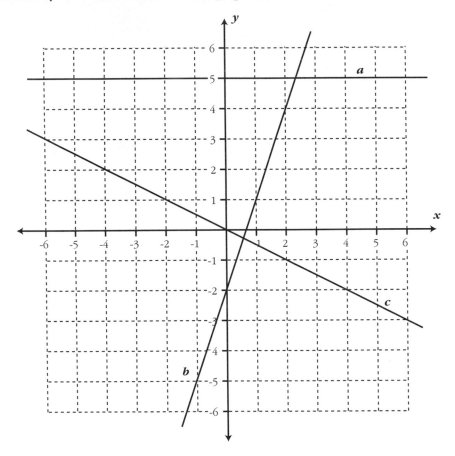

For each graph

- find four points that lie on that graph

- put the four points into an In-Out table

- write an equation for that table

- check that your equation seems to work for all of the points on the graph

Homework 23   Graphs in Search of Equations II

As with *Homework 22: Graphs in Search of Equations I,* the coordinate system below shows three graphs, labeled a, b, and c.

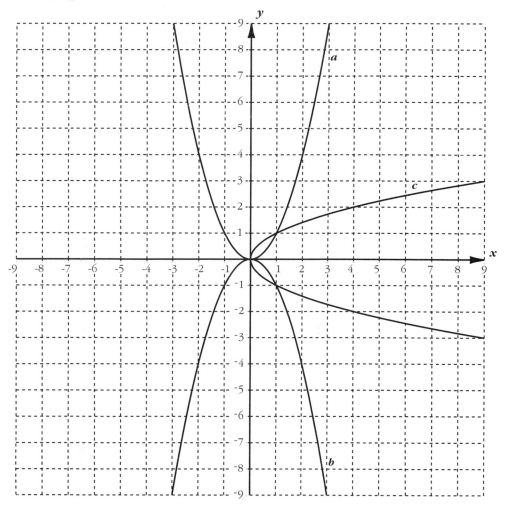

For each graph

- find four points that lie on that graph
- put the four points into an In-Out table
- write an equation for that table
- check that your equation seems to work for all of the points on the graph

Homework 24   Graphing Summary

Through your work on *Graphing Free-for-All*, you should now have a collection of information about different equations and their graphs.

Your task now is to organize and summarize this information.

Create a summary document that will help you in the future to find an equation that fits a particular graph or to sketch the graph for a particular equation.

**Days
25-28**

Measuring and Predicting

Almost there! You're about to gather some data about the periods for pendulums of different lengths. That sets the stage for the final task—analyzing the data and making a prediction for the 30-foot pendulum.

You might want to think about how you will test your prediction.

Principal Robert Embertson makes a special appearance as the bob for the final pendulum experiment.

The Period and the Length

Based on earlier work, you have determined that the period of a pendulum seems to be a function of its length.

Now you are going to gather some data about that function. Use the standard weight (one washer) and standard amplitude (20°), but vary the length.

For each length that you examine, find the time for *twelve* periods, since the prisoner in Poe's story thought there were about twelve swings remaining when he created his plan to escape.

Homework 25

Graphs in Search of Equations III

For each of the graphs *a* and *b* below

- find four points that lie on that graph
- put the four points into an In-Out table
- write an equation for that table
- check that your equation seems to work for all of the points on the graph

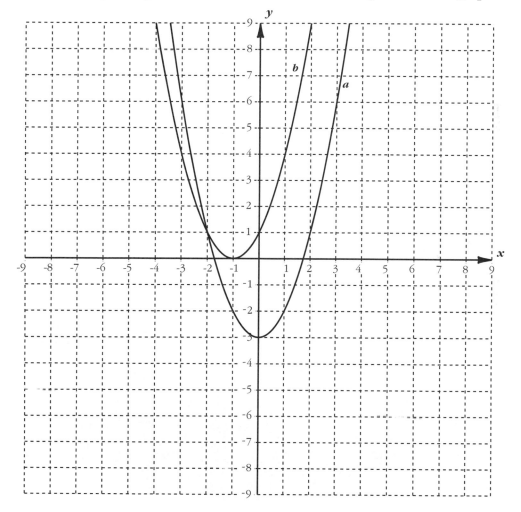

The Thirty-Foot Prediction

Now that you have the data on the time required for 12 swings for pendulums of several different lengths, your task is to make a prediction for a 30-foot pendulum.

Look for a function *f* that fits all of your data as well as possible. You probably won't find a function that fits the data perfectly, but do the best you can.

Once you are satisfied with your choice of function, find *f*(30). That is, find out what your function would predict as the time required for 12 swings of a 30-foot pendulum.

Homework 26

Mathematics and Science

Think about what you have learned in this unit, both in mathematics and in science.

Choose what you consider to be the two or three most important ideas or concepts.

Then, for each of those ideas or concepts

- write what you learned about that idea or concept

- write about a problem for which it might be useful to know that idea or concept

Homework 27 Beginning Portfolios

1. State the central problem for this unit in your own words. Then write a careful description of how you arrived at a solution for the problem. This description will serve as the cover letter for your portfolio for this unit.

2. In *Homework 26: Mathematics and Science,* you identified two or three key ideas or concepts from this unit.

   a. Describe the role that those ideas played in solving the unit problem.

   b. Select a class activity or homework that helped you to understand each of those ideas. Describe what you learned in those assignments.

"The Pit and the Pendulum" Portfolio

Now that *The Pit and the Pendulum* is completed, it is time to put together your portfolio for the unit.

Cover Letter for "The Pit and the Pendulum"

Your work on Question 1 of *Homework 27: Beginning Portfolio Work* will serve as your cover letter for this unit.

Selecting Papers from "The Pit and the Pendulum"

Your portfolio for *The Pit and the Pendulum* should contain these items.

- Activities selected in *Homework 27: Beginning Portfolios*

  Include your written work for Question 2 of this assignment as well as the activities from the unit that you selected.

- *Homework 26: Mathematics and Science*

- *Homework 24: Graphing Summary*

- A Problem of the Week

  Select one of the four POWs you completed during this unit (*The Big Knight Switch, Corey Camel, Eight Bags of Gold,* and *Twelve Bags of Gold*).

- Other quality work

  Select one or two other pieces of work that represent your best efforts. (These can be any work from the unit—Problem of the Week, homework, classwork, presentation, and so on.)

Continued on next page

Other Thoughts

In addition to the papers selected above, discuss these issues.

- How you liked doing science experiments in a mathematics class

- What ideas you learned about in the unit but would like to understand better

- How you felt about grading yourself and others on group work

- Any other thoughts you might like to share with a reader of your portfolio

Appendix

Supplemental Problems

Many of the activities in *The Pit and the Pendulum* involve experiments and data-gathering. In analyzing data from these experiments, you use the concepts of normal distribution and standard deviation. Another important theme of the unit is the study of functions and their graphs. Experiments, data analysis, and functions are some of the themes in the supplemental problems as well. These are some examples.

• In *Height and Weight* you are asked to plan and carry out an exploration of the relationship between two variables.

• *Making Better Friends* and *Mean Standard Dice* strengthen your understanding of mean and standard deviation.

• In *Family of Curves,* you look at how changes in a function lead to changes in its graph.

Poe and "The Pit and the Pendulum"

Learn more about Edgar Allan Poe, the author of the short story "The Pit and the Pendulum."

What was his life like? What else did he write?

Also, read the entire story, to discover how the prisoner came to find himself strapped to the table, and what happened to him after he freed himself from the danger of the descending pendulum. (You may recall that the excerpt closes with the words "For that moment, at least, *I was free*.")

Report on what you learned about Poe and the story.

Getting in Synch

Al and Betty are taking a break from their probability games, and have gone to the circus to ride on the Ferris wheels.

There are actually several different Ferris wheels at the circus. Al chose one of them, and Betty chose another.

Al and Betty each get on at the bottom of the Ferris wheels' cycles, and the two Ferris

wheels start at the same time. The period of Al's Ferris wheel is 40 seconds; that is, it takes 40 seconds for it to make a complete turn. Betty's Ferris wheel has a period of 30 seconds.

1. How long will it be until the next time they are at the bottom together again?

2. Now redo Question 1 using each of the following combinations of periods for the two Ferris wheels.

    a. Al's, 40 seconds; Betty's, 25 seconds

    b. Al's, 31 seconds; Betty's, 25 seconds

    c. Al's, 23 seconds; Betty's, 18.4 seconds

3. Is it possible to find periods for the two Ferris wheels for which Al and Betty will never be at the bottom at the same time again?

4. What generalizations can you come up with?

Octane Variation

Elizabeth and her dad decided to find out if the number of miles per gallon their car got was affected by the type of gasoline they used. They decided to try three different grades of gasoline and measure the car's mileage for each.

When they began the experiment, the tank was filled with 87-octane gasoline. Elizabeth's dad drove until the tank was nearly empty. When he filled up the tank, he wrote down the octane of the gasoline he'd just been using, the number of gallons he'd used since the last fill-up, and the number of miles he had driven since the last fill-up.

He then went through the same procedure for each of the other two types of gasoline. Here is the information he presented to Elizabeth.

Octane used	Number of gallons used	Number of miles traveled
87	9.5	304
89	8.6	292
92	9.2	322

1. Given this information, do you think that the higher-octane gasoline yields better mileage? Explain your reasoning.

2. Elizabeth's brother Zeke thought there might be some other explanations for the variation in miles per gallon besides the octane of the gasoline. List all the other possibilities you can think of.

3. In what ways could Elizabeth and her dad have carried out a better experiment?

Height and Weight

In class, you are seeing that the period of a pendulum may be affected when different variables, such as length and weight, are changed.

In this activity, you will deal with variables in a different context. Specifically, you are to choose some setting in which to examine the relationship between *weight* and *height*. You are to design and carry out a plan for exploring how weight might depend on height in that context.

1. State the context of your exploration. (For instance, you may want to study how the weight of an animal depends on its height.)

2. Describe a plan for this exploration. For example:

   a. How will you gather information?

   b. What other variables will you take into account?

   c. What methods will you use to analyze your data?

3. Carry out your plan. That is, gather and study your data and come to some conclusions.

4. Describe your conclusions, evaluate the strengths and weaknesses of your plan, and discuss the difficulties involved in developing a connection between height and weight.

More Knights Switching

If you liked *POW 12: The Big Knight Switch,* here is a similar problem that is a bit more challenging.

This time there are three white and three black knights instead of two and two, and they are sitting on a board with four rows and three columns, as in the diagrams at the right.

The knights start in the positions shown in the top diagram. The goal is for the three black knights to change places with the three white knights, so that they end up as shown in the bottom diagram.

The knights are allowed to make only the same types of moves that they could make in the POW.

The big questions again are these.

1. Can they do it?

2. If so, what is the least number of moves it will take them to switch, and how do you know your answer is the least?

3. If it is not possible, explain why you are sure it is not.

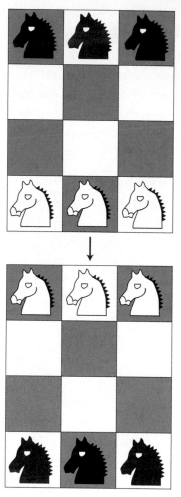

Adapted from *aha! Insight,* by Martin Gardner, Scientific American, Inc./ W. H. Freeman and Company, San Francisco, © 1978.

A Knight Goes Traveling

End here
↓

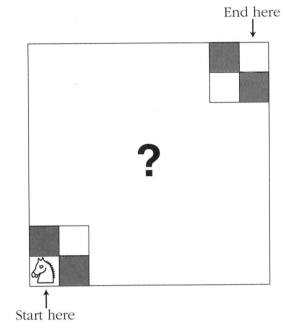

?

Start here
↑

If you like playing around with knight moves, here's one more problem for you.

In *POW 12: The Big Knight Switch*, you worked with four knights on a 3-by-3 chessboard, and in *More Knights Switching,* you worked with six knights on a 4-by-3 chessboard.

Now look at a single knight, and imagine placing that knight in one corner of a square chessboard of some unknown size, as shown at the left.

Here is the question for this problem.

> *How many moves will it take for the knight to get to the diagonally opposite corner?*

Of course, the answer depends on the size of the chessboard, and it may even be impossible for some cases.

Begin with a 2-by-2 board, then look at a 3-by-3 board, and gradually work your way up. Keep track of what the fewest possible moves is in each case, and look for patterns.

Data for Dinky and Minky

In *Homework 12: The Best Spread*, you were asked to make up two data sets, set X and set Y, that together fit these two conditions.

• Set X was to have a larger standard deviation than set Y.

• Set Y was to have a larger range than set X.

In other words, based on standard deviation, set X was to be more spread out, but based on Rinky's method, set Y was to be more spread out.

In this activity, you are to find two other pairs of data sets. In each case, deciding which set is more spread out will depend on the method used for measuring data spread.

1. Make up a pair of data sets, R and S, so that both of these statements are true.

   • Based on standard deviation, set R is more spread out than set S.

   • Based on Dinky's method, set S is more spread out than set R.

   Reminder: Dinky measures the spread of a set of data by finding the distance from each number to the mean and then adding those distances.

2. Make up another pair of data sets, U and V, so that both of these statements are true.

   • Based on standard deviation, set U is more spread out than set V.

   • Based on Minky's method, set V is more spread out than set U.

   Reminder: Minky measures the spread of a set of data by ignoring the highest and lowest data items, and then finding the largest distance from any remaining data item to the mean.

Making Better Friends

In *Making Friends with Standard Deviation*, you explored what happened to the mean and the standard deviation of a set of data when you added the same number to each member of the set or multiplied each member of the set by the same number.

In this activity you are asked to explore some other questions about mean and standard deviation. Here are some ideas to start you off.

1. How can you add new data items to a set so that you don't change the mean or the standard deviation?

2. How can you add new data items to a set so that you can keep the mean the same but make the standard deviation as large as you like?

Don't restrict yourself to these two questions. Make up some questions of your own and explore them. Report on everything you have discovered.

Mean Standard Dice

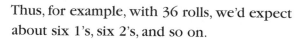

You know that, in the long run, a normal die will come up 1 one-sixth of the time, 2 one-sixth of the time, and so on.

Thus, for example, with 36 rolls, we'd expect about six 1's, six 2's, and so on.

1. Find the mean and standard deviation for the data represented by this "ideal result" for 36 rolls (six 1's, six 2's, and so on), and explain the computations you used.

2. Suppose the die were rolled 360 times, with the "ideal result" of 60 1's, 60 2's, and so on.

   a. Write down a guess about what the mean and the standard deviation would be for this set of data, and explain your guess.

   b. Actually find the mean and the standard deviation for this situation, and explain the computations you used.

   c. Are the actual mean and the actual standard deviation the same as in Question 1? Explain why you think they came out the same or different.

3. Now suppose you used a pair of fair dice, rolling them together and each time finding the sum of the numbers on the two dice.

   a. What would be the "ideal result" for these sums if the pair of dice were rolled 36 times? (That is, how many 12's would you get, how many 11's, and so on, as the sum of the pair of dice?)

   b. Write down a guess about what the mean and the standard deviation would be for this "ideal result" of 36 sums for a pair of dice, and explain your guess.

   c. Find the actual mean for this "ideal result." How does it compare to your mean in Question 1?

   d. Find the actual standard deviation for this "ideal result." How does it compare to your standard deviation in Question 1?

Are You Ambidextrous?

In this activity, you will compare the reflexes of your two hands. Here's how.

Have a partner hold a ruler vertically between your thumb and forefinger, so that the lower end of the ruler is level with your fingers. Spread your thumb and forefinger as wide apart as possible. Your partner should hold the ruler from its upper end.

Your partner will say "Drop" at the moment he or she drops the ruler. As the ruler falls past your fingers, you try to pinch it as quickly as you can.

1. Do the experiment with one of your hands 20 times, each time recording the place where you grab it.

2. Find the mean and the standard deviation of your data.

3. Draw a normal curve, with a horizontal scale, that has the same mean and standard deviation as your data. Show where the standard deviation marks are located.

4. Now do the ruler experiment one time with your other hand.

5. How many standard deviations from the mean was the experiment result from your "other" hand? What percent of the time do you think you would get a result that far from the mean using your "first" hand? Explain.

6. Do you think you are ambidextrous? Why or why not? (If you don't know what the word *ambidextrous* means, ask someone or look it up in a dictionary.)

Family of Curves

You've seen that functions based on similar algebraic expressions often have similar graphs. For example, certain equations have graphs that are straight lines.

In this activity, your goal is to explore such **families of curves**.

Start with a simple function, such as $y = x^2$, and examine carefully how its graph changes as you make various changes in the equation itself.

Make a poster showing your results.

More Height and Weight

In the supplemental activity *Height and Weight*, you did a preliminary investigation of the relationship between the height and weight of objects.

In this problem, you will follow up with a more detailed investigation that looks specifically at the relationship between height and weight for people.

1. Find out the heights and weights for various people. Try to use individuals with a wide range of different heights, from small children to adults.

2. Make an In-Out table of your data, using height as the *In* and weight as the *Out.* Then make a graph of your data.

3. Try to find a formula that comes close to fitting your data.

4. Use what you've learned to estimate how much a 10-foot-tall person might weigh. Explain your reasoning.

Shadows

Days 1-5

What is a Shadow?

This unit asks the question, "How long is a shadow?" But before you can answer this question, you need to think about some others, such as, "What is a shadow?" "Where do

shadows come from?" and "Are there different kinds of shadows?"

If you see some resemblance to *The Pit and the Pendulum* in the early days of this unit, don't be surprised. But *Shadows* has its own set of mathematical ideas for you to learn, and the two units are really quite different.

Cody Boling, Ethan Fitzhenry, and Nikki Robinson measure the length of the shadow in the "Shadow Data Gathering" experiment.

Shadows

A Riddle

As you walk around, I stay with you.

I'm sometimes ahead of you and sometimes behind you.

If you were smaller, I would be too.

If you come toward me, I often get bigger (especially at night).

If you shine a light on me, I disappear.

What am I?

Since the title of this unit is *Shadows,* you probably were able to guess the answer to this simple riddle.

Continued on next page

The Real Riddle

But there are some riddles about shadows that are not so clear. The big riddle for the unit is this:

> *How long is a shadow?*

It's easy to answer by saying, "It depends," but what does it depend on? You might consider these comparisons with previous work:

- In *The Pit and the Pendulum,* you saw that the period of a swinging pendulum is primarily determined by the pendulum's length. What variable or variables determine the length of a shadow?

- In *The Pit and the Pendulum,* you developed a formula based on experiments that estimated the period as a function of the pendulum's length. What kind of formula can you develop for the length of a shadow? And how should it be developed? Is there a better way than experimentation?

Your central task in this unit is to develop answers to these and similar questions.

POW 16   *Spiralaterals*

This POW is about spiralaterals. A spiralateral is a sequence of line segments that forms a spiral-like shape. It is easiest to draw spiralaterals if you use grid paper.

Each spiralateral is based on a sequence of numbers. To give an example, let's suppose your sequence is 3, 2, 4. To draw the spiralateral, you need to choose a starting point. The starting direction is always "up" on the paper.

The first number is 3, so the spiralateral begins with a segment that goes up 3 spaces, as in diagram A.

Before each new number, the spiralateral turns clockwise 90° (that is, a quarter turn to the right). So the second segment of the spiralateral will go to the right. The second number is 2, so the spiralateral moves 2 spaces in that direction. This gives diagram B.

Next, the spiralateral again turns clockwise 90° (so it's now facing "down"), and this time goes 4 spaces (because the third number in the sequence is 4), giving diagram C.

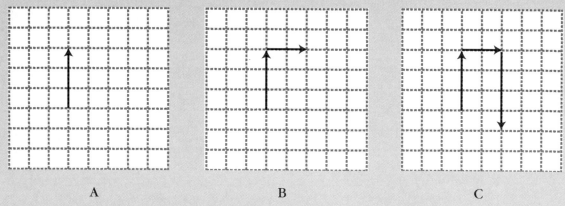

| A | B | C |

You've now gotten to the end of the original three-number sequence.

But this is where it gets interesting. Instead of stopping, you go back to the beginning of the sequence and continue where you left off.

That is, make another 90° clockwise turn (so you're now going to the left), and move 3 spaces. And then another 90° turn and 2 up, a 90° turn and 4 right, a 90° turn and 3 down, and so on. Continue until you get back to the place where you started (if you ever do!). In other words, it's as if your sequence, instead of just being 3, 2, 4, was 3, 2, 4, 3, 2, 4, 3, 2, 4, 3, 2, 4, . . . , and so on, as long as necessary.

Continued on next page

In our example, the diagram will look like this after ten steps:

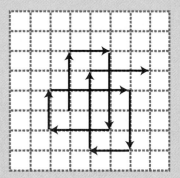

As you can see, in two more steps, you'll be back to the start. So the complete spiralateral for this sequence looks like this:

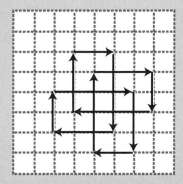

Your assignment for this POW is to explore the idea of spiralaterals. Here are some things you can do as part of your exploration.

- Make some spiralaterals, using your own sequences of numbers.

- Look for patterns.

- Make up questions about spiralaterals.

- Try sequences of different lengths.

- Make up new rules.

Whenever you come to a conclusion about spiralaterals, try to explain why your conclusion is true.

Reminder: Save your notes as you work on the problem. You will need them to do your write-up.

Continued on next pc

Write-up

1. *Problem statement:* Explain what a spiralateral is and how it is formed.

2. *Process*

3. *Results and conclusions:*

   a. Show the results of some of the specific examples that you investigated, including diagrams as appropriate.

   b. What patterns did you notice among your results in part a? Summarize what you concluded from your examples, stating your conclusions clearly.

   c. Justify your conclusions as fully as you can. In other words, for any patterns that you found in your examples, explain why you believe that those patterns hold in general.

   d. What questions occurred to you as you worked on this problem that you did not discuss yet?

4. *Evaluation*

Homework 1

Shadows and Spiralaterals

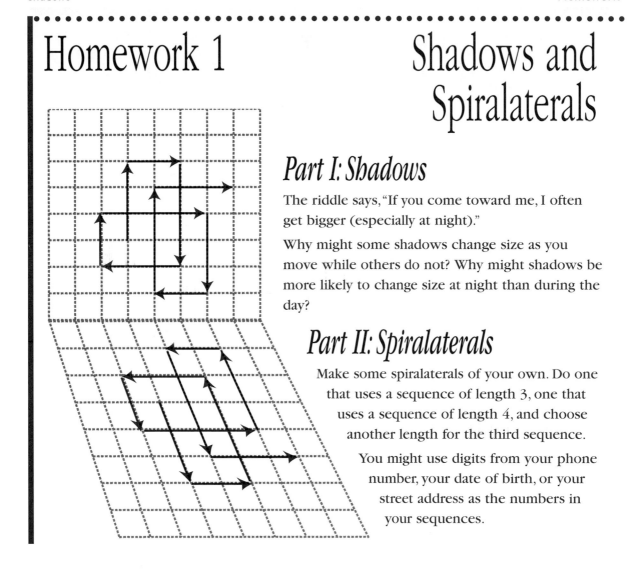

Part I: Shadows

The riddle says, "If you come toward me, I often get bigger (especially at night)."

Why might some shadows change size as you move while others do not? Why might shadows be more likely to change size at night than during the day?

Part II: Spiralaterals

Make some spiralaterals of your own. Do one that uses a sequence of length 3, one that uses a sequence of length 4, and choose another length for the third sequence.

You might use digits from your phone number, your date of birth, or your street address as the numbers in your sequences.

How Long Is a Shadow?

When you stand between a source of light and another object, your body blocks part of the light and casts a shadow on that other object.

For example, if you stand near a street lamp, as illustrated in the diagram above, your body casts a shadow on the ground.

The length of this shadow may depend on various **parameters** or **variables**, that is, on characteristics of the situation that can change from one example to another.

The central problem of the unit is to find out what variables the shadow length depends on and how the shadow length is determined by the values of those variables.

Part I: Defining Variables

Think of as many variables as possible that could affect the length of a shadow. (You may already have some ideas about this.)

Make a *written list* of these variables. Be very specific in describing your variables. For example, if you think a certain distance might be important, state exactly what that distance measures—*from* where *to* where.

When you have compiled a list, you can begin thinking about Part II.

Continued on next page

Part II: Preparation for "Homework 2: Experimenting with Shadows"

As a group, choose *one* of the variables that can be measured and write a careful plan for a set of experiments concerning this variable. The purpose of the experiments is to explore whether your variable really affects the length of a shadow and, if so, how changing the value of the variable affects shadow length.

Each person should make a copy of the plan your group creates. You will use this plan in doing the homework and will need to attach it to your write-up of the homework assignment.

Here are some ideas to keep in mind as the group puts the plan together.

- You should change only the variable that you are working with, keeping everything else constant. Your plan should state which variables you are keeping constant as well as the one you are changing.

- Think about the materials you might use in your experiment. For example, what will be your light source? What kind of object will cast the shadow? Include that information in your plan.

- Think about how you will change the value of the variable you are studying. You should try at least three different numerical values for this variable.

Homework 2   Experimenting with Shadows

In *How Long Is a Shadow?* your group planned an experiment to investigate how a particular variable might affect the length of a shadow. Your homework assignment is to carry out this experiment.

1. As closely as you can, carry out that plan, recording the results. (You may need to change the plan once you actually try to carry it out.)

2. Describe the results of your experiment, giving all the numerical data you collected. Include a diagram of your experiment. Make note of the specific values you used for the fixed variables.

3. Write about what you learned concerning the effect the variable you studied had on the length of shadows. State your conclusions clearly. Use the data you collected as evidence for your conclusions.

Attach to this homework your copy of the plan set up by your group.

Homework 3   Poetical Science

Augusta Ada Byron (1815–1852) was the daughter of the famous English poet George Gordon Byron (usually known by his title as Lord Byron) and a mathematician, Anne Isabella Milbanke Byron. Augusta Ada Byron is known today as Ada Lovelace, having married Lord Lovelace.

At the time she lived, people thought there was a sharp separation between the kinds of skills needed for the sciences and the type of ability involved in creative arts like poetry.

This conflict between science and poetry was an 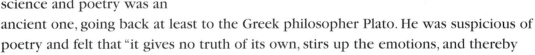 ancient one, going back at least to the Greek philosopher Plato. He was suspicious of poetry and felt that "it gives no truth of its own, stirs up the emotions, and thereby blinds mankind to the real truth."

Ada Lovelace was unusual for her time, perhaps because of her parents' combination of interests. Her formal education was traditional in its emphasis on "the facts," but her father's imaginative influence kept appearing. Her teacher thought that studying mathematics would "cure" Ada of being too imaginative, but Ada responded that she had to use her imagination in order to understand mathematics.

Lovelace was herself a mathematics teacher and encouraged her students to use their imagination. She emphasized metaphors and visual images, and suggested that they use colored pens, rulers, and compasses (which were then considered "vulgar instruments") to make drawings that would help their understanding.

Continued on next page

She wrote, "Imagination is the *Discovering* Faculty preeminently. It is that which penetrates into the unseen worlds around us, the worlds of Science. It is that which feels & discovers what *is*, the REAL which we see not, which *exists* not for our *senses*."

At the age of 18, she met Charles Babbage, who was then in the process of inventing what became the world's first computer. Working with him was the realization of a dream, because it allowed her to combine her imagination with her analytical skills. She was able to work on mathematics as a joy, not as the duty it had been when her mother made her study it.

Lovelace played an important role in the development of computer science by explaining Babbage's inventions to a larger audience. In her written *Notes*, she created a unified vision of their usefulness, combining metaphors about the creative power of the machines with detailed technical descriptions of their operation.

In honor of these contributions, a modern computer language has been named after her. The language Ada is one of the most sophisticated tools for studying artificial intelligence and is used by the military.

This article is adapted from the preface "Poetical Science" in the book *Ada, The Enchantress of Numbers* by Betty Alexandra Toole, Strawberry Press, Mill Valley, CA. The book contains Ada's letters and her description of the first computer.

Your Assignment

1. The article talks about the use of imagination in understanding mathematics. Think about two situations this year when your imagination helped you *in this class*. Write about those experiences.

2. Do you agree or disagree with what Plato said about poetry? Write what you think about poetry and truth.

Shadow Data Gathering

In *The Pit and the Pendulum*, you used experiments to find a relationship between the length of the pendulum and the pendulum's period.

The general approach in that unit was to gather data and then look for a function that fit the data.

In this activity and in *Looking for Equations*, you will be using the same approach for the shadow problem.

Continued on next page

You have seen that the length of a shadow seems to depend on three parameters or variables:

- The height of the light source (L)
- The distance from the object to the light source (D)
- The height of the object (H)

Using S for the length of the shadow, the central problem of the unit might be stated in this way:

> *What formula can be used to express S as a function of the variables L, D, and H? That is, how can you get a formula for a function f so that S = f(L, D, H)?*

Your Task

Your task in this assignment is to focus on just *one* of these three variables, keeping the other two fixed. For example, if your chosen variable is H, then you would pick specific values for L and D, and gather data about how S changes as you change H.

Your data should be organized into an In-Out table in which the input is your chosen variable and the output is the length of the shadow.

Your group will need to prepare a report on its work. The report should include your In-Out table, in a form appropriate for display.

The report should also include

- identification of your chosen variable
- a diagram of your experiment, which includes the *fixed values* used in your experiments for the other variables

For example, if *height of the light source* is your chosen variable, then you should keep the height of the object and the distance from the object to the light source fixed throughout the experiments. The values used for these other variables should be stated in your report and shown on your diagram.

Homework 4 An *N*-by-*N* Window

The central problem of this unit is to find a formula relating shadow length to certain other variables, either based on experiments or using some other method.

This problem also involves finding a formula, although the setting is completely different.

The diagram to the right shows the frame for a window 3 feet by 3 feet.

The frame is made of wood strips that separate the glass panes. Each glass pane is a square that is 1 foot wide and 1 foot tall.

As the numbering in the diagram shows, it would take 24 feet of wood strip to build a frame for a window 3 feet by 3 feet.

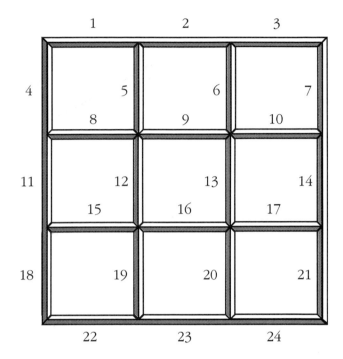

Your task is to develop a formula for the total length of wood strip needed to build square windows of different sizes.

You may want to do this by gathering data and making an In-Out table from different examples. Or you may prefer to study the window looking for insights that lead directly to a formula. (Or you may do a combination of both.)

In either case, generalize the problem to a window *N* feet by *N* feet. As usual, include all drawings, In-Out tables, and graphs.

Looking for Equations

You now have an In-Out table that shows data relating one of the shadow variables, *L, D,* or *H,* to the shadow length, *S.* Other groups have made similar tables.

Your next task is to analyze these In-Out tables, looking for equations connecting the *Out* values to the *In* values.

Start with your own In-Out table.

You might choose to look at the table directly, examining the pairs of numbers and looking for patterns. You can organize the entries in any way that makes sense to you. If you think it would be helpful to have additional pairs for your table, do the necessary experiments to find the appropriate information.

You might also try graphing your data, either by using pencil and paper or by entering the data in a graphing calculator. If you make a graph, choose scales for the axes that seem suitable to your data. Examine whether the points on your graph form a familiar shape.

When you find an equation that describes your data well, or if you decide that you are unable to find a reasonable rule to fit the data, you should move on to another group's set of data.

Homework 5   More About Windows

In *Homework 4: An N-by-N Window,* you investigated the length of wood strip needed for window frames like the one at the right.

In that assignment, your goal was to find a general formula for the amount of wood strip needed for a square window frame of any size.

Now, try to generalize to an arbitrary rectangular window frame. That is, get a formula in terms of *M* and *N* for the amount of wood strip needed for the frame of an *M*-by-*N* window.

As in *Homework 4: An N-by-N Window,* you may want to gather data about a variety of examples into an In-Out table and then look for a pattern in your data. If so, once you gather data, look for an algebraic rule that describes your table.

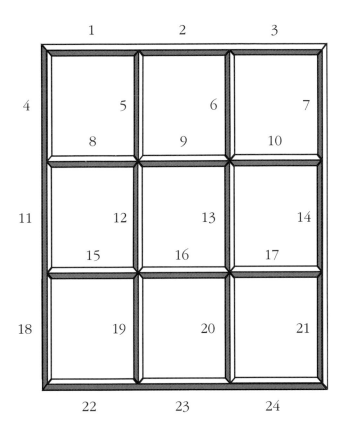

Or you may prefer a more analytic approach, in which you reason through why such a window frame should use a particular amount of wood strip. If you find a rule this way, verify it using some examples.

Days 6-9

The Geometry of Shadows

You've done some measurements involving shadows, and now it's time to try a different approach.

For a while, you're going to leave the world of shadows and enter the more abstract realm of geometry. Angles, polygons, lengths of sides—these will be the focus of your attention for much of the unit, but eventually these ideas will fit together to answer the shadowy questions that are lurking in the background.

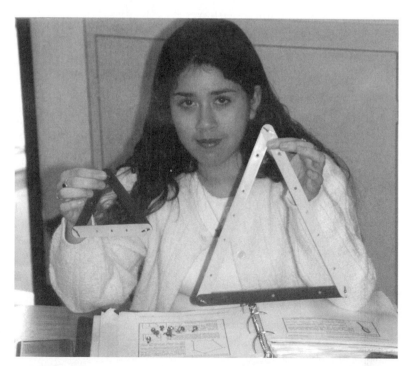

Jackie Hernandez shows the class possible counterexamples.

Homework 6   Draw the Same Shape

1. Draw a small, simple picture on a sheet of grid paper.

   Then draw another version of your picture that is *exactly the same shape* as the first one. Your second drawing should be *larger* than the original. (You have to decide what "exactly the same shape" means to you.)

2. Renata was making illustrations for a book on basic drawing technique. She came up with the figure below as the first step for drawing a house.

   Kim decided he liked this shape, but needed a bigger version of the house for his work.

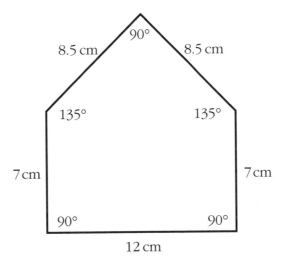

   a. Give a set of length and angle measurements that you think Kim might be able to use in place of those shown in the diagram above.

   b. Carefully draw a diagram that has your suggested measurements and compare it to Renata's. Does it have the same shape?

Continued on next page

3. Consider the following pairs of figures. In each case, state whether you consider them to be the same shape or not, and why.

a.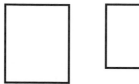

b.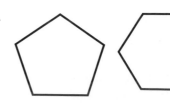

c.

d.

4. Based on your experience with Questions 1 through 3, write your ideas in response to this question:

How can you create a diagram that has exactly the same shape as a given one?

How to Shrink It?

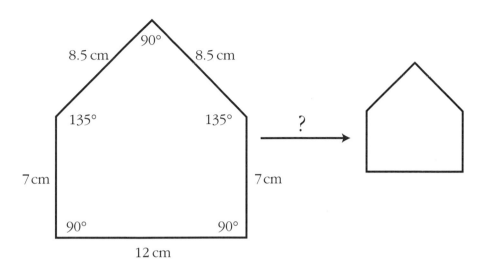

Lola, Lily, and Lulu love Renata's house, but find it a little too large for their liking.

In other words, they want to shrink the house down to a smaller size while keeping it exactly the same shape.

After a long discussion, each came up with a strategy for drawing the smaller house.

Lola's Way: Keep all the angles as they are and subtract five centimeters from the length of each side.

Lily's Way: Keep all the lengths as they are and divide all the angles by two.

Lulu's Way: Keep all the angles as they are and divide the lengths of all the sides by two.

Try to shrink the house by using each of the methods above. Show what result each method produces. Explain why the method does or does not work.

Homework 7

The Statue of Liberty's Nose

Consider this problem:

> The Statue of Liberty in New York City has a nose that is 4 feet 6 inches long.* What is the approximate length of one of her arms?

1. Solve the problem. (*Hint:* Think about your own nose and arms.)

2. Pick two other body parts and find the approximate length that these parts should be on the Statue of Liberty.

3. Examine what you did with the three examples from Questions 1 and 2. How was your work the same in the three cases? How did it change from case to case?

4. State how this problem is similar to the problem of drawing a house that has the same shape as another house (Question 2 from *Homework 6: Draw the Same Shape*).

5. What connection do you see between this problem and the shadow problem?

*Measurement taken from *How They Built the Statue of Liberty* by Mary Shapiro (Random House, 1985).

Homework 8   Make It Similar

You have seen that two polygons are called **similar** if their corresponding angles are equal and their corresponding sides are proportional.

The phrase "corresponding sides are proportional" means that if you compare each side of the first polygon to the corresponding side in the second polygon, the ratios of those lengths are all the same.

Here's a problem where you need to think carefully about which sides are corresponding.

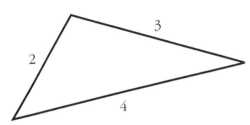

First, suppose you have one triangle whose sides have lengths of 2 inches, 3 inches, and 4 inches, as shown at the right.

Next, suppose there is a second triangle that is known to be similar to the first one.

And suppose you know that one of the sides of this larger triangle is 6 inches long.

Unfortunately, you don't know which side of the large triangle has this length.

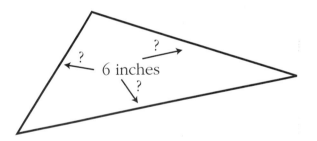

What can you say about the lengths of the other sides of the larger triangle? Try to find all the possibilities. (There's more than one answer. Don't assume that the triangles shown are drawn to scale.)

POW 17   Cutting the Pie

You can sometimes organize information from experiments into In-Out tables to help you understand what's happening in the experiment.

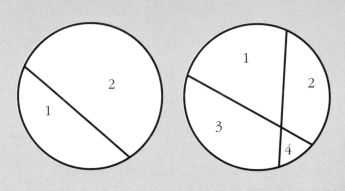

The diagrams to the left show the results of a pie-cutting experiment. In the first picture, one cut across the pie has created two pieces. In the next diagram, two cuts have created a total of four pieces.

Notice that the cuts do not necessarily go through the center of the pie, but they do have to be straight and go all the way across the pie. Also, the pieces do not have to be the same size or shape.

The two diagrams below show different possible results from making three cuts in the pie.

In the first case, the three cuts produced six pieces, while in the second case, the three cuts produced seven pieces. (It's also possible to produce five or even only four pieces from three cuts.)

You should be able to convince yourself that seven is the largest number of pieces that can be created by three cuts across the pie.

The purpose of the pie-cutting experiment is to find out:

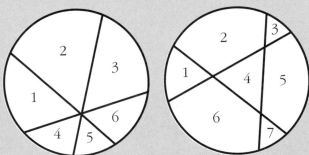

What is the largest number of pieces that can be produced from a given number of cuts?

Continued on next page

The information from the diagrams on the previous page has been organized into the In-Out table below. Your task is to extend and analyze this table.

1. Find the largest number of pieces you can get from four cuts and from five cuts. Include those numbers in your table.

Number of cuts	Maximum number of pieces
1	2
2	4
3	7
4	?
5	?

2. a. Try to find a pattern describing what is happening in the table.

   b. Use your pattern to find the largest possible number of pieces from ten cuts.

   c. Try to explain *why* this pattern is occurring.

3. Try to find a rule for the In-Out table. That is, if you used a variable for the input, how could you write the output as a formula in terms of that variable?

Write-up

1. *Problem statement*

2. *Process:* Include important diagrams you used while working on this problem.

3. *Solution:* This should include

   • your In-Out table (as far as you took it)

   • any patterns you found in the table, expressed either in words or in symbols (or both)

   • your answer for the largest possible number of pieces from ten cuts

   • explanations for your answers

4. *Evaluation*

Is There a Counterexample?

Try to find counterexamples for each of the statements below by creating appropriate pairs of polygons.

If you think you have found a counterexample, explain why your pair of polygons disproves the given statement.

If you think that there is no counterexample for a given statement, explain why you think so.

Reminder: Not every polygon is a triangle, so be sure to consider figures with more than three sides.

Statement 1

If two polygons have their corresponding angles equal, then the polygons are similar.

Statement 2

If two polygons have their corresponding sides proportional, then the polygons are similar.

Statement 3

Every triangle with two equal sides also has two equal angles.

Homework 9

Triangular Counterexamples

Attempt to draw counterexamples to each of the following statements. Be sure to show all your work, including any appropriate diagrams.

If you don't think a counterexample exists, then explain why you think there isn't one.

Statement 1

If two triangles have their corresponding angles equal, then the triangles are similar.

Statement 2

If two triangles are both isosceles, then the triangles are similar.

(*Reminder:* An isosceles triangle is a triangle with at least two sides of equal length.)

Statement 3

If two triangles have their corresponding sides proportional, then the triangles are similar.

Days 10–16

Triangles Galore

The unit now moves from polygons in general to triangles in particular, but algebra starts playing an important role as

well. You will be investigating the special case of triangles in more detail, using angles, parallel lines, and ratios.

While you investigate these ideas, you might keep thinking about the unit problem that's waiting for you in the shadows, and ask yourself what triangles and equations have to do with it.

Tamika Greene demonstrates how she might make a specific triangle using straws.

Why Are Triangles Special?

You have seen that triangles seem to be different from other polygons with regard to similarity.

In this activity, you will investigate why triangles are special.

1. Pick four lengths and form a quadrilateral using those lengths for the sides of a quadrilateral.

   Then try to use the same four lengths to form a quadrilateral that is not similar to the first. Can you?

2. Repeat Question 1 starting with more than four lengths. That is, pick some lengths and form a polygon using those lengths; then, using the same lengths, try to form a polygon that is not similar to the first.

3. Start with three lengths and use them to form a triangle. As in Questions 1 and 2, try to use the same lengths to form a triangle that is not similar to the first. Can you?

Homework 10   Similar Problems

In each of the four pairs of figures below, assume that the second polygon is similar to the first. In each case, do these steps:

- Set up equations to find the lengths of any sides labeled by variables.

- Find the length that solves each equation.

- Explain how you found the solutions to the equations.

Note: Measuring the diagrams will probably not give correct answers, because the diagrams may not be drawn exactly to scale.

1.

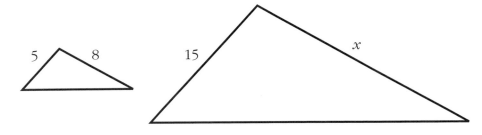

2.

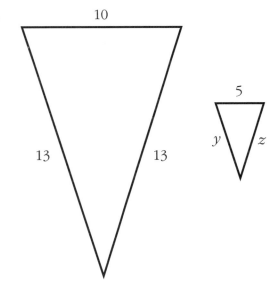

Continued on next page

3.

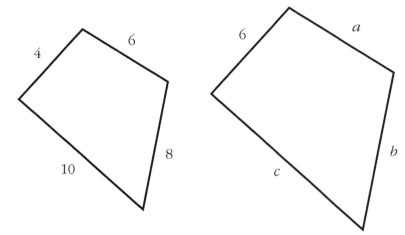

4.

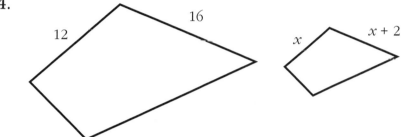

(*Note*: The side labeled *x* + 2 must be 2 units longer than the side labeled *x*.)

Are Angles Enough?

You've seen that the lengths of the sides of a triangle *determine* the triangle. Another way to say this is

If the lengths of the three sides of one triangle are the same as the lengths of the three sides of a second triangle, then the two triangles are congruent.

What about angles? Do the *angles* of a triangle determine the triangle? In other words, what happens if two triangles have the same three angles as each other?

1. Start with angles of 40°, 60°, and 80°. Each group member should try to draw a triangle using these three angles.

   Did the triangles all come out congruent? Were they all similar? Why or why not?

Continued on next page

2. Next, do the same thing starting with a different set of angles. You might just draw some arbitrary triangle and then have each group member use the same angles as that triangle.

   Did the triangles all come out congruent? Were they all similar? Why or why not?

3. Now go back to the angles of 40°, 60°, and 80°. This time, decide as a group on the length each group member will use for the side connecting the angles of 40° and 60°. As before, have each group member try to draw a triangle using angles 40°, 60°, and 80°, but also using the given length in the given position.

   Did the triangles all come out congruent? Were they all similar? Why or why not?

4. What do these experiments suggest concerning Statement 1 of *Homework 9: Triangular Counterexamples*? Explain.

Homework 11   From Top to Bottom

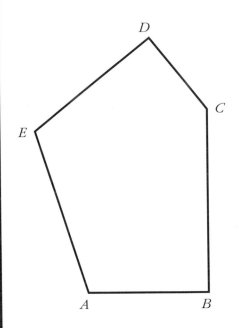

A scale drawing of a figure or object is a drawing that is *similar* to the original. In this assignment, you are to make two scale drawings of the pentagon *ABCDE,* which is shown at the left.

In each of your drawings, you are to keep the pentagon facing the same way it is shown at the left.

Make your two drawings on an $8\frac{1}{2}$-inch by 11-inch sheet of paper (standard binder paper), with one drawing on each side of the sheet.

Use a ruler and protractor to measure the sides and the angles carefully, in order to make your drawings as accurate as you can.

1. First make a scale drawing of the pentagon so that the bottom of it is one inch from the bottom of the sheet and the top of it is one inch from the top of the paper. Your drawing should be positioned roughly like the diagram at the right.

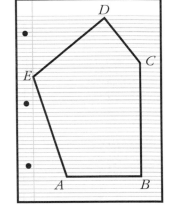

2. For your second drawing, flip the sheet of paper over and turn it sideways. With the paper in this position, again make a scale drawing of the pentagon.

   Again, the bottom of the pentagon should be one inch from the bottom of the sheet and the top of the pentagon should be one inch from the top of the paper, so that the pentagon is positioned roughly like the diagram at the right.

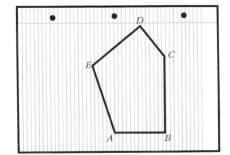

3. a. For each of your two drawings, find the ratio between the length of a side of your drawing and the length of the corresponding side in the actual pentagon in this assignment.

   b. How might you find these ratios before you start the drawings?

What's Possible?

This activity starts with triangles and has two initial parts—one on angles and one on sides. Parts III and IV ask about generalizations to other polygons.

Work with your group. Play around with scissors, straws, paper, protractors, and pencils. If you think other materials might help, ask if they arc available.

Tomorrow, your group will give a presentation on part or on all of this activity. Chart paper will help with your presentation.

Part I: Angles

Can any three angles be the angles of a triangle?

Experiment to find the answer to this question. Start with three angles, say 30°, 50°, and 80°. Can you draw a triangle whose angles are these sizes?

Try three other values, say 50°, 60°, and 70°. Keep making up numbers and trying them. Keep track of which sets of angles are possible and which are not. What conclusions can you reach about the three angles of a triangle?

Note: You may believe that you already know the answer to the question for Part I. If so, then state what you know and how you know it.

Continued on next page

Part II: Sides

Can any three numbers be the lengths of the sides of a triangle?

Experiment to find the answer to this question. Start with three numbers, say 2, 3, and 4. Can you draw a triangle whose sides are these lengths? (You have to choose a unit of length.)

Try three other values, say 3 , 6, and 11. Keep making up numbers and trying them. Keep track of which sets of lengths are possible and which are not. What conclusions can you reach about the three sides of a triangle?

Part III: Quadrilaterals

What if you were considering quadrilaterals (four-sided polygons) instead of triangles? What would be possible for the angles of a quadrilateral? What would be possible for the sides of a quadrilateral? Find conditions for quadrilaterals that are similar to those you found in Parts I and II for triangles.

Part IV: Other Polygons

How can you generalize your observations to apply to all polygons?

Homework 12   Very Special Triangles

You saw in *Why Are Triangles Special?* that triangles are special within the category of polygons.

Some triangles are even more special than others.

You've already met the *isosceles* and *equilateral* triangles, which require either two or all three of the sides to be equal. (An equilateral triangle is a special type of isosceles triangle.)

Another special category of triangle is the **right triangle**, which is a triangle with one right angle.

1. Why must the other two angles of a right triangle be acute (that is, less than 90°)?

2. Why do you think right triangles are considered important?

Continued on next page

Triangle *ABC* shown here is a right triangle with a
right angle at vertex *C*. (The small square inside that vertex
is a standard symbol indicating a right angle.)

There are special names for the sides of a right triangle.

The two sides of the triangle that form the right angle, $\overline{AC}$
and $\overline{BC}$, are called the **legs** of the triangle, and the third
side, $\overline{AB}$, is called the **hypotenuse**.

Note: The notation $\overline{AC}$ as used here (with a line above the
letters) indicates the **line segment** from *A* to *C*. The
notation *AC* (with neither the line above the letters nor the
word *segment*) means the **length** of this segment. The
line through *A* and *C* is represented by the notation $\overleftrightarrow{AC}$,
and the **ray** from *A* through *C* is writte $\overrightarrow{AC}$.

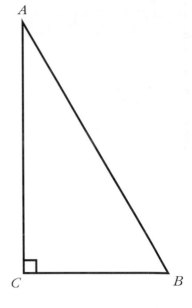

3. What statements can you make about how the
   lengths of the sides of a right triangle compare
   to each other? Explain your reasoning.

4. Draw a right triangle, measure the legs, and then draw a right triangle whose
   legs are twice as long.

   a. How does the hypotenuse of the new triangle compare to the hypotenuse
      of the original?

   b. How do the acute angles of the new triangle compare to the acute angles
      of the original?

   c. What do your answers to Questions 4a and 4b tell you about the two
      triangles?

Each of the acute angles of a right triangle is formed by the hypotenuse and one of the
legs. For example, angle *A* is formed by the hypotenuse, $\overline{AB}$, and by the leg $\overline{AC}$. The leg
that helps form an acute angle is said to be **adjacent to** that angle. For example, $\overline{AC}$ is
the leg (or side) *adjacent to* angle *A*.

That same leg is said to be **opposite** the other acute angle. For example, $\overline{AC}$ is the leg
opposite angle *B*.

5. Draw a right triangle in which the acute angles are different sizes. Is the longer
   leg *opposite* or *adjacent to* the larger of the acute angles? Do you think this is
   true for all right triangles?

6. Is it possible for a right triangle to be isosceles? Equilateral? Explain your
   answers.

Homework 13   Inventing Rules

In working with similar triangles, you often have to solve equations involving proportions.

For example, suppose one triangle has sides of lengths 6, 9, and 14, and there is a similar triangle whose shortest side has length 15. If you use x to represent the longest side of the second triangle, then the value of x has to satisfy an equation like

$$\frac{6}{15} = \frac{14}{x}$$

(This is one of several possible equations for x.)

Continued on next page

Some such equations are easier to solve than others. Sometimes the particular numbers involved suggest tricks or shortcuts that make them easy to solve.

In each of the equations below, the letter x stands for an unknown number. Use any method you like to find the number x stands for, but write down *exactly how you do it*.

Be sure to check your answers and write down in detail how you find them.

$$\frac{x}{5} = 7 \qquad \frac{x}{6} = \frac{72}{24} \qquad \frac{x}{8} = \frac{11}{4} \qquad \frac{x}{7} = \frac{5}{3}$$

$$\frac{x+1}{3} = \frac{4}{6} \qquad \frac{5}{13} = \frac{19}{x} \qquad \frac{2}{x} = 6 \qquad \frac{9}{x} = \frac{x}{16}$$

Homework 14   What's the Angle?

You've seen that angles play a very important role in similarity. So it's useful to know when two angles are sure to be equal.

The diagram at the right is made up of three line segments: $\overline{AG}$, $\overline{AH}$, and $\overline{BE}$.

$\overline{BE}$ intersects $\overline{AG}$ at point C and intersects $\overline{AH}$ at point D.

There are also lots of angles in the diagram. Your first task in this assignment is to explore the relationships between those angles. Then test whether your observations apply to similar diagrams.

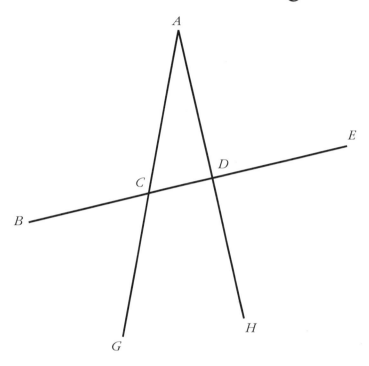

Note: Some of these angles can be described easily by a single letter, such as $\angle A$. In other cases, you need three letters to specify the angle you mean. For example, writing $\angle C$ would be ambiguous. That is, it would be unclear which angle was meant because there are several angles in the diagram that have C as the vertex. If you write $\angle ACD$, there shouldn't be any confusion. Be sure to express all your angles using notation that is clear.

You may want to use a protractor to gather some information, but you should also find explanations for *why* certain angle relationships hold. That will allow you to generalize your results.

1. Based on your exploration of the specific diagram above, answer questions like these:

   • Which angles are equal to which other angles?

   • What angle sum relationships can you find?

2. Draw some other diagrams to test whether the relationships you found in Question 1 were specific to that diagram or examples of a general principle.

3. Generalize from your work in Questions 1 and 2, and justify your general conclusions.

POW 18

Trying Triangles

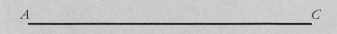

Suppose you have a straight pipe cleaner of a given length.

For convenience, label the two ends of the pipe cleaner A and C, as shown at the left.

Now suppose that the pipe cleaner is bent into two portions, with one portion twice as long as the other. Label the place where the bend is made B, as shown at the left, so that the segment from B to C is twice as long as the segment from A to B.

Then a fourth point, X, is chosen at random somewhere on the longer section, and the pipe cleaner is bent at that place as well. So now the pipe cleaner might look like the illustration below.

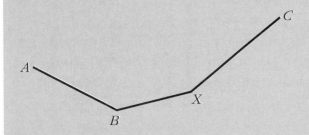

Can the three segments of the pipe cleaner be made into a triangle by changing the angles at the two bends? As you might suppose, the answer depends on the location of point X.

So here's the question.

> *If point X is chosen at random along the section from B to C, what is the probability that the three segments of the pipe cleaner can be made into a triangle?*

(Recall that "chosen at random" means that all positions between B and C are equally likely to be selected as the location for point X.)

Continued on next page

As part of your investigation of this problem, you will probably first need to come up with the answer to this question:

> *Suppose three lengths, a, b, and c, are given. What condition must these lengths satisfy for it to be possible to make a triangle whose sides have these three lengths?*

Note: You may find it helpful to assume that the original pipe cleaner has a specific length.

Write-up

1. *Problem Statement*

2. *Process*

3. *Solution:* Your solution should include answers to both questions posed above.

4. *Evaluation*

Adapted from *Mathematics Teacher* (November 1989), National Council of Teachers of Mathematics, Volume 82, Number 6.

More About Angles

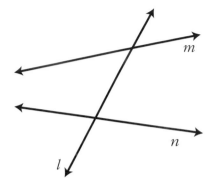

In this activity, you will continue your investigation of the angles formed when lines intersect.

In general, a line that intersects two or more other lines is called a **transversal** for those other lines.

For example, in the diagram at the left, the line labeled *l* is a transversal for the pair of lines labeled *m* and *n*.

The case where the two lines *m* and *n* are parallel is especially important, and that's the subject of this activity.

In the second diagram at the left, $\overleftrightarrow{BD}$ and $\overleftrightarrow{EG}$ are parallel lines. $\overleftrightarrow{AH}$ is a transversal that intersects $\overleftrightarrow{BD}$ at C and intersects $\overleftrightarrow{EG}$ at F.

Investigate the angles in this diagram, focusing on these two questions:

- Which angles are equal to which other angles?

- What angle sum relationships can you find?

Pay special attention to the angle relationships that occur because $\overleftrightarrow{BD}$ and $\overleftrightarrow{EG}$ are parallel.

Homework 15   Inside Similarity

How do you make small triangles inside larger ones so that the small ones are similar to the large ones?

The diagram below shows two triangles that are congruent to the top triangle. In each case, a dotted line has been drawn that connects two sides of the triangle and cuts off a smaller (shaded) triangle.

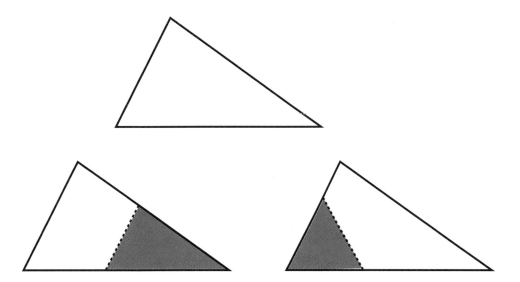

In the first case, the smaller triangle appears to be similar to the larger one. In the second case, the smaller triangle seems not to be similar to the larger one.

Your task is to investigate and report on the difference between these two cases. That is, if you connect points on two sides of a triangle, when does the smaller triangle created in this way come out similar to the original?

You may want to begin your investigation by tracing the original triangle and experimenting by drawing some lines on your tracing. Find as many ways as you can to draw lines to cut off small triangles that are similar to the original triangle.

Then describe in words those lines that can be used to cut off a small triangle that is similar to the larger one, and explain your answer.

A Parallel Proof

For some time, you've known from measurement that the sum of the angles of any triangle seems to be 180°. Now it's time to see why this must be true.

In this activity, you will be given a diagram involving an arbitrary triangle. Your task will be to show how to use this diagram to prove the angle sum property for triangles.

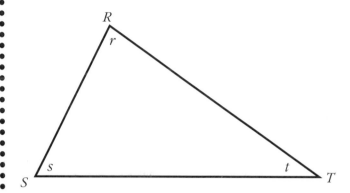

To get started, suppose *RST* is any triangle, such as the one shown at the left.

For convenience, the angles of this triangle are labeled *r, s,* and *t.*

Next, draw a line through vertex *R* that is parallel to the opposite side. This is the line $\overleftrightarrow{AB}$ shown in the diagram below, in which $\overleftrightarrow{AB}$ is parallel to $\overleftrightarrow{ST}$. The angles *ARS* and *BRT* have been labeled *x* and *y* in this new diagram.

Your task is to show how this diagram can be used to prove the angle sum property for triangles. In other words, prove that the angles labeled *r, s,* and *t* add up to 180°.

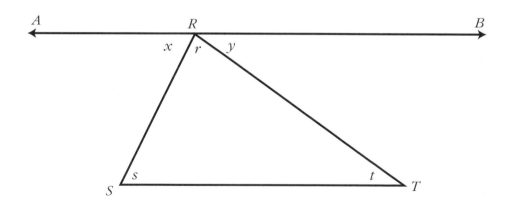

Continued on next page

Interactive Mathematics Program

Hint: You may find it helpful to extend the sides of the original triangle, as shown below. In this diagram, both $\overleftrightarrow{EF}$ and $\overleftrightarrow{GH}$ are transversals for the parallel lines $\overleftrightarrow{AB}$ and $\overleftrightarrow{CD}$. Think about how to use the transversals to get information about angles.

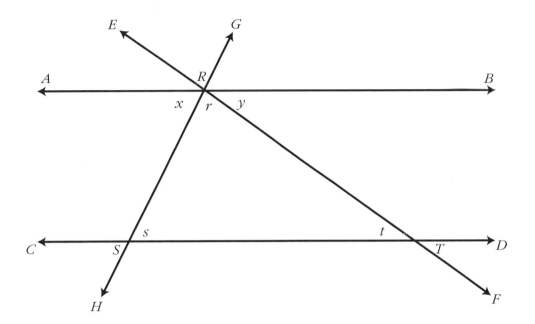

Homework 16   Ins and Outs of
                                              Proportion

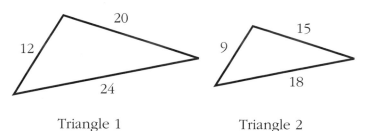

Triangle 1   Triangle 2

The two triangles above are similar, since the ratios between a side of Triangle 1 and the corresponding side of Triangle 2 are the same for all three sides.

In other words, the three ratios $\frac{12}{9}$, $\frac{20}{15}$, and $\frac{24}{18}$ are equal. For triangles, having corresponding sides proportional guarantees similarity.

What about ratios of sides *within* a triangle? For example, the ratio of the longest to the shortest side in Triangle 1 is $\frac{24}{12}$, while the corresponding ratio in Triangle 2 is $\frac{18}{9}$. These two ratios are also equal, since both fractions are equal to 2.

1. Compare the other ratios within each triangle. In other words, find a different ratio of two sides of Triangle 1, and find the corresponding ratio in Triangle 2, and compare. Do this for all possible pairs of sides.

   What do you conclude?

2. Form another pair of similar triangles. (To get corresponding sides in proportion, you can use any convenient set of lengths for the sides of the first triangle, and multiply those numbers by a fixed value to get the lengths of the sides of the second triangle.)

   Now repeat Question 1 for your new pair of triangles. That is, find the ratio of a pair of sides of your first new triangle, find the corresponding ratio in your second new triangle, and compare.

3. Form a third pair of triangles, but this time make them not similar. Examine the ratios of sides within one triangle to the ratios of sides within the other. What do you conclude?

Continued on next page

4. Now consider the two triangles at the right. Assume that they are similar, so the ratios $\frac{r}{x}$, $\frac{s}{y}$, and $\frac{t}{z}$ are all equal.

   a. Based on your results in Questions 1 through 3, identify a pair of ratios—one using sides of Triangle 3 and one using sides of Triangle 4—that you think are equal to each other.

   b. Find as many pairs of equal ratios as you can.

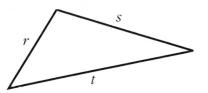

Triangle 3

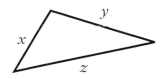

Triangle 4

Days 17-20

Lights and Shadows

You know that shadows have something to do with light (or lack of it). You're almost ready to solve the lamp shadow problem, but first you will look at some fascinating situations that involve light in a different context. Similar triangles continue to be the main theme.

Lydia Garcia measures Michelle France's shadow to compare it to the shadow of a light pole.

Interactive Mathematics Program

Bouncing Light

If you take a flashlight and shine it into a mirror, the light will "bounce off" the mirror. In this activity, you will look at the angles involved in such "bouncing light."

Set up your flashlight and mirror in a way similar to that shown in the sketch below.

That is, one person can hold the mirror, another can shine the flashlight at the mirror, and a third can mark the path along which the reflection of the light leaves the mirror.

The angle between the mirror and the incoming ray of light from the flashlight is called the **angle of approach**. The angle between the mirror and the ray bouncing off the mirror is called the **angle of departure**.

Continued on next page

1. Use a protractor to measure the angle of approach and the angle of departure. (You may want to trace the path of the flashlight's beam to and from the mirror onto chart paper.)

   What do you notice about the relationship between the two angles?

2. Repeat this experiment but change the angle at which the beam goes into the mirror. Do this two more times to see whether the relationship that you observed between the angles always seems to hold true. Write down what you've noticed about the relationship.

3. Hold the mirror in different positions to look at other things in the classroom. What do you notice about the position of the mirror? Write about the relationship between your observations in Question 2 and how you have to hold the mirror. Try to explain what looking at something in a mirror has to do with bouncing light.

Homework 17   Now You See It, Now You Don't

Use the principle of light reflection and your protractor to answer the following problems. You will need to trace each of the diagrams in this assignment.

1. A person is standing at point *A*, looking toward the mirror. Which letters of the alphabet can this person see?

A
•

B C D E F G H I J K L M

2. Two spiders are on opposite walls. A large mirror is placed on the floor.

Copy the diagram below, and show exactly where on the floor the spiders should look to see each other. Can you find two triangles that are similar in your drawing? Why must they be similar?

Mirror

Mirror Magic

You can actually use a mirror and the principle of light reflection to measure the heights of objects. All that is needed is a flat surface on which to place your mirror.

The method uses similar triangles, and it begins like this:

> You lay the mirror on the ground some distance from the object. Then you move slowly backwards, away from the object, while looking down at the mirror. At some point, you should be able to see the object in your mirror.

Continued on next page

You then measure some things that are easier to measure than the height of the given object and apply ideas of geometry.

1. Find the height of an object in the classroom using this method.

2. Make a diagram that shows your method. Label the distances that you measured, and show how you used these measurements to find the height of the object.

3. Assign variables to the distances you measured, and set up an In-Out table in which these variables are labels for the input columns. Assign a variable for the height of your object and use that as the label for the output column.

   Enter your actual measurements as the first row of inputs of your table, and put the height you got as the first output.

4. Next, make up some numbers for your input variables. Then, based on your made-up numbers, find the new height of the object.

   In other words, find some more rows for your table, calculating the output (the height) in terms of the numbers you made up. The geometric situation in your diagram should serve as the basis for your calculation.

5. Give a description in words or write an equation that shows the relationship between the height of the object and your input variables.

Homework 18

Mirror Madness

A family of spiders has found a bunch of mirrors on the ground, and they have been positioning themselves to see each other in the mirrors.

They are dangling in the order shown below, although their distances from each other, their heights off the ground, and the positions of the mirrors are not necessarily drawn to scale.

Sister spider, who is 48 inches off the ground, can see Momma spider in a mirror that is on the ground between them. This mirror is 20 inches from the point directly below Sister spider and 30 inches from the point directly below Momma.

Momma spider can see Uncle spider in a mirror that is 10 inches from the point below Momma and 5 inches from the point below Uncle.

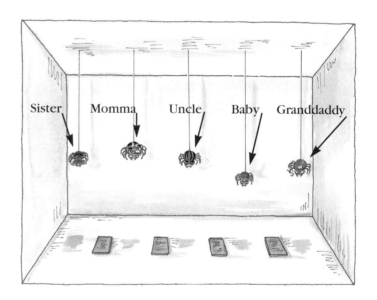

Uncle spider can see Baby spider in a mirror that is 8 inches from the point below Uncle and 6 inches from the point below Baby.

Finally, Baby spider can see Granddaddy spider in a mirror that is 12 inches from the point below Baby and 16 inches from the point below Granddaddy.

Your Assignment

Find the height of each spider. (You already know the height of Sister spider.)

Show your equations and how you solved them.

Homework 19   To Measure a Tree

This unit started with a problem about finding the length of a shadow. But other measurement ideas have come up as well.

You've seen how to measure the height of an object using a mirror. Now you will look at measuring the height of a tree.

One straightforward way to find the height of a tree is to climb to the tippy top and drop a long tape measure to the ground (while still holding one end) and have a friend on the ground read off how tall the tree is.

Although straightforward, that method has many potential difficulties (and dangers).

Fortunately, there's a less hazardous method—one that uses similar triangles.

Continued on next page

Your task in this assignment is to use your knowledge of similar triangles to invent a method for measuring a tree. Use the illustration above for ideas.

Write down what you'd have to know and how you'd use that information to figure out how high the tree is.

Identify clearly what similar triangles there are in the situation, and explain how they would fit into your method.

POW 19   *Pool Pockets*

Imagine a modified pool table in which the only pockets are those in the four corners.

The diagram at the right shows such a table as viewed from above.

This POW will use the view from above all the time, with different parts of the table labeled as in the next diagram.

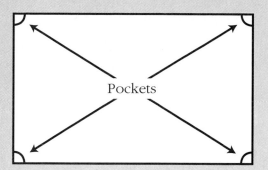

Pockets

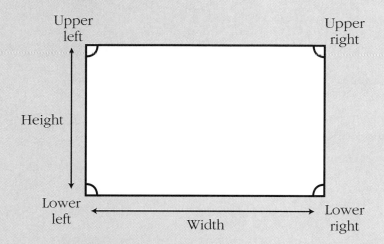

Upper left

Upper right

Height

Lower left

Width

Lower right

Next, imagine that a ball is hit from the lower left corner in a diagonal direction that forms a 45° angle with the sides, as shown in the diagram at the right.

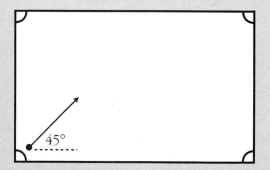

45°

Continued on next page

Finally, imagine that every time the ball hits an edge of the table, it bounces off, again at a 45° angle, and that it continues this way until it hits one of the corner pockets perfectly.

For example, using the previous diagram, the first few bounces of the ball would look like the diagram at the right.

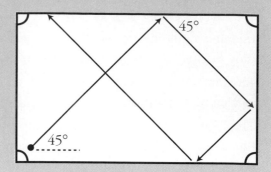

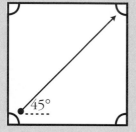

Of course, the path of the ball will depend on the shape of the table. For example, with a square table, the ball would go directly into the opposite corner without bouncing at all, as shown in the diagram at the left.

Your task in this POW is to investigate what happens to the ball and how this depends on the dimensions of the table.

You should make these assumptions.

- Both the height and the width of the table are whole number distances.
- The ball is always shot at an angle of 45°.
- The ball is always shot from the lower-left corner.

For example, you might look at these questions.

- Does the ball always hit a pocket eventually?
- If so, which pocket does it hit?
- If it does hit a pocket, how many times does it bounce before it hits the pocket?

You may have some other questions of your own.

You will probably find it very useful to have grid paper for your investigation, using the width of the squares on the grid paper as your unit of length. In that way, you'll be able to keep track more easily of the exact path of the ball.

Continued on next page

For example, the diagram to the right illustrates how you might use grid paper to show the path of the ball for a 3-by-5 table. The dotted lines represent the lines of the grid paper and the solid rectangle is the outline of the table. The diagonal lines with arrows show the path of the ball. At the end of the path, the ball is about to go into the pocket in the upper-right corner of the table.

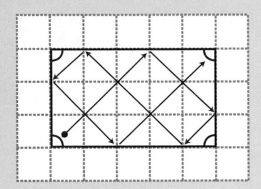

Happy bouncing!

Write-up

1. *Subject of Exploration:* Describe the subject that you are investigating. What questions do you want to explore?

2. *Information Gathering:* Basing your comments on your notes (which should be included with your write-up), state what happened in the specific cases you examined.

3. *Conclusions, Explanations, and Conjectures:* Describe any general observations you made or conclusions that you reached. Wherever possible, explain why the particular conclusions are true. That is, try to *prove* your general statements. But also include *conjectures*, that is, statements that you only *think* are true.

4. *Open Questions:* What questions do you have that you were not able to answer? What other investigations would you do if you had more time?

5. *Evaluation*

A Shadow of a Doubt

Can you now use the ideas of similarity to predict the length of a shadow without a shadow of a doubt?

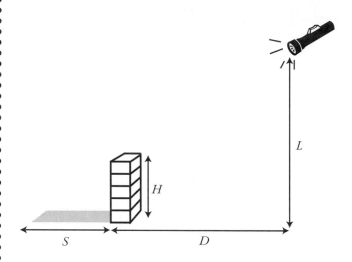

Recall these variables, shown in the diagram:

- L = the distance from the light source to the ground

- D = the distance along the ground from the light source to the object casting the shadow

- H = the height of the object casting the shadow

- S = the length of the shadow

Of course, in order to use similarity, you're going to have to find some triangles. They're hiding somewhere in the diagram above.

1. What triangles do you see in the diagram? Which of them are similar? Why must these triangles be similar?

2. Use your knowledge of similar triangles to write an equation that expresses a relationship between these four variables.

3. Students at Mystery High School did some experiments set up like the one above. As usual, there's a mystery about their work, because they forgot to write down the lengths of the shadows. Find the length of the shadow in each situation below.

   a. $L = 11, H = 5,$ and $D = 12$

   b. $L = 15, H = 5,$ and $D = 12$

   c. $L = 15, H = 5,$ and $D = 60$

4. Write a description in words of how to find the length of a shadow when L, H, and D are given.

Homework 20   A Few Special Bounces

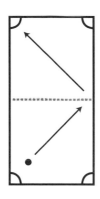

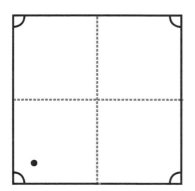

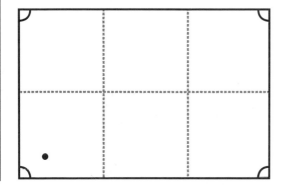

POW 19: Pool Pockets asks you to consider all possible tables with whole-number dimensions.

That's a lot of cases, so this assignment will get you started with a simpler version.

Specifically, you will consider all tables that have a height of exactly two units. (Remember that the width is supposed to be a whole number.)

The first three such tables are shown at the left, and the path of the ball has been drawn for the first of these tables.

Be sure to consider not just these three, but all tables with a height of two units.

What happens to the ball on these tables? Consider the specific questions posed in the POW and make up some others of your own.

Days 21-26

The Lamp and the Sun

You're about to solve the lamp shadow problem, and get a rather nice formula expressing the length of the shadow in terms of other variables.

But here comes another problem—the sun shadow! As you solve this problem, you will be finishing the unit and Year 1 as well.

Your portfolio for this unit asks you to look back over the entire year.

Mike Dominguez experiments with trigonometric functions on his calculator.

More Triangles for Shadows

By now, you have probably developed a diagram similar to the one shown here in order to represent the shadow problem.

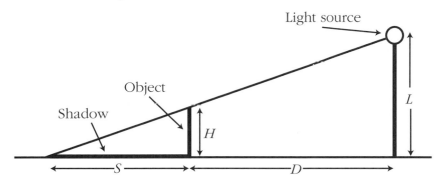

In terms of this diagram, the length of a shadow (*S*) depends on the height of the light source (*L*), on the height of the object casting the shadow (*H*), and on the distance along the ground from that object to the light source (*D*).

Your goal is to develop an algebraic expression for *S* in terms of *L, H*, and *D*. In other words, you would like to find a function *f* so that $S = f(L, D, H)$.

You may have used similar triangles to develop an equation involving these four variables. For example, if you compare the small triangle in the diagram to the large triangle, you might get the equation

$$\frac{S}{S+D} = \frac{H}{L}$$

The fact that *S* appears in two places in this equation complicates the process of using this equation to get a general expression for *S* in terms of the other variables.

So in this assignment, your task is to find another way to use similar triangles so that using proportions gives you a simpler initial equation.

In particular, see if you can find a pair of similar triangles in the diagram so that the variable *S* appears in only one place in the equation for proportionality. Once you get that simpler equation, use it to find the long-sought expression for *S* in terms of *L, H*, and *D*.

Homework 21

The Sun Shadow Problem

At night or if you are indoors, shadows are likely to be caused by lamps or streetlights. But during the day, the shadows you see outdoors usually come from blocking off the light from the sun.

For such a "sun shadow," it doesn't make much sense to talk about the height of the light source off the ground or the distance along the ground from the light source to the object casting the shadow.

In other words, the variables L and D are pretty meaningless for sun shadows.

So what does the length of a sun shadow depend on? What are the relevant variables? At what time of day would a shadow be the longest and when would it be the shortest?

Speculate on these questions (and any others you want to add). Think about how one might go about expressing the length of a shadow in terms of those variables.

Write down any conjectures or ideas you have on these issues.

The Return of the Tree

Woody is really interested in trees, and he was pretty excited when he learned the ideas from *Homework 19: To Measure a Tree.*

Now Woody has found a new way to measure a tree. (You probably can't wait to hear about it!)

First he measured the height from the ground to his eye. That was 5 feet.

Then he used a protractor to measure the angle between the horizontal and his line of sight up to the top of the tree. That turned out to be 70°.

Finally, he measured his distance from the tree. That was 12 feet.

That's all the information that Woody needed. Using these measurements, he figured out how tall the tree was. So you, with the help of your trusty protractor and your understanding of similarity, should be able to figure it out also.

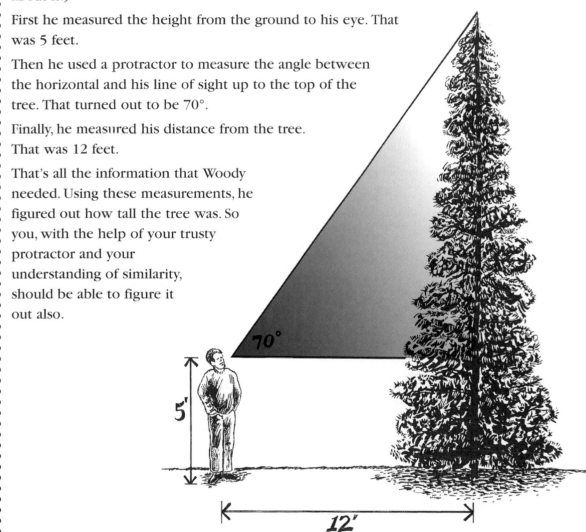

Homework 22   Right Triangle Ratios

Many of the problems you've worked on, including the basic diagram for the shadow problems, have involved right angles.

You've also seen that ideas of similarity involve ratios of sides of triangles.

So it's natural to think about ratios of sides within right triangles.

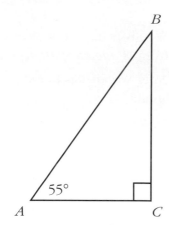

1. Carefully draw a right triangle *ABC* with a right angle at *C* and with a 55° angle at *A*, such as the one at the right. (You should make your triangle larger than the one at the right so your measurement error will be less significant.)

   Record the lengths of the three sides of your triangle.

In *Homework 12: Very Special Triangles*, you were introduced to this terminology:

- Side $\overline{AB}$ is called the **hypotenuse** of this right triangle.

- Side $\overline{BC}$ is called the leg **opposite** angle *A*.

- Side $\overline{AC}$ is called the leg **adjacent to** angle *A*.

2. Find each of the ratios below. If your measurements in Question 1 involved fractions of a unit, convert your fractions to decimals and use those decimal values to compute the ratios.

$$\frac{\text{length of leg opposite angle } A}{\text{length of hypotenuse}}$$

$$\frac{\text{length of leg adjacent to angle } A}{\text{length of hypotenuse}}$$

$$\frac{\text{length of leg opposite angle } A}{\text{length of leg adjacent to angle } A}$$

3. Do you think that your classmates will get the same results for Questions 1 and 2 that you got? Explain in detail why or why not.

Sin, Cos, and Tan Buttons Revealed

Did you ever wonder what those keys on your calculator that say "sin," "cos," and "tan" are all about? Well, here's where you find out.

You've seen that, whenever two right triangles have another angle in common, the triangles must be similar, and so the corresponding ratios of lengths of sides within those triangles are equal.

These ratios depend only on that common acute angle, and each ratio of lengths within the right triangle has a name. The study and use of these ratios is part of a branch of mathematics called **trigonometry.**

Suppose you are given an acute angle (in other words, an angle between 0° and 90°).

You can create a right triangle in which one of the acute angles is equal to that given angle. Suppose you label that triangle as shown in the diagram below, so that ∠A is equal to the acute angle you started with.

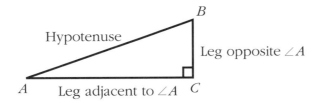

The trigonometric ratios are then defined as explained on the following pages. The principles of similarity guarantee that these ratios will be the same for *every* right triangle that has an acute angle the same size as ∠A.

Continued on next page

Sine of an Angle

The **sine** of $\angle A$ is the ratio of the length of the leg opposite $\angle A$ to the length of the hypotenuse. The sine of $\angle A$ is abbreviated as **sin A**. For example, in $\triangle RST$ below, the leg opposite $\angle R$ has length 4, and the hypotenuse has length 7, so $\sin R = \frac{4}{7}$.

In summary

$$\sin A = \frac{\text{length of leg opposite } \angle A}{\text{length of hypotenuse}}$$

or simply,

$$\sin A = \frac{\text{opposite}}{\text{hypotenuse}}$$

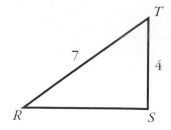

Cosine of an Angle

The **cosine** of $\angle A$ is the ratio of the length of the leg adjacent to $\angle A$ to the length of the hypotenuse. The cosine of $\angle A$ is abbreviated as **cos A**. For example, in $\triangle UVW$ below, the leg adjacent to $\angle U$ has length 3, and the hypotenuse has length 5, so $\cos U = \frac{3}{5}$.

In summary

$$\cos A = \frac{\text{length of leg adjacent to } \angle A}{\text{length of hypotenuse}}$$

or simply,

$$\cos A = \frac{\text{adjacent}}{\text{hypotenuse}}$$

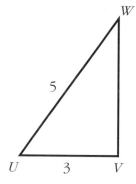

Tangent of an Angle

The **tangent** of $\angle A$ is the ratio of the length of the leg opposite $\angle A$ to the length of the leg adjacent to $\angle A$. The tangent of $\angle A$ is abbreviated as **tan A**. For example, in $\triangle HKL$ on the following page, the leg opposite $\angle H$ has length 2, and the leg adjacent to $\angle H$ has length 6, so $\tan H = \frac{2}{6}$.

Continued on next page

In summary

$$\tan A = \frac{\text{length of leg opposite } \angle A}{\text{length of leg adjacent to } \angle A}$$

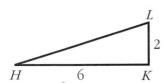

or simply,

$$\tan A = \frac{\text{opposite}}{\text{adjacent}}$$

Trigonometric Functions on a Calculator

Any scientific calculator or graphing calculator has keys that will give you the values of these functions for any angle.

In some calculators, you enter the size of the angle and then push the appropriate trigonometric key, while for other calculators, you do the opposite.

Caution: You have been measuring angles using *degrees* as the unit of measurement, but there are other units for measuring angles. Most calculators that work with trigonometric functions have a *mode* key that you can set to "deg."

The Other Ratios

There are three other ratios of side lengths within a right triangle, in addition to the sine, the cosine, and the tangent. These other ratios are used less often and usually do not have their own calculator keys.

Each is the reciprocal of one of the three ratios already defined. Here are the definitions of those other ratios.

$$\text{cotangent } A = \frac{1}{\text{tangent } A}$$

$$\text{secant } A = \frac{1}{\text{cosine } A}$$

$$\text{cosecant } A = \frac{1}{\text{sine } A}$$

They are abbreviated, respectively, as **cot A, sec A,** and **csc A.**

The Tree and the Pendulum

1. Now that you have been introduced to the definitions of the trigonometric functions, it's time to look again at the situation described in *The Return of the Tree*.

   Here are the key facts again.

   • Woody was 12 feet from the tree.

   • Woody's line of sight to the top of the tree was at an angle of 70° up from horizontal.

   • Woody's eye was 5 feet off the ground.

   Describe how Woody could find the height of the tree using trigonometry and these measurements.

Continued on next page

Interactive Mathematics Program

2. You can also apply trigonometry to the pendulum from *The Pit and the Pendulum*.

For example, suppose a 30-foot pendulum has an initial amplitude of 30°, as shown at the right.

How far is the bob from the center line when the pendulum starts? In other words, what is the distance labeled *d*?

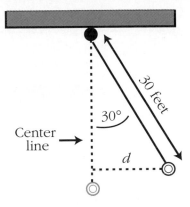

(By the way, although the last syllable of the word *trigonometry* sounds like "tree," the origin of the word really has nothing to do with trees. The word comes from Greek and combines the word *trigonon*, which means "triangle," and the suffix *-metria*, which means "measurement.")

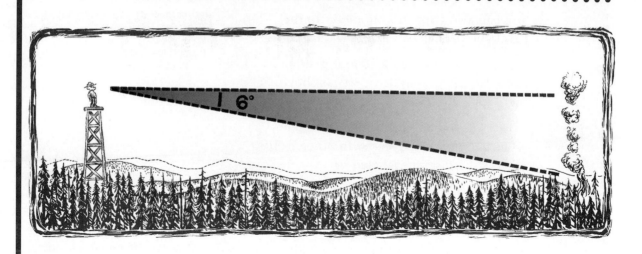

Homework 23   Smokey and the Dude

Reminder: Be sure to check that your calculator is set to use *degrees*. (There is probably a *mode* key to fix this setting.)

1. *Smokey the Bear*

Smokey the Bear is atop a 100-foot tower, looking out over a fairly level area for careless people who might start fires.

Suddenly, he sees a fire starting. He marks down the direction of the fire, but he also needs to know how far away from the tower the fire is.

To figure out this distance, Smokey grabs his handy protractor. Since he is high up on top of the tower, he has to look slightly downward toward the fire. He finds that his line of sight to the fire is at an angle of 6° below horizontal, as shown in the diagram above. (*Note:* This diagram is not to scale.)

      a. How far is Smokey from the fire?

      b. How far is the base of Smokey's tower from the fire?

Continued on next page

2. *Dude on a Cliff*

Shredding Charlene is out surfing and catches the eye of her friend, Dave the Dude, who is standing at the top of a vertical cliff. The angle formed by Charlene's line of sight and the horizontal measures 28°. Charlene is 50 meters out from the bottom of the cliff. Charlene and Dave are both 1.7 meters tall. They are both 16 years old. The surfboard is level with the base of the cliff. How high is the cliff?

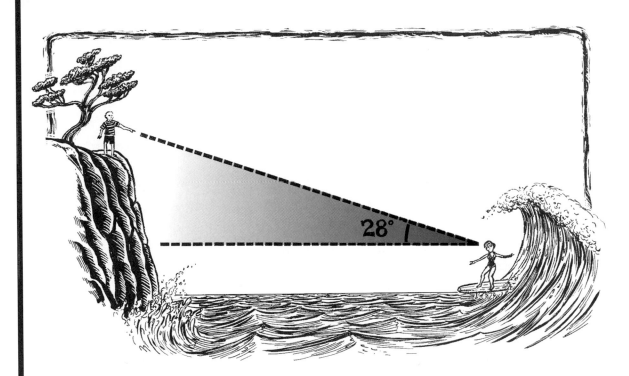

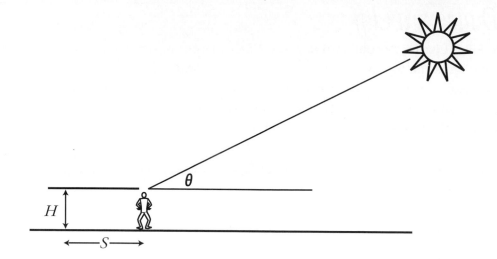

The Sun Shadow

Suppose you are standing outdoors on a bright, sunny day.

You look up toward the sun and estimate the angle of the sun's elevation.

In other words, you measure the angle shown as θ in the diagram above.

How can you find the length of your shadow (S) using this angle and your own height (H)?

Homework 24

Your Opposite Is My Adjacent

Every right triangle has two acute angles. You can learn some interesting facts about trigonometry by using both of them.

Use the labeling in $\triangle ABC$ below to answer the questions.

1. What relationship must exist between angles *A* and *B*? (*Hint:* If you know one of these two angles, how can you find the other?)

2. Express the ratio $\frac{BC}{AB}$ in two ways:

   a. as the sine, cosine, or tangent of $\angle A$

   b. as the sine, cosine, or tangent of $\angle B$

3. a. Use your results from Questions 1 and 2 to write a general formula for the sine of an angle as the cosine of a related angle.

   b. Write a similar general formula for the cosine of an angle as the sine of a related angle.

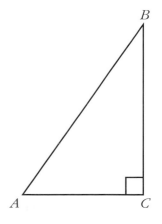

Homework 25 Beginning Portfolio Selection

As the first step in assembling your portfolio for *Shadows,* look back over the main unit problem.

One of the key ideas in this unit is the concept of *similarity*.

1. Explain what similarity means, both by giving an intuitive description and by using the formal definition.

2. Choose two or three activities in the unit that helped you understand this concept and use it. Explain why you chose those activities and how they contributed to your ideas about similarity.

"Shadows" Portfolio

In addition to writing a cover letter and choosing papers, your portfolio work for *Shadows* includes looking back over the entire first year of your IMP experience.

Cover Letter for "Shadows"

Look back over *Shadows* and describe the central problem of the unit and the main mathematical ideas. This description should give an overview of how the key ideas were developed and how they were used to solve the central problem.

As part of the compilation of your portfolio, you will be selecting some activities that you think were important in developing the key ideas of this unit. Your cover letter should include an explanation of why you select the particular items you do.

Selecting Papers from "Shadows"

Your portfolio for *Shadows* should contain the items described below.

- *Homework 25: Beginning Portfolio Selection*

  Include the activities from the unit that you selected in *Homework 25: Beginning Portfolio Selection*, along with your written work about the concept of similarity and about the activities.

Continued on next page

- Other key activities

  Include two or three other activities that you think were important in developing the key ideas of this unit.

- A Problem of the Week

  Select one of the four POWs you completed during this unit (*Spiralaterals, Cutting the Pie, Trying Triangles,* and *Pool Pockets*).

- Other quality work

  Select one or two other pieces of work that demonstrate your best efforts. (These can be any work from the unit—Problem of the Week, homework, classwork, presentation, and so forth.)

End-of-Year Review

Because this is the final unit of the year, you should take this chance to look back over your overall experience. Here are some of the issues you might want to examine.

- How was this experience different from your previous work in mathematics

  - in terms of *how* you learned the mathematics?

  - in terms of the mathematics itself?

- How have you changed personally as a result of your experience

  - in terms of your confidence in your own ability?

  - in terms of your work with others?

- What are your mathematics goals for the rest of your high school years? How have those goals changed over the past year and why?

You should include here any other thoughts you might like to share with a reader of your portfolio.

Appendix

Supplemental Problems

Many of the supplemental problems for *Shadows* focus on similarity, but other problems look at logic and counterexamples, at the use of proportions, or at the history underlying concepts from the unit. These are some examples.

- *Fit Them Together* and *Similar Areas* examine the connection between area and similarity.

- *Is It Sufficient?* and *Triangular Data* look at the conditions needed for similarity and congruence, and ask you to find counterexamples or generalizations.

- *Proportions Everywhere* uses proportionality in a geometric setting. *What If They Kept Running?* looks at proportionality in the context of a track competition.

- *The Parallel Postulate* gives you a glimpse into the historical development of ideas about parallelism. Reading on your own, you'll learn how these ideas led to the development of non-Euclidean geometry.

Crates

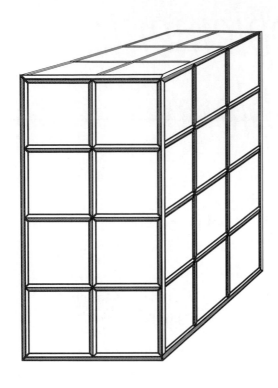

In *Homework 4: An N-by-N Window* and in *Homework 5: More About Windows,* you looked for formulas for the amount of wood strip needed to create a window frame.

Now suppose that instead of building a window frame, you are building a frame for a wooden crate, such as the one shown at the left.

Keep in mind that the wood strip is just used to make a *frame* for the crate. Cardboard has been placed between the strips to make the crate into a solid box.

Because of the cardboard, you can't see the bottom or the back sides of the crate in the diagram.

1. First find the amount of wood strip needed if the crate is 2 feet wide, 3 feet long, and 4 feet high, as shown above.

   Remember that only three sides of the crate are shown here, so you'll need to imagine the other three sides. Also remember that some of the wood strips are shared by two sides of the crate.

2. Now look for a general formula, using a crate that is *w* feet wide, *l* feet long, and *h* feet high.

Some Other Shadows

The central problem in this unit involves finding the length of a shadow cast on the floor by a lamp or streetlight.

But what if the shadow is cast along a surface that isn't horizontal? For example, the picture below shows someone using a lamp to create shadows on a wall.

These other kinds of shadows may be difficult to study, but give it a try. You don't have to look at the length of the shadow—you can investigate any aspect you like.

Investigation

In *The Pit and the Pendulum,* you experimented with pendulums of different weights to see if changing the weight of the bob caused a change in the length of the pendulum's period.

In this unit, you began by experimenting with shadows, studying how changing certain lengths or distances affected the length of the shadow.

In each of these investigations, it was important that everything was the same in each experiment except for the variable you were testing. In other words, each experiment had one variable (such as the weight of the bob) that you were changing, and one result (such as the length of the period) that you looked at to see if there was an effect.

For this assignment, you are to think of your own topic of investigation. In your investigation, as before, there should be one variable that changes (the **independent variable**) and one result (the **dependent variable**) where you look for an effect.

You are to create an experiment on your topic that will provide data for you to analyze. Your goal is to come up with some kind of formula that will describe your data. (There may not be an exact formula. In that case, you should either look for an approximate formula or come up with a verbal description of what is happening.)

Continued on next page

Here is a suggested plan:

1. Decide on a topic to investigate. You should pick a topic that can be organized so that there is one independent variable and one dependent variable. Everything else should remain constant.

2. Design the experiment.

3. Do one or two trial runs of your experiment and refine it as necessary.

4. Collect and organize the data.

5. Try to use your data to come up with a formula or verbal description of what is happening.

You will need to turn in a summary of your work. You can use the steps above as an outline.

The Golden Ratio

There is a ratio that often comes up in art and nature called the **golden ratio** (or the **golden section**). Many people think that structures that make use of this ratio are visually appealing.

Research the golden ratio and write a paper on what it is and where it occurs. The paper should be at least two pages in length and should include a list of the sources of your information.

Rigidity Can Be Good

You saw in *Why Are Triangles Special?* that if you "build" a triangle using specific lengths for the sides, then the triangle is *rigid*. That is, once the sides are put together, there is no flexibility.

For polygons with more than three sides, though, the polygon can be "flexed" at the corners, which changes the shape without changing the lengths of the sides.

Of course, in many situations, it's important to be flexible. But in architecture, it can be important that a building keep its shape.

Investigate the significance of rigidity for architecture and construction. You may want to do some construction of your own, or you may want to read about how triangles can be used to make buildings stable.

Suggestion: Look up the work of R. Buckminster Fuller.

Is It Sufficient?

As you already know, you can conclude that two triangles are similar whenever you know that two angles of one triangle are equal to two angles of the other triangle.

Mathematicians express this by saying that having two pairs of equal angles is **sufficient** for concluding that two triangles are similar.

Your goal in this problem is to investigate what other information about two triangles can be considered sufficient to conclude that the triangles are similar.

For each of the conditions stated below, start out as a skeptic. Use your ruler and

Continued on next page

protractor to make sketches, and try to find two triangles that fit the condition but that *are not* similar. In other words, look for a counterexample. If you find such triangles, you will have shown that the particular combination is not sufficient to conclude that the triangles are similar.

On the other hand, you may decide a given condition *is* sufficient; that is, that there are no counterexamples. In that case, try to explain why any two triangles that fit the condition must be similar.

Condition 1

An angle of one triangle is equal to an angle of the other triangle.

Condition 2

A side of one triangle is proportional to a side of the other triangle.

Condition 3

A pair of sides of one triangle is proportional to a pair of sides of the other triangle.

Condition 4

The three sides of one triangle are proportional to the three sides of the other triangle.

Condition 5

An angle of one triangle is equal to an angle of the other triangle, and a side of one triangle is proportional to a side of the other triangle.

Condition 6

A pair of sides of one triangle is proportional to a pair of sides of the other triangle, and the angles between these pairs of sides are equal.

Condition 7

A pair of sides of one triangle is proportional to a pair of sides of the other triangle, and an angle not between the pair in one triangle is equal to the corresponding angle of the other triangle.

How Can They Not Be Similar?

You know that two polygons are similar if they satisfy both of these conditions.

- The angles of the first polygon are equal to the corresponding angles of the second.

- The sides of the first polygon are proportional to the corresponding sides of the second.

But what if the word "corresponding" is omitted? Do the polygons still have to be similar?

The answer is no, but constructing a counterexample is not easy. To make life simpler for you, look at the special case where the ratio of sides is 1.

In other words, your task in this activity is to try to construct two polygons that satisfy both of the following conditions but that are not similar.

- The angles of the first are equal (as a group) to the angles of the second.

- The lengths of the sides of the first polygon are equal (as a group) to the lengths of the sides of the second.

Triangular Data

You saw in *Why Are Triangles Special?* that if you were given three lengths, there would be at most one way to build a triangle whose sides had those lengths.

Mathematicians express this property by saying that the lengths of the sides **determine** the triangle.

Here's another way to express this property.

> *If the sides of one triangle have the same lengths as the sides of another triangle, then the two triangles must be congruent.*

We sometimes think of a triangle as having six parts—three sides and three angles. As just discussed, three sides determine a triangle. You saw in *Are Angles Enough?* that three angles do *not* determine a triangle, since two triangles with the same angles might be similar but not congruent.

In Part I of this activity, you will explore through examples what other combinations of information determine a triangle. In Part II, you will try to generalize your discoveries.

Continued on next page

Part I: Exploring Triangles

In each of the problems below, you are given the values for three of the six parts of a possible triangle, $\triangle ABC$. You are to try to draw a triangle that fits the conditions. In each case you have to answer two questions:

    a. Is it possible to draw a triangle that fits the conditions?

    b. If so, will two triangles that both fit the conditions have to be congruent to each other?

In other words, your task is to find out if the given information determines a triangle.

Each of Questions 1 through 8 is a separate problem. Answer both part a and part b for each example and justify your answers.

Note: You will probably find it helpful to use a ruler and a protractor on this assignment.

1. $AC = 5$ inches, $\angle ABC = 50°$, and $\angle CAB = 110°$

2. $BC = 7$ inches, $\angle ABC = 70°$, and $\angle BCA = 80°$

3. $AB = 5$ inches, $BC = 8$ inches, and $\angle ABC = 70°$

4. $AB = 7$ inches, $AC = 11$ inches, and $\angle CAB = 130°$

5. $AB = 7$ inches, $AC = 6$ inches, and $\angle ABC = 50°$

6. $AB = 2$ inches, $BC = 4$ inches, and $\angle BCA = 60°$

7. $AB = 3$ inches, $AC = 5$ inches, and $\angle ABC = 90°$

8. $AB = 4$ inches, $BC = 6$ inches, and $\angle CAB = 100°$

Part II: Generalizing Triangles

Look at the examples above, and consider these questions.

- How many lengths and how many angles were provided in each case?

- How were the lengths and angles situated in relation to each other in the triangle?

Based on these examples and others you might create on your own, try to develop some general principles. The central question to explore is

    What type of information determines a triangle?

Scale It!

Scale drawings and scale models are used for many purposes, such as map-making and testing new inventions.

Here are a few options you might consider for an investigation of scaling.

- Make a scale drawing of some aspect of your school or neighborhood.

- Build a scale model of some object.

- Interview someone who uses scale drawings or scale models in his or her work.

If you have other ideas for learning more about scaling, that's fine too.

Whatever you do, write a report about your work and discuss how the ideas of this unit were connected to your investigation.

Proportions Everywhere

Polygons *ABCDE* and *PQRST* at the right are similar, so the ratios of the lengths of corresponding sides are the same.

For example, the ratio $\frac{AB}{PQ}$ is the same as the ratio $\frac{CD}{RS}$, because $\overline{AB}$ corresponds to $\overline{PQ}$ and $\overline{CD}$ corresponds to $\overline{RS}$.

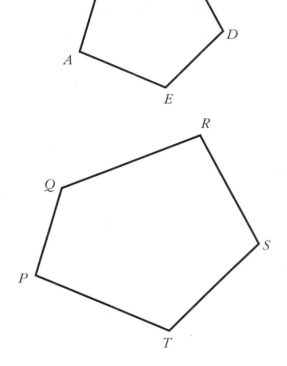

What about other lengths in these diagrams? Does every part of the first figure have a corresponding part in the second? Do other ratios of corresponding parts come out the same as the ratios above? First look at some examples.

1. Consider the diagonal $\overline{BE}$ in the first polygon.

   a. What segment in the second polygon corresponds to this diagonal?

   b. Is the ratio of the length of $\overline{BE}$ to the length of its corresponding part the same as the ratio of *AB* to *PQ?* Why or why not?

2. Use *F* to represent the midpoint of side $\overline{AE}$.

   a. What segment in the second polygon corresponds to $\overline{CF}$?

   b. Is the ratio of the length of $\overline{CF}$ to the length of its corresponding part the same as the ratio of *AB* to *PQ?* Why or why not?

Now make up your own examples and think about generalizing. State clearly any general principles you think must hold true.

What If They Kept Running?

Mandy, Callie, and Kate were running a race of 1500 meters. Mandy won.

At the moment when Mandy crossed the finish line, she was 300 meters ahead of Callie and 420 meters ahead of Kate.

If Callie and Kate keep running at the same rates as they have run so far, how many meters ahead of Kate will Callie be when Callie crosses the finish line?

Adapted from *Mathematics Teacher* (January 1990), National Council of Teachers of Mathematics, Volume 83, Number 1.

Fit Them Together

The illustration below shows how to start with one triangle (the top triangle) and fit four copies of it together to make a "double-size" version of that triangle.

Such a diagram shows that the large triangle is similar to the original triangle, because each side is twice as long. The diagram also shows that the area of the "double-size" triangle is four times the area of the original triangle.

1. Can you do this "fitting together" starting with any triangle? Try either to find a triangle for which you can't put four copies together this way, or to explain why this diagram works for any initial triangle.

2. Now move on to quadrilaterals. If you start with any initial quadrilateral, can you fit four exact copies of it together to make a "double-size" version of that quadrilateral?

   This may depend on the initial quadrilateral. Start with squares, then move on to rectangles, parallelograms, trapezoids, and others. In each case, explore whether four exact copies can be put together to make a "double-size" version.

   If you think that this can be done with a given category of quadrilaterals, show how. If you find quadrilaterals for which this "fitting together" cannot be done, show some of them.

3. That still leaves a question about area. If you start with an arbitrary quadrilateral and make a similar quadrilateral whose sides are twice as long as those of the original, will the area of this "double-size" quadrilateral always be four times the area of the original?

   Either explain why this is so, or give a counterexample.

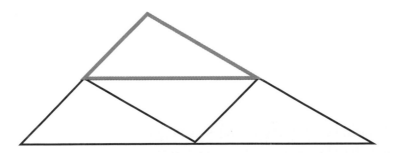

Similar Areas

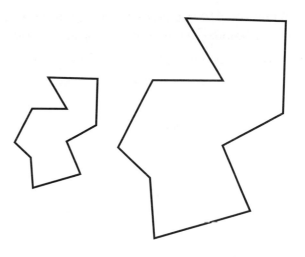

In *Fit Them Together,* you saw that you could double the lengths of the sides of a triangle to create a new triangle that was similar to the original and that had an area four times that of the original.

What more can you say about areas of similar figures?

Specifically, how does the ratio of the area of two similar figures depend on the ratio of the lengths of corresponding sides?

The Parallel Postulate

When the Greek mathematician Euclid wrote his *Elements* (about 300 B.C.E.), he made certain fundamental geometric assumptions, called **postulates** and **axioms**.

For example, his first postulate says

> A straight line may be drawn between any two points.

That's pretty reasonable. Most of his postulates are just as simple as this first one.

But Euclid's fifth postulate is quite complicated. It says

> If two straight lines lying in a plane are met by another line, and if the sum of the interior angles on one side is less than two right angles, then the straight lines if extended sufficiently will meet on the side on which the sum of the angles is less than two right angles.

1. What does this mean? Draw a diagram to explain what Euclid was talking about. (*Hint:* The phrase "another line" corresponds to what was called a *transversal* in the activity *More About Angles*. In other words, this line crosses each of the other two lines.)

2. Explain how this postulate is related to the principles about parallel lines that you found in *More About Angles*. In particular, discuss the connection between Euclid's fifth postulate and the statement

   > Given a line *L* and a point *P* not on *L,* there is a unique line through *P* that is parallel to *L*.

   This statement is sometimes called **Playfair's axiom**, after the Scottish mathematician John Playfair (1748-1819).

Mathematicians were intrigued by Euclid's fifth postulate, partly because it was so complicated. A long history developed in which they tried to prove this statement without making any assumptions except for Euclid's other postulates. They were never successful.

In the nineteenth century, three mathematicians in three different countries showed that this challenge was impossible. A German mathematician, Carl Friedrich Gauss (1777-1855), a Russian mathematician, Nicolai Ivanovitch Lobachevsky (1793-1856), and a Hungarian mathematician, János Bolyai (1802-1860), all explored the idea of a geometric system in which Euclid's postulate was false. Quite independently of each

Continued on next page

other, they discovered that such a system was logically possible. The system they developed is called **hyperbolic geometry**.

Another geometric system, which required changing some of Euclid's other postulates, was developed by the German mathematician Georg Friedrich Bernhard Riemann (1826–1866), and this is called **elliptic geometry**.

Both are examples of geometrical systems that describe the geometry of surfaces other than a plane, and both are examples of a broader field called **non-Euclidean geometry**. It turns out that Albert Einstein made use of the ideas of non-Euclidean geometry in developing his concepts of space and time that are part of the theory of relativity.

3. Read about and report further on the history of Euclid's fifth postulate and the development of non-Euclidean geometry.

Exterior Angles and Polygon Angle Sums

In *A Parallel Proof,* you saw how to use principles about parallel lines to prove that the sum of the angles of any triangle is exactly 180°. You also know that this fact for triangles can be used to develop an angle sum formula for arbitrary polygons. It turns out that these facts about angle sums can also be proved by using a concept called **exterior angles.**

This activity will explain that concept and then give a sequence of questions to help you develop that proof.

Exterior Angles

Generally, when we talk about the angles of a polygon, we mean the angles *inside* the figure. For example, in the first pentagon, we might mean $\angle ABC$ or $\angle DEA$, among others.

But you get some other interesting angles by extending the sides of the polygon. For example, the diagram at the right shows the same polygon with $\overline{BC}$ extended beyond C to point F.

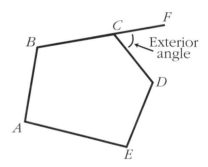

The angle *FCD* is called an **exterior angle** of the polygon. For emphasis, we sometimes call an angle inside a polygon, such as $\angle BCD$, an **interior angle.**

There are actually two exterior angles at each vertex of a polygon. For example, at C, in addition to extending $\overline{BC}$ as above, you could also extend $\overline{DC}$ past C, as shown at the right. Both $\angle BCK$ and $\angle FCD$ are considered exterior angles at C for polygon *ABCDE*.

In this activity, you will only be considering one exterior angle at each vertex.

Note: Since angles *FCD* and *BCK* are vertical angles, they are equal, and it won't matter which one is used.

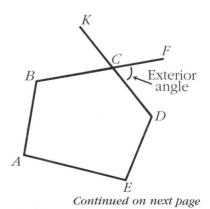

Continued on next page

Polygon Angle Sums

The proof of the angle sum formula for polygons combines two ideas:

- The relationship between each interior angle and the corresponding exterior angle

- A general formula about exterior angles

In this activity, you will develop the two ideas separately and then put them together.

Step 1. Interior and Exterior Angles

Step 1 is the easier of the two parts, and it has two stages. First you need to answer this question.

> *What is the relationship between an interior angle of a polygon and the corresponding exterior angle?*

For example, how are angles *BCD* and *FCD* related?

Write a formula or equation relating two such angles, and explain why that relationship must hold for every such pair of angles.

Your answer to the question above should give you a formula for the sum of each interior angle and the corresponding exterior angle. Basing your response on that result, answer this question.

> *If you combine all the interior angles with their corresponding exterior angles (using only one exterior angle for each vertex), what is the sum of all of these angles?*

Hint: The answer depends on the number of sides of the polygon.

Step 2. Total Turns

The second key idea involves just the exterior angles of a polygon, choosing one at each vertex, as shown in the diagram at the right.

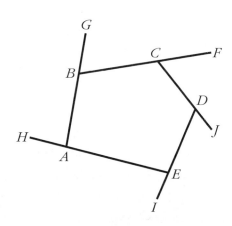

Imagine that you are standing at point *C*, facing toward *F*. From that position, turn toward *D*, turning through an angle equal to the exterior angle *FCD*.

Now move along $\overline{CD}$ to point *D*. When you get there, turn toward *E*, this time turning through an angle equal to exterior angle *JDE*.

Continued on next page

Next, move along $\overline{DE}$ to E, and again make a turn. Continue around the polygon in this way, moving along each side and then turning through the exterior angle.

Your final turn will occur when you are at point B, facing toward G. You will turn toward C, going through a turn equal to the last of the exterior angles. You are now facing in the same direction in which you started.

The key question here is

> *What is the total number of degrees in all of your turns?*

In other words, what is the sum of all the exterior angles of the polygon (taking one exterior angle at each vertex)?

Would your result work for any polygon? Explain.

Step 3. Putting It All Together

In Step 1, you should have found a formula for the sum of an interior angle and its corresponding exterior angle, and from that you should have found a formula for the sum of all the interior and exterior angles.

In Step 2, you should have found a formula for the sum of all the exterior angles.

The final step of the process is

> *What is the sum of the interior angles of the polygon?*

Exactly One-Half!

You may have observed that, according to your calculator, sin 30° = 0.5000.

You might wonder whether this is just an approximation or if sin 30° is really *exactly* one-half.

Your task in this activity is to show, beyond any doubt, that the sine of 30° is exactly, precisely one-half.

Hint: Use an equilateral triangle and the fact that the sum of the angles of a triangle is 180°.

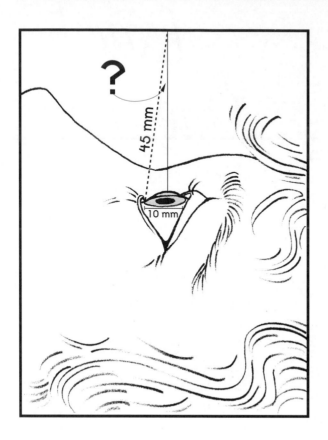

Eye Exam

An eye surgeon must perform an operation on a person who has pressure behind the cornea. (The cornea is the shaded area in the picture.) The surgeon will use a laser to make small holes along the edge of the cornea.

The patient will be lying on the operating table and the laser will be above her. More precisely, it will be directly above her pupil (the center of her eye). The laser is 45 millimeters from the outer edge of the cornea. The diameter of the cornea is 10 millimeters.

The surgeon needs to find the angle at which to set the laser. This is the angle shown in the diagram as "?"

1. Using trigonometry, set up an equation that could be used to find this angle.

2. Use your scientific calculator to get an approximate solution to this equation (by trial and error).

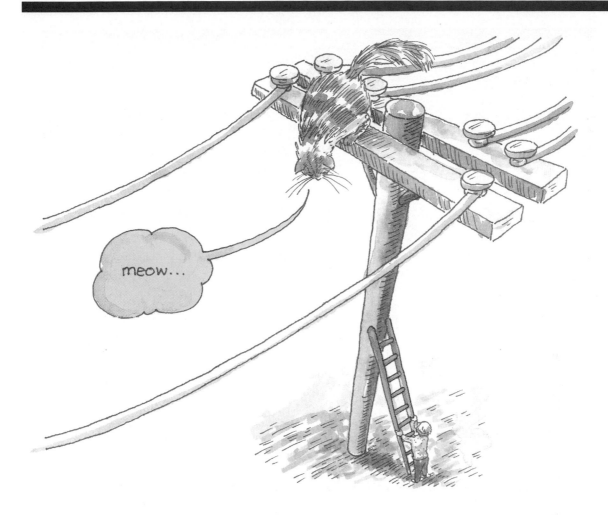

Pole Cat

Poor Diane. Her cat, Wanda Ann, has climbed up a telephone pole and can't get down.

The crossbar of the telephone pole is 20 feet high. Diane is 5 feet 6 inches tall and can reach a foot above her head. She has a 15-foot ladder.

In order to keep the ladder from tipping, Diane must lean it against the pole at an angle of 70° with the ground. Can Diane save Wanda Ann?

Dog in a Ditch

Oscar and Rasheed are identical twins. They are both 6 feet tall. They are on opposite sides of a ditch that is 30 feet wide. Their dog, Earl, is at the bottom of the ditch.

Earl can get out if he wants to. When Oscar looks at Earl, his line of sight makes a 75° angle below the horizontal. When Rasheed looks at Earl, his line of sight makes a 40° angle below horizontal. How deep is the ditch?

(*Hint:* Trigonometry may not be very useful in this problem.)

Glossary

This is the glossary for all five units of IMP Year 1.

Absolute value   The distance a number is from 0 on the number line. The symbol | | stands for absolute value.

Examples: $|{-2}| = 2$; $|7| = 7$; $|0| = 0$

Acute angle   An angle that measures more than 0° and less than 90°.

Acute triangle   A triangle whose angles are all acute.

Adjacent angles   Two angles with the same vertex and formed using a shared ray.

Example: Angles A and B are adjacent angles.

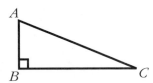

Adjacent side   (for an acute angle of a right triangle) The side of the right triangle which, together with the hypotenuse, forms the given angle.

Example: In the right triangle ABC, side $\overline{BC}$ is adjacent to $\angle C$, and side $\overline{AB}$ is adjacent to $\angle A$.

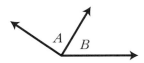

Alternate interior angles   If two lines are intersected by a transversal, then the inside angles that are on opposite sides of the transversal are alternate interior angles.

Example: Angles *K* and *L* are one pair of alternate interior angles, and angles *M* and *N* are another pair.

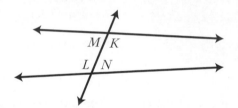

Amplitude

(for a pendulum) The angle of a pendulum's swing, measured from the vertical to the most outward position of the pendulum during its swing.

Example: The pendulum in the diagram has an amplitude of 20°.

Angle

Informally, an amount of turn, usually measured in **degrees.** Formally, the geometric figure formed by two **rays** with a common initial point, called the **vertex** of the angle.

Angle of elevation

The angle at which an object appears above the horizontal, as measured from a chosen point.

Example: The diagram shows the angle of elevation to the top of the tree from point *A*.

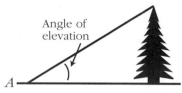

Area

Informally, the amount of space inside a two-dimensional figure, usually measured in square units.

Area model

For probability, a diagram showing the possible outcomes of a particular event. Each portion of the model represents an outcome, and the ratio of the area of that portion to the area of the whole model is the probability of that outcome.

Axis	(plural: **axes**) See **Coordinate system.**
Coefficient	Usually, a number being used to multiply a variable or power of a variable in an algebraic expression.
	Example: In the expression $3x + 4x^2$, 3 and 4 are coefficients.
Complementary angles	A pair of angles whose measures add to 90°. If two complementary angles are adjacent, together they form a right angle.
Composite number	A counting number having more than two whole-number divisors.
	Example: 12 is a composite number because it has the divisors 1, 2, 3, 4, 6, and 12.
Conclusion	Informally, any statement arrived at by reasoning or through examples.
	See also **"If . . . , then . . ." statement.**
Conditional probability	The probability that an event will occur based on the assumption that some other event has already occurred.
Congruent	Informally, having the same shape and size. Formally, two polygons are congruent if their corresponding angles have equal measure and their corresponding sides are equal in length. The symbol ≅ means "is congruent to."
Conjecture	A theory or an idea about how something works, usually based on examples.
Constraint	Informally, a limitation or restriction.
Continuous graph	Informally, a graph that can be drawn without lifting the pencil, in contrast to a **discrete graph.**
Coordinate system	A way to represent points in the plane with pairs of numbers called **coordinates**. The system is based on

Example: This frequency bar graph shows, for instance, that 11 times in 80 rolls, the sum of two dice was 6.

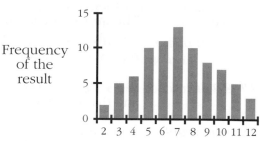

Function   Informally, a process or rule for determining the numerical value of one variable in terms of another. A function is often represented as a set of number pairs in which the second number is determined by the first, according to the function rule.

Graph   A mathematical diagram for displaying information.

Hexagon   A polygon with six sides.

Hypotenuse   The longest side in a right triangle, or the length of this side. The hypotenuse is located opposite the right angle.

Example: In right triangle *ABC*, the hypotenuse is $\overline{AC}$.

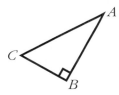

Hypothesis   Informally, a theory about a situation or about how a certain set of data is behaving. Also, a set of assumptions being used to analyze or understand a situation.

See also **"If . . . , then . . ." statement.**

"If . . . , then . . ."
statement   A specific form of mathematical statement, saying that if one condition is true, then another condition must also be true.

Example: Here is a true "If . . . , then . . ." statement.

If two angles of a triangle have equal measure, then the sides opposite these angles have equal length.

The condition "two angles of a triangle have equal measure" is the **hypothesis.** The condition "the sides opposite these angles have equal length" is the **conclusion.**

Independent events

Two (or more) events are independent if the outcome of one does not influence the outcome of the other.

Integer

Any number that is either a counting number, zero, or the opposite of a counting number. The integers can be represented using set notation as

$$\{\ldots -3, -2, -1, 0, 1, 2, 3, \ldots\}.$$

Examples: -4, 0, and 10 are integers.

Interior angle

An angle inside a figure, especially within a polygon.

Example: Angle *BAE* is an interior angle of the polygon *ABCDE.*

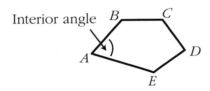

Isosceles triangle

A triangle with two sides of equal length.

Leg

Either of the two shorter sides in a right triangle. The two legs of a right triangle form the right angle of the triangle. The longest side of a right triangle (the hypotenuse) is not considered a leg.

Line of best fit

Informally, the line that comes closest to fitting a given set of points on a discrete graph.

Line segment

The portion of a straight line between two given points.

Mathematical model

A mathematical description or structure used to represent how a real-life situation works.

Mean

The numerical average of a data set, found by adding the data items and dividing by the number of items in the set.

Example: For the data set 8, 12, 12, 13, and 17, the sum of the data items is 62 and there are 5 items in the data set, so the mean is 62 ÷ 5, or 12.4.

Measurement variation   The situation of taking several measurements of the same thing and getting different results.

Median   (of a set of data) The "middle number" in a set of data that has been arranged from smallest to largest.

Example: For the data set 4, 17, 22, 56, and 100, the median is 22, because it is the number in the middle of the list.

Mode   (of a set of data) The number that occurs most often in a set of data. Many sets of data do not have a single mode.

Example: For the data set 3, 4, 7, 16, 18, 18, and 23, the mode is 18.

Natural number   Any of the counting numbers 1, 2, 3, 4, and so on.

Normal distribution   A certain precisely defined set of probabilities, which can often be used to approximate real-life events. Sometimes used to refer to any data set whose frequency bar graph is approximately "bell-shaped."

Observed probability   The likelihood of a certain event happening based on observed results, as distinct from **theoretical probability.**

Obtuse angle   An angle that measures more than 90° and less than 180°.

Obtuse triangle   A triangle with an obtuse angle.

Octagon   An eight-sided polygon.

Opposite side   The side of a triangle across from a given angle.

Order of operations   A set of conventions that mathematicians have agreed to use whenever a calculation involves more than one operation.

Example: 2 + 3 · 4 is 14, not 20, because the conventions for order of operations tell us to multiply before we add.

Ordered pair	Two numbers paired together using the format *(x, y)*, often used to locate a point in the coordinate system.
Origin	See **Coordinate system.**
Parallel lines	Two lines in a plane that do not intersect.
Pentagon	A five-sided polygon.
Perimeter	The boundary of a polygon, or the total length of this boundary.
Period	The length of time for a cyclical event to complete one full cycle.
Perpendicular lines	A pair of lines that form a right angle.
Polygon	A closed two-dimensional shape formed by three or more line segments. The line segments that form a polygon are called its sides. The endpoints of these segments are called **vertices** (singular: **vertex**).

Examples: All the figures below are polygons.

Prime number	A whole number greater than 1 that has only two whole number divisors, 1 and itself.

Example: 7 is a prime number, because its only whole number divisors are 1 and 7.

Probability	The likelihood of a certain event happening. For a situation involving equally likely outcomes, the probability that the outcome of an event will be an outcome within a given set is defined by a ratio:

$$\text{Probability} = \frac{\text{number of outcomes in the set}}{\text{total number of possible outcomes}}$$

Example: If a die has 2 red faces and 4 green faces, the probability of getting a green face is

$$\frac{\text{number of green faces}}{\text{total number of faces}} = \frac{4}{6}$$

Proof   An absolutely convincing argument.

Proportion   A statement that two ratios are equal.

Proportional   Having the same ratio.

Example: Corresponding sides of triangles *ABC* and *DEF* are proportional, because the ratios $\frac{4}{6}$, $\frac{8}{12}$, and $\frac{10}{15}$ are equal.

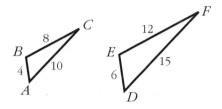

Quadrant   One of the four areas created in a coordinate system by using the *x*-axis and the *y*-axis as boundaries. The quadrants have standard numbering as shown below.

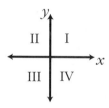

Quadrilateral   A four-sided polygon.

Random   Used in probability to indicate that any of several events is equally likely or that an event is selected from a set of events according to a precisely described distribution.

Range   (of a set of data) The difference between the largest and smallest numbers in the set.

Example: For the data set 7, 12, 18, 18, and 29, the range is 29 – 7, or 22.

Ray	The part of a line from a single point, called the **vertex,** through another point on the line and continuing infinitely in that direction.
Rectangle	A four-sided polygon whose angles are all right angles.
Regular polygon	A polygon whose sides all have equal length and whose angles all have equal measure.
Rhombus	A four-sided polygon whose sides all have the same length.
Right angle	An angle that measures 90°.
Right triangle	A triangle with a right angle.
Sample standard deviation	The calculation on a set of data taken from a larger population of data, used to estimate the standard deviation of the larger population.
Sequence	A list of numbers or expressions, usually following a pattern or rule. Example: 1, 3, 5, 7, 9, . . . is the sequence of positive odd numbers.
Similar	Informally, having the same shape. Formally, two polygons are similar if their corresponding angles have equal measure and their corresponding sides are proportional in length. The symbol ~ means "is similar to."
Simulation	An experiment or set of experiments using a model of a certain event that is based on the same probabilities as the real event. Simulations allow people to estimate the likelihood of an event when it is impractical to experiment with the real event.
Slope	Informally, the steepness of a line.
Solution	A number that, when substituted for a variable in an equation, makes the equation a true statement. Example: The value $x = 3$ is a solution to the equation $2x = 6$ because $2 \cdot 3 = 6$.
Square	A four-sided polygon with all sides of equal length and with four right angles.

Square root   A number whose square is a given number. The symbol $\sqrt{}$ is used to denote the nonnegative square root of a number.

Example: Both 6 and –6 are square roots of 36, because $6^2 = 36$ and $(-6)^2 = 36$; $\sqrt{36} = 6$.

Standard deviation   A specific measurement of how spread out a set of data is, usually represented by the lowercase Greek letter sigma (σ).

Straight angle   An angle that measures 180°. The rays forming a straight angle together make up a straight line.

Strategy   A complete plan about how to proceed in a game or problem situation. A strategy for a game should tell a person exactly what to do under any situation that can arise in the game.

Supplementary angles   A pair of angles whose measures add to 180°. If two supplementary angles are adjacent, together they form a straight angle.

Term   (of an algebraic expression) A part of an algebraic expression, combined with other terms using addition or subtraction.

Example: The expression $2x^2 + 3x - 12$ has three terms: $2x^2$, $3x$, and 12.

Term   (of a sequence) One of the items listed in a sequence.

Example: In the sequence 3, 5, 7, . . . , the number 3 is the first term, 5 is the second term, and so on.

Theoretical probability   The likelihood of an event occurring, as explained by a theory or model, as distinct from **observed probability.**

Transversal   A line that intersects two or more other lines.

Example: The line *l* is a transversal that intersects the lines *m* and *n*.

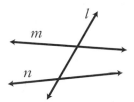

Trapezoid   A four-sided polygon with exactly one pair of parallel sides.

Example: Quadrilateral *PQRS* is a trapezoid, because $\overline{QR}$ and $\overline{PS}$ are parallel and $\overline{PQ}$ and $\overline{SR}$ are not parallel.

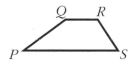

Triangle   A polygon with three sides.

Triangle inequality principle   The principle that the lengths of any two sides of a triangle must add up to more than the length of the third side.

Trigonometric function   Any of six functions defined for acute angles in terms of ratios of sides of a right triangle.

Vertex   (plural: **vertices**) See **Angle, Polygon,** and **Ray.**

Vertical angles   A pair of "opposite" angles formed by a pair of intersecting lines.

Example: Angles *F* and *G* are vertical angles.

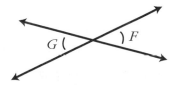

Whole number   A number that is either zero or a counting number.

x-intercept   A place on a graph where a line or curve crosses the *x*-axis.

y-intercept   A place on a graph where a line or curve crosses the *y*-axis.

Photographic Credits

Classroom Photography

3 Lincoln High School, Lori Green; **14** Lincoln High School, Lori Green; **27** Lincoln High School, Lori Green; **36** Lincoln High School, Lori Green; **42** San Lorenzo Valley High School, Kim Gough; **55** Lincoln High School, Lori Green; **95** Foothill High School, Sheryl Dozier; **104** Foothill High School, Sheryl Dozier; **114** Mendocino Community High School, Lynne Alper; **127** Mendocino High School, Lynne Alper; **150** Lake View High School, Carol Caref; **157** West High School, Janice Bussey; **189** Whitney Young High School, Carol Berland; **210** Pleasant Valley High School, Michael Christensen; **222** Lynne Alper; **238** East Bakersfield High School, Susan Lloyd; **252** Lincoln High School, Lynne Alper; **274** Colton High School, Sharon Taylor; **281** Foothill High School, Sheryl Dozier; **307** Santa Cruz High School, Lynne Alper; **324** Foothill High School, Cheryl Dozier; **352** Santa Maria High School, Mike Bryant; **366** Santa Cruz High School, Lynne Alper; **373** Shasta High School, Dave Robathan; **397** Santa Cruz High School, Lynne Alper; **414** Santa Maria High School, Mike Bryant; **424** Bartram Communications Academy, Robert Powlen; **446** Santa Maria High School, Mike Bryant; **460** Ranum High School, Rita Quintana